UPSOLD

UPSOLD

Real Estate Agents, Prices, and
Neighborhood Inequality

MAX BESBRIS

The University of Chicago Press ▪ *Chicago and London*

The University of Chicago Press, Chicago 60637
The University of Chicago Press, Ltd., London
© 2020 by The University of Chicago
Published 2020

29 28 27 26 25 24 23 22 21 20   1 2 3 4 5

ISBN-13: 978-0-226-72123-1 (cloth)
ISBN-13: 978-0-226-72137-8 (paper)
ISBN-13: 978-0-226-72140-8 (e-book)
DOI: https://doi.org/10.7208/chicago/9780226721408.001.0001

Library of Congress Cataloging-in-Publication Data

Names: Besbris, Max, author.
Title: Upsold : real estate agents, prices, and neighborhood inequality / Max Besbris.
Description: Chicago : University of Chicago Press, 2020. | Includes bibliographical references
and index.
Identifiers: LCCN 2020004956 | ISBN 9780226721231 (cloth) | ISBN 9780226721378 (paperback) |
ISBN 9780226721408 (ebook)
Subjects: LCSH: Housing—New York (State)—New York—Finance. | Discrimination in
housing—New York (State)—New York. | Real estate agents—New York (State)—New York.
Classification: LCC HD7304.N4 B473 2020 | DDC 333.33/8097471—dc23
LC record available at https://lccn.loc.gov/2020004956

CONTENTS

VALUE, PREFERENCES, AND INEQUALITY IN THE HOUSING MARKET

Ben, a corporate accountant in his mid-thirties, grew up in what he described as an affluent suburb of Minneapolis. His father, a doctor, and his mother, a nurse, had bought a house before Ben was born. They still lived there and had recently paid off their standard thirty-year mortgage. "That's obviously not the kind of house I think I'll ever want to buy," Ben said, referring to the three-bedroom tract-style home familiar to suburban subdivisions across the United States. Ben had moved to New York City right after graduating from an elite East Coast university and said he didn't want to live anywhere else.

For the past six years Ben had been renting a one-bedroom apartment in Williamsburg, a neighborhood in Brooklyn on the East River that provided relatively easy access to Ben's work in downtown Manhattan. He told me he had had enough of renting. "It's the right time for me to buy," he said. "I have the money to get something for myself." After studying his finances, he decided his price ceiling was $600,000. With the property market in Williamsburg extremely hot, Ben knew he might have to leave the neighborhood. "But I want to stay in Brooklyn," he said, "I've been here the whole time and I like it."

A coworker of Ben's who had recently bought in Williamsburg referred him to Liz, a real estate agent. Ben's coworker had praised Liz's thoroughness and attentiveness. Liz, a white woman in her mid-forties, prided herself on knowing the housing market in northern Brooklyn, including Williamsburg, as well as the intimacy she cultivated with her clients. "It's good for business," she told me. "If I know you really well, I'm going to get you the place you really want." Most of Liz's clients over the past few years looked like Ben—white people in their twenties, thirties, and forties who worked in industries like finance, tech, public relations, publishing, and advertising.

Ben and Liz hit it off. I trailed along over the next four months as the two attended open houses and scheduled showings. As they walked through one newly renovated kitchen after another, they discussed what Ben saw in his future. How was his life going to unfold? Would he stay at his current job for long time? Did he ever want to get married? have kids? Liz shared details about her own life as they grabbed coffees and quick meals in between apartment viewings.

But something else was happening during their interactions. Liz would often bring up the tightness of the market—high prices and low inventory—and the need to make offers quickly. Although Ben had said he wanted to spend less than $600,000, Liz consistently brought him to open houses at apartments priced between $640,000 and $700,000. When they were visiting these pricier places, Liz would talk about how it was worth spending just a little bit more to get a lot more—an apartment in a new building with an elevator instead of one in a prewar walk-up, for instance. More importantly, if Ben spent a little more he'd get the status that came with owning an apartment in a new building and, as Liz put it, the "ability to start a brand-new life."

Liz also frequently mentioned other buyers she had recently represented who she said shared similar tastes with Ben—in restaurants, bars, and other amenities—and she would reference their occupations and share details about their housing searches. She would say how these other clients were living great lives in the neighborhoods where they had bought homes and told Ben that he too would soon find the right apartment in the right part of town.

On one visit to an apartment in a newer building with an elevator, listed at $660,000, Liz and Ben both seemed excited. They talked about the view, the size of the unit, and the loveliness of the Lower East Side, the neighborhood in Manhattan where the apartment was located. "This place is just so you," Liz said. A day later, Ben called Liz and told her to make an offer on the apartment for $650,000. Ben would not be living in Williamsburg, and he paid significantly more than his stated budget of $600,000. And yet he seemed thrilled.

Where do preferences come from? How do consumers decide that certain goods and services are worth their cost? How do these decisions aggregate into broader market patterns and produce inequality?

Upsold addresses these questions by looking at the housing market. In examining how real estate agents guide buyers through the process of searching for a home, *Upsold* provides insights into economic decision-making, including how buyers come to pay the prices they do, and the role of market intermediaries in shaping taste preferences in unequal ways. More broadly, it shows how face-to-face interactions between buyers and agents produce neighborhoods, some which are or are soon to become elite and exclusive places where aspiring residents can expect ever-rising housing prices.

WHY STUDY HOUSING?

Houses are important to the people who live in them for many reasons. They provide shelter from the elements, privacy from others, and proximity to schools, labor markets, social networks, and various other amenities. Housing is a fundamental human right, enshrined by the United Nations as part of a package of goods and services necessary for the maintenance of an adequate and humane standard of living. Housing is also a source of debt and an opportunity to accumulate wealth that can be passed down to future generations. Scholars have been trying to understand the contradictions of the housing market—is housing a commodity or is it a right?—for hundreds of years. In 1872 Friedrich Engels published a set of essays, *The Housing Question*, in which he argued that any market for housing was unjust and that the only solution was collective ownership not only of housing but of all means of production. As he pointed out, people need, and have the right to, a place to live, and yet a commodified housing market creates incentives that prevent universal access to housing.[1]

Today houses are status symbols for individuals, and the housing market itself—as the financial crisis of 2008 demonstrated so dramatically—is integral to the national and international economies. Houses are also fixed in place; unlike our favorite type of candy bar, which we eat immediately after buying, or even a highly sentimental article of clothing, which we can take wherever we go, houses have a permanent location. Given the material and symbolic importance of houses, as well as their spatial permanence, it is not surprising that they provide residents with an overarching sense of place, identity, and security. As Don, a real estate agent working in Brooklyn, once said to his clients at an open house, "Houses are just everything. They are your life."

Houses are also uncommon purchases. Most Americans buy a house only once or twice in their lives.[2] In the United States, homeownership is both a stratified financial product that perpetuates wealth inequality and a stratified cultural product that distributes claims to citizenship and belonging unequally.[3] No wonder, then, that houses are imbued with multiple meanings since they are the largest asset and expenditure for the majority of Americans and satisfy the essential needs of life. Reflecting on the multiple meanings of housing, sociologists John Logan and Harvey Molotch (1987:17) write that homes are infused with a "preciousness for their users that is not part of the conventional concept of a commodity."[4] Houses are, after all, not just investments; they are also physical locations where we spend time with loved ones among many other daily activities necessary for reproduction—eating, childcare—seemingly unrelated to the dollar value of the house.

Despite the importance of a home in grounding our everyday lives, the desire to *own* a home is not an inherent disposition. That Americans frequently refer to it as such is partially a political construction born largely in response to demographic trends in the early twentieth century. Immigration rapidly increased the size and changed the look of cities, worrying nativist politicians who feared social unrest as the number of renters skyrocketed and tenancy became commonplace. In response, political and economic elites created pro-ownership campaigns intended to root individuals within communities as well as create profits for certain sectors of the economy.[5] As these campaigns continued through the postwar era, they were complemented with tax incentives encouraging homeownership.[6]

These pro-ownership campaigns, and the accompanying policies meant to spur homebuying, were very effective. In large part because of these campaigns, the single-family residence became the marker of middle-class status in the United States, tied to values of patriotism, traditional gender roles, and economic prudence.[7] Houses are reflections not just of the people that live in them but of neighborhood character and economic provision.[8] Indeed, while about two-thirds of all US households are owner occupied, homeownership remains the stated goal of many more people; the vast majority of Americans consider homeownership an integral part of achieving the American dream.[9] Notably, support for homeownership remains extremely high despite the bursting of the housing market bubble and subsequent global recession in 2008—highlighting the strength and durability of much of the ideology about homeownership.[10]

So how do homeseekers make their decisions? How does a buyer choose one particular housing unit over others? What are the processes that lead potential buyers to decide that a single, particular house is worth such a huge sum of money? The answer, as this book shows, is found in interaction.

MAKING ECONOMIC DECISIONS

Understanding how individuals form preferences, make economic choices, and establish the worth of goods is of great importance to both everyday life and macroeconomic structures. Accordingly, these questions have attracted much attention from scholars, who have answered them in dramatically different ways. In recent decades, attention has shifted toward the networks that constitute markets and the institutions and cultural beliefs that give products meaning and value.

Scholars of economic networks—the web of relationships that any given individual or firm has in a market—posit that actors are linked by their previous transactions with each other. These links vary in their strength and the kinds of obligations they create. The fact that actors become more familiar with each other over multiple transactions matters because it increases trust and reduces cheating, price gouging, and other bad behavior. Lacking perfect information, actors will think back to their previous dealings with others as a guide when making economic decisions.[11] Buyers' willingness to pay a certain price will depend on their familiarity with the seller and some assurance that they're getting a good deal.[12] Put another way, economic transactions and the worth of goods more generally depend on actors' interests in keeping up their own reputations as honest dealers in a given market. Some individuals or firms have particularly good reputations that allow them to charge higher prices or pay lower ones.[13]

By and large, this approach to understanding value has proved incredibly productive, but it has attracted criticism for ignoring other parts of social life that affect why we value the things we do. In particular, it does not account for our shared ideas and beliefs about the worth of goods and services. These collective understandings are often referred to as culture.[14]

To understand how culture matters for how we assign value, consider the following. Today most Americans would likely say that the labor of children is not economically valuable because it is immoral; it cannot be valued because it ought not exist. Such distaste for child labor is, however, a relatively recent historical development. At the dawn of the industrial revolution, child labor had value that it lost only through shifts in cultural attitudes about the role of children in society. Making something more or less valuable, or even commodifying or decommodifying something, depends on culture and ideology.[15] Broad shifts in sentiment and belief can change economic preferences and create or destroy entire markets.[16] But once markets are established, making economic decisions within them can become rote or habitual. Established markets have experts and institutions that determine how products are compared and priced.[17] Understanding the value of goods therefore requires attention not only to networks within markets but also to the cultural history of the commodity; the multiple mechanisms by which goods are categorized, compared, and judged; and differences in the power and ability to say what is or is not valuable.

Together, the network and cultural approaches to understanding economic action go a long way toward explaining why we are willing to pay the prices we do. Yet one aspect of social life that is widely understood to be consequential for many other outcomes is still typically overlooked when it comes to studying economic decisions: social interaction. *Upsold* uses the case of real estate markets to explicitly ask how value is formed through interaction. Put another way, this is a study of how interaction with market intermediaries affects how individuals value products within an existing economic market, and it shows how interactions, replicated in aggregate, reproduce inequality.

Upsold focuses on a particular kind of consumer—affluent home buyers—and a specific kind of market intermediary—real estate agents. Broadly defined, market intermediaries are individuals or organizations tasked with facilitating economic transactions. They intervene between supply and demand in a professional or expert capacity, and their work has some effect on the value of the good or service being exchanged.[18] When individuals enter most markets, particularly unfamiliar ones in which they have little experience, intermediaries aid them in searching for and differentiating between products. In the existing literature on value, the relationships between consumers and market intermediaries—and interactions more generally—are not thought to be as relevant as network positions and culture in explaining market outcomes.[19] But in many other aspects of social life, including the formation of identities, the direction and failure or success of social movements, and the accomplishment of group and organizational goals, scholars *do* understand interaction to be causal, in that particular interactional sequences produce one outcome while others do not.[20] *Upsold* adopts this interactional perspective to reveal how interactions between consumers and market intermediaries are key for understanding outcomes in a given market.

Real Estate Agents

Purchasing a house is a process dense with face-to-face encounters. Many of these are mediated by real estate agents, who sort available units on buyers' behalf, schedule visits and accompany buyers to open houses, and ultimately make offers and negotiate deals.

Since the 1950s, the majority of homebuyers in the United States have used real estate agents to aid them in their housing search. By 2016, 88 percent of home buyers purchased their houses using a real estate agent, up from 69 percent in 2001.[21] Despite real estate agents' wide involvement in the market, sociologists know surprisingly little about them and how their work affects the valuation of houses. In his ethnographic study of Canadian real estate agents in the 1970s, the sociologist J. D. House (1977:10) explains why such a gap in knowledge is potentially problematic: "Where a person lives, what kind of house he wants, and how much he will pay are subjective opinions that other people can influence."[22] Over forty years later, House's findings remain useful for framing new questions about real estate agents and their role in the housing market, particularly as the nature of the market has changed. Indeed, for almost a century of their existence, real estate agents maintained relatively exclusive access to listed properties.[23] In recent years, however, the rise of shared databases and real estate websites have made basic information on real estate inventory available to anyone with an internet connection. Real estate agents are no longer mandatory, yet more buyers use them now than before these resources were available.

House's orienting ideas about the malleability of individuals' housing decisions and real estate agents' influence over the process parallels concerns in two more recent books about how to conceptualize economic activity and inequality. In *Phishing for Phools* (2015), the Nobel Prize winning economists George Akerlof and Robert Shiller argue that economic markets are inherently spaces of manipulation. That is, sellers and market intermediaries like real estate agents are often trying to get consumers to pay more, and they do so by appealing to certain psychological biases we all have. Like House, Akerlof and Shiller believe that the housing search and payment processes are highly influenced by real estate agents, particularly because consumers participate in housing transactions so infrequently. Homeseekers lack the knowledge and experience that might prevent them from being ripped off.

The sociologist Pierre Bourdieu also wrote about the influence real estate agents might have over the sales process. In *The Social Structures of the Economy* (2005)—both an examination of the French housing market and a call to understand the market as a socially constructed object of analysis— Bourdieu argues that individuals can conceive of themselves as rationally acting consumers in a market only when they have had the economic security, education, and experience to understand themselves as such. In other words, through early and protracted experience with economic markets, individuals learn how to be consumers. Becoming economically rational means believing others who seem to have more market experience. Real estate agents are familiar with the housing market in a way that the vast majority of consumers are not, and therefore they appear as experts to most homeseekers.[24] Studying interactions between agents and buyers should go long way toward seeing how potential buyers decide where to live and how much to pay.[25]

Interaction and Preferences

Individuals do not have fixed ways of acting; rather, they observe what is going on around them and act accordingly. Situations demand certain types of behaviors and ways of being, so it is impossible to understand why people do what they do without examining the contexts in which action is occurring.[26] Interactions can change how individuals behave and even the types of people they imagine themselves to be. As the sociologist Mustafa Emirbayer (1997:296) puts it, "Individual identities are not preconstituted and unproblematic; parties to a transaction do not enter into mutual relations with their attributes already given." The methodological implication is that understanding why individuals do what they do requires attention to occasions—measuring resources, patterns, and properties in interactions instead of as a coherent set of entities that move from one interaction to another.[27]

This interactional perspective has deep implications for how we understand economic outcomes, since it highlights how indeterminate exchanges can be. Instead of thinking of individuals' wants or desires—their preferences for particular outcomes in an economic transaction—as fixed, we should theorize them as malleable and dependent on the flows of interaction. In the specific instance of real estate, this perspective implies that the interactions between real estate agents and home buyers actively shape housing markets. Potential buyers may begin the search process thinking they want one thing, but their preferences, including what they are willing to spend and where they want to live, can change through the course of interacting with agents and the market more generally.

This way of understanding preferences contrasts with classical models of economic behavior that conceive of actors as utility-maximizing and rational in their pursuits of their stated preferences, preferences that are generally consistent through transactions. Since the 1980s a robust research agenda within economics, largely influenced by psychology, has similarly come to view preferences as unstable and individual action as motivated by more than the desire to maximize profit. Broadly called behavioral economics, this work has shown how contextual factors like the availability of other options, other individuals' choices, and time constraints all shape decision-making in economic markets.[28] Individuals tend to rely on established heuristics when making economic decisions, and these heuristics are not free of bias. Preferences are not stable, consistent, or even mentally retrievable through different contexts. Instead consumers construct their preferences as they are being elicited.[29] This includes preferences for the prices consumers are willing to pay.[30]

Upsold draws on this work in behavioral economics but attends more to the interactional dynamics and power relations that structure economic transactions and lead to unequal outcomes in markets.[31] Decision-making happens through interaction. Interaction is where individuals solve the pragmatic problem of completing a transaction, where they reflect on past experiences, weigh the cultural values that might be part of their decision-making, and imagine a future where their purchase brings them some kind of satisfaction. Put another way, consumers do not make decisions in a vacuum; their choices stem from how interactions unfold. The buyers I observed constantly changed their minds about where they wanted to live and how much they wanted to spend during interactions with agents. *Upsold* therefore emphasizes the role of interaction—particularly interaction with market intermediaries—in determining the prices buyers are willing to pay and their preferences in economic decision-making more broadly.[32]

OBSERVING AGENTS AND BUYERS

Viewing and subsequently analyzing interaction requires witnessing how individuals engage with each other at specific times and in particular contexts.[33] In other words, we cannot fully understand what individuals do and why they do it without observing when, where, and how they do it.[34] Researchers can use ethnographic data—observations of a particular group, place, or process over time—to make claims about why particular outcomes happen.[35] Systematic observation of the same type of interaction with different participants will reveal patterns. With enough data, an observer can build a theory of why and how interactions produce particular outcomes.

To answer questions about consumers' preferences and decision-making in the context of purchasing homes, I observed interactions between real estate agents and prospective home buyers. Since the housing market is so central to stratification in the United States, uncovering how individuals make choices in this particular market should also reveal something about spatial inequality—why it is that some places have high and rising housing prices and some places do not. My efforts to understand agents' role in the market began in late 2011 with interviews of real estate agents in New York State and continued with ethnographic fieldwork conducted in the residential real estate market in the New York City metropolitan area. Respondents came from both my social network and a randomized list of all licensed real estate agents in the state.[36] In order to see how interactions with real estate agents affect buyers' perceptions and valuations of houses, I observed interactions between twelve real estate agents and fifty-seven buyers (twenty-eight individuals and twenty-nine couples) in New York City over the course of twenty-seven months, beginning in January 2012. These observations included agent–buyer interaction during the process of searching for a home, from the initial meetings where agents and clients discussed finances, buyer requirements, desires, and expectations; to showings where agents and buyers jointly viewed units for sale and discussed their merits; through to subsequent meetings and communications where agents and buyers thrashed out their experiences and formed plans for making offers. Of these fifty-seven potential buyers, forty-nine made offers on units during my fieldwork, ranging from $415,000 to $13,000,000. The earliest offers came only three weeks after buyers started their search, but the average length of time from visiting the first open house to making an offer was a little under two months. Throughout the sales process I asked buyers to reflect on the search and their experiences of the housing market.

I conducted additional interviews with twenty-one of the buyers who had made offers on houses. I reinterviewed almost all of these buyers four to five years after they had made an offer, since I wanted to know if their assessments of their purchases—and of the search process more generally—had changed over time. Did they think they had paid the right price? Looking back, were they satisfied with their real estate agent? I also interviewed prospective buyers who did not make offers, as well as buyers who were friends of friends or friends of other participants in the research who had bought houses without using real estate agents. I asked all buyers to share their feelings about the search process and the overall experience of purchasing ,and I asked them whether their real estate agent (if they used one) had been helpful and respectful of their preferences.

While these buyers and agents came from all over New York City, my

fieldwork concentrated on Manhattan and Brooklyn—particularly downtown Manhattan and northern and central Brooklyn. These areas are,
broadly, considered some of the most desirable parts of the city, with
accordingly very high housing prices. Race, class, and neighborhood are
highly correlated in the United States, and the buyers I observed were
mostly white (over three-quarters) and mostly well-off (only three buyers
had initially stated price ceilings below $500,000). Most of the buyers were
a lot like Ben—they were professionals, and over three-quarters of them
were first-time buyers. Of the few buyers who had school-aged children
(under 10 percent of my sample), all sent their kids to private school.[37] The
homogeneity of the buyers is likely the result of referrals.[38] As I discuss
in chapter 1, referrals are the most important way that agents find clients,
and since social networks are extremely segregated in the United States,
agents' clients tend to be demographically homogenous—especially by race
and ethnicity.[39] In addition, as I discuss in chapters 1 and 4, agents often
concentrate their work in particular neighborhoods, which further narrows
their client pools.

I also interviewed forty-five other agents working in a variety of other
locations, including other parts of New York City, wealthy areas of Long
Island, rural parts of the Hudson Valley, and neighborhoods in smaller cities
like Albany, Buffalo, and Syracuse. Of these, twenty-five were drawn ran-
domly from a list of all licensed agents in New York State, while the remaining twenty were agents working in New York City who were introduced to
me by other agents or friends/acquaintances. I asked these agents a set of
questions about their work, including how they assessed buyers, their fair
housing practices, and how recent economic and technological changes in
the housing market affected their work. Respondents described the sales
process and reported on the best ways to complete purchases. I also asked
them questions related to residential segregation and racial and ethnic steering, including why they thought segregation existed. Additionally, I asked
them questions about if and how clients changed their price preferences
during the housing search.[40]

As part of my fieldwork, I also visited eighty-seven open houses in New
York and New Jersey and attended real estate salesperson licensing classes
at three different licensing schools, where I learned what agents are taught
about valuation, the laws of agency, building trust with clients, and abiding
by fair housing laws. Appendix A provides further details on all qualitative data.

As a mixed-methods study, *Upsold* also incorporates some quantitative
analyses. I built regression models with data on the geographic distribution

of agents, house prices, and changes in house prices over time in New York State to understand how the interactions I was seeing in my ethnographic fieldwork aggregate into larger patterns of socio-spatial inequality. These models show how agents concentrate in already hot markets and drive increases in house prices in neighborhoods that are already expensive. Appendix B provides detailed information on all quantitative data and methods.

All of these sources of information ground my main arguments about the importance of interactions during the sales process and intermediaries in shaping demand preferences and determining outcomes in housing market.

WHY STUDY NEW YORK?

In 2012 the median price of a single housing unit in the United States was slightly under $200,000. In New York City as a whole it was slightly over $400,000. Although New York has a reputation for high housing prices—and astronomical prices in parts of Manhattan and Brooklyn—the median is similar to that of other coastal cities in the United States, including Boston, San Francisco, Los Angeles, and Seattle. In fact, at the time my fieldwork began, buyers faced *less* affordable housing markets in some West Coast metropolitan areas like San Francisco and San Jose.[41] In terms of affordability, the New York City housing market was comparable to that of other cities, including Los Angeles, Seattle, Boulder, and Boston.[42] As my fieldwork continued, more and more places in the United States came to mirror the New York market's level of unaffordability.[43] By 2017 New York's market was *more* affordable than markets in Miami, San Diego, Los Angeles, San Francisco, and San Jose, and only slightly less affordable than Denver, Seattle, Boston, Sacramento, and Portland, Oregon.[44] While no single housing market is representative of all housing markets, New York City's is in some ways similar to other parts of the United States that are experiencing price increases and diminishing affordability in the aftermath of the Great Recession. My goal was to see what on-the-ground processes both reflected and drove these changes.

Studying agents' effects on buyers' decisions in a relatively low-inventory and high-priced urban housing market provided other empirical and theoretical advantages. First, doing so expands empirical knowledge on the housing market since studies of housing search outcomes tend to focus on low-income individuals—often in the market for rental leases—who do not use real estate agents.[45] If we are to understand how housing searches play out, we need to examine a wider portion of the market—even the very high end—particularly since so many housing searches in the United States do involve a real estate agent.

Second, attention to high-price housing transactions should also tell us something about inequality and the geography of opportunity in cities. Cities in the contemporary United States are defined by stratification. Some neighborhoods are good places to live—they are safe, with good schools, high levels of social and political organization and efficacy, and low levels of environmental pollution. The people that live in them are relatively healthy, and children who grow up in them are more likely to attend college and earn more money than their parents when they become adults. Other neighborhoods are less safe, are more polluted, and have higher rates of poverty, a greater likelihood of encounters with the criminal justice system, and poorer outcomes in terms of health and economic mobility.[46] Housing prices are a key driver of increasing income segregation and the uneven distribution of resources across neighborhoods.[47] Indeed property taxes—assessed through home value—are an important source of funding for municipal services. Housing prices are also clearly linked to racial and ethnic residential segregation, which is increasing in cities with rapidly rising housing prices.[48]

Observing how potential home buyers come to pay the prices they do shows how it is that neighborhoods are differentiated, valorized, and deemed worthy of a certain price. Unpacking the processes that maintain spatial boundaries, spatial hierarchies, and resource differences across places is key to understanding how places are stratified.[49] While *Upsold* reveals how individuals' preferences are highly dependent on interaction, it also shows that interactions between agents and buyers produce neighborhood reputations and define places by price, with dramatic effects on the housing market overall.

WHAT FOLLOWS

Chapter 1, "Benevolence, Interest, and Establishing Authority," examines agents' work in the context of the rise of real estate websites.[50] If agents are no longer the only source of information on available units, how do they establish their occupational authority? How do buyers come to trust the decisions agents make for them? How, in short, do agents become so influential in the housing search and selection process? In this opening chapter I show that the answer lies in how agents framed their own labor to clients. Real estate agents claimed expertise by contrasting their own benevolent motives with the more suspicious or ethically problematic intentions of other agents, disparaging the information available for free on real estate websites, and deemphasizing their own economic interests. The chapter reveals how market intermediaries with already weak claims to expertise try to attract referrals and, more broadly, how agents become taste- and place-making authorities in their relationships with buyers.[51]

Chapter 2, "Romancing the Home," and chapter 3, "Malleable Prices," address questions of interaction and preference formation directly. Chapter 2 examines how market intermediaries like real estate agents cultivate certain emotional reactions in consumers, which in turn affect those consumers' decisions. Agents were generally adept at linking aspects of buyers' identities to particular neighborhoods and particular housing units. Chapter 2 reveals how agents treated buyers differently depending on buyers' class, gender, occupation, and taste preferences. This work helped to singularize the products buyers were purchasing—after all, at any given moment, urban real estate markets contain many units that are broadly similar in size, location, and price. The work agents did to link buyers to particular houses and neighborhoods created and reified place reputations, making certain neighborhoods appropriate for some kinds of residents but not others. Interactions with real estate agents also elicited emotions from buyers—feelings of confidence in their choices, excitement over particular units, or anxiety and fear of missing opportunities to make a purchase—that altered buyers' stated preferences. These observations reveal how individual preference and consumption decisions are subject to situational structuring by market intermediaries like real estate agents.

Chapter 3 extends this argument by looking at how interactional patterns between agents and buyers produced buyers' price preferences. Every single buyer in this study was upsold, meaning that they ended up offering a price above their initially stated price ceiling. But upselling played out differently for buyers at different price points. Interactions between agents and very wealthy buyers lacked overt discussions of price, while price was a common point of discussion in interactions between agents and less wealthy buyers. The result was that after interacting with agents, very wealthy buyers offered amounts far above their initially stated price ceilings, while less wealthy buyers offered amounts much closer to their stated price preferences. In other words, wealthier buyers were upsold at higher rates.

These differences reveal how the prices buyers pay are conditioned not only by their access to capital but also by their interactions with agents.

Chapter 4, "Real Estate Agents and Neighborhood Inequalities," considers how agents' work in shaping the preferences of their clients has broader consequences for the geography of opportunity in cities. I draw on observations from real estate licensing schools, interviews with agents about their fair housing practices, and statistical models to show how real estate agents contribute to neighborhood inequality. A great deal of past research has examined racial steering and agents' relationship to racial segregation in American cities. The classic *Black Metropolis* (1945) by St. Clair Drake and Horace R. Cayton, for instance, details how Chicago real estate agents engaged in "blockbusting" or "panic peddling" by steering a small number of black buyers to a predominantly white block in order to stir white residents' racial anxieties so as to heighten their desire to move. Agents could then buy white residents' properties for low prices only to sell them for higher amounts to more incoming black homeseekers.[52] At a time when federal and state laws were outlawing discrimination in the housing market, Rose Helper (1969) dedicated an entire book to revealing how agents largely believed in residential racial segregation and worked to maintain it. Decades of audit studies have revealed that agents steer nonwhite home buyers to certain neighborhoods, show them fewer homes than comparable white home buyers, and are less likely to discuss possible financing options with nonwhites.[53] In addition to describing some of the interactional mechanisms behind racial steering, Chapter 4 shows how upselling is a driving force behind increasing levels of income segregation in the metropolitan United States. Real estate agents play an integral part in producing inequality both in the US housing market and across neighborhoods more generally.

Upsold takes the work of market intermediaries seriously. It does so because market intermediaries are present in many markets. Our consumption choices are constantly being shaped by myriad actors who interpret the value of available products and services we might purchase. Sommeliers describe the flavor of wines to restaurant patrons, financial advisers recommend mutual funds and stocks to investors, and doctors list the benefits and potential side effects of different medical procedures and prescription drugs to their patients. In all of these situations, consumers' preferences are being made and remade. This book makes the case for understanding our consumer preferences as highly malleable and dependent on interaction with market intermediaries. In the housing market, this means that buyers' choices are heavily influenced by the work of real estate agents who shape what it means to live in a particular place and how much living in that place is worth. In helping define buyers' preferences, agents define neighborhoods and the price we have to pay to live in them.

1

BENEVOLENCE, INTEREST, AND ESTABLISHING AUTHORITY

Why do real estate agents still exist?
LYDIA DEPILLIS, *WASHINGTON POST*

A computer pricing algorithm does not know if those countertops were put in correctly, or what lies beneath those new floorboards, or if that third bedroom used to be a garage. It most likely doesn't know the motivations of the previous owner, upcoming development changes that may affect property values, and it certainly cannot negotiate.
BRET CALLTHARP, INMAN.COM

Americans consistently use real estate agents to purchase property, but they don't trust them. At no point since 1977, when Gallup began measuring public opinion on the subject, have more than 20 percent of Americans rated the honesty and ethical standards of real estate agents as "high" or "very high."[1] While they generally enjoy more goodwill and trust than car and insurance salespeople, telemarketers, and members of Congress, real estate agents are less trusted by Americans than nurses, bankers, pharmacists, and journalists among many other occupations and professions.[2]

Home buyers are not necessarily wrong to question their agents' trustworthiness.[3] During my research, I came across news stories about agents accused of racial steering, creating Ponzi lending schemes, illegally raising commissions, misleading buyers about prices, using listed houses to film sexual encounters, lying about the square footage of a listing, and even laundering money for a drug cartel.[4] Perhaps home buyers are right to be suspicious of agents. So what do agents do to assure their clients that they are worth their commission? How do agents manage their relationships with clients and guard against their occupation's negative reputation? How have real estate agents become so influential in buyers' housing decisions given that the public does not trust them?

These were some of the questions I had in mind as I began to meet with and observe real estate agents in 2011 and 2012. Over time I noticed patterns in how agents attempted to shake the stigma associated with their occupation. Individual agents contrasted their own benevolent behavior to vague descriptions of other agents. These other agents served as placeholder projections for the bad and nefarious activities often ascribed to the occupation more generally. Agents also justified their role in the housing market by disparaging online and free sources of information as unreliable or untrue. Real estate websites, agents claimed, do not accurately reflect the market because no one at the website is taking the time to walk around particular neighborhoods and experience them firsthand.

Throughout their interactions with buyers, agents consistently sought to shift focus away from their own interests in housing sales. Clients are obviously aware that real estate agents make money off a completed transaction—agents don't work for free—and yet agents tried very hard to avoid talking about their commissions. Instead they spoke about the benefits of their work to their clients and to local communities and neighborhoods. They did so in part because experts or professionals in a given market are *supposed* to be economically disinterested problem solvers.[5] Yet the process of becoming a real estate agent does not much resemble that of becoming, say, a doctor or a lawyer. The requirements to become a licensed real estate salesperson (agent) vary from state to state but are, in general, far from onerous. All states establish a minimum age (eighteen in most states, but occasionally nineteen or twenty-one), and most require a high school diploma or GED. All require some in-person classroom instruction, but the levels vary between 40 and 180 hours. Some states do not grant licenses to individuals who have been convicted of a felony. The rules governing appropriate behavior of real estate agents are also quite variable across states.[6] Real estate agents, in other words, occupy an ambiguous occupational position in which the barriers to entry are low and their responsibilities are unclear. In this context, agents often felt the need to deemphasize their own economic interests in order to seem professional and trustworthy.

In doing so they established themselves as friendly and knowledgeable confidants who were serving buyers' interests. As we shall see, this relationship allowed them to more easily shape buyers' preferences as the search progressed.

A SHORT HISTORY OF REAL ESTATE AGENTS

While there have always been individuals who brokered the sale of land, real estate agents are a product of mass urbanization in the United States. The outlines of the occupation as we know it today—maintaining knowledge about multiple units for sale in a given area, a standardized commission fee, and government licensure—began to form in the late 1800s. Owing in part to their reputation as swindlers and crooks, groups of land brokers formed local real estate boards as a means of reframing their occupation as an honorable one, as well as a way to share information about listings.[7]

For most of the twentieth century, real estate agents kept close guard over their knowledge of inventory. Local boards created multiple listing systems (MLS) to address the problem of information in the housing market. No one agent could possibly know every house for sale in a given neighborhood, let alone in an entire city or county, so boards established mechanisms for their members to share information on their properties. Members paid an extra fee beyond their annual membership dues to submit and view properties on the MLS, and agents established conventions for sharing commissions on cross-listed properties.[8] The existence of local MLS meant that while home buyers and sellers did not *have* to use real estate agents, there was a clear advantage to doing so. The MLS, in other words, established a fundamental asymmetry in who had access to information about the housing market.

In 1908 a national board (the National Association of Real Estate Boards, which would later become the National Association of Realtors) was formed to further professionalization.[9] In 1916 the national board adopted the term *Realtor* to distinguish between members and nonmembers. The board also recognized the need to change Americans' attitudes toward housing. Before 1920 the vast majority of urban residents did not own property. Local boards marketed homeownership as a public as well as personal good and partnered with developers and builders to advocate for policies that would expand the real estate market. By the 1920s the national board was highly active in promoting homeownership across the nation.[10] Today the National Association of Realtors is a massive and highly active professional group with a large lobbying budget and a host of resources for members.[11]

Professional bodies also created rules that shaped real estate transactions in ways familiar to today's homeseeker.[12] As a result of the boards' efforts, the lease between a renter and landlord morphed from a simple

agreement between individuals to a complex legal document, eviction procedures became codified into law, local governments began to keep records
on land sales, states instituted licensing exams, and listing agents and buyers' agents agreed to split commissions on sales evenly. For home buyers in
particular, these changes complicated the housing market. Residential real
estate transactions necessarily entail some legal paperwork. At minimum,
the sale of a property requires the seller to transfer their deed—the legal
document that affirms the owner's right to use the land and the built structure on it—to buyers for some agreed-upon sum of money. However, as almost anyone who has ever bought or sold a house can attest, contemporary
residential real estate transactions involve plenty of other people. The other
parties may include mortgage brokers, real estate attorneys, appraisers,
inspectors, co-op boards, neighborhood councils, and insurance agents.
One of the benefits of hiring real estate agents is that they provide buyers
with connections to many of the other individuals necessary to complete
the transaction—transactions that have become more complicated in part
because of the lobbying of the real estate industry. Indeed real estate agents
often "come with" mortgage brokers, lawyers, and appraisers.

By the 1950s, real estate agents had become an institutionalized part of
the housing market, participating in the majority of land sales in the United
States. Agents' state-regulated licenses gave them a veneer of professionalism, and their connection to mortgage lenders allowed the buyers they
represented to access federally backed bank loans. Agents' mobilization
through professional organizations also changed housing policy, encouraging federal subsidies for more home construction, suburbanization, and
the creation of the secondary mortgage market.[13] At the same time, Americans' ideas about homeownership changed dramatically: the vast majority
of Americans now aspired to own their own homes, and they were willing
to take on massive amounts of debt to attain that goal.

"THAT'S NOT LIKE ME"

Despite a century's worth of success in integrating themselves into the process of buying and selling houses, today's real estate agents still feel the need
to establish their authority and prove their worth. In early meetings with
potential clients, agents often explained how their approach to their work
differed from mainstream conceptions of the occupation as well as that of
other agents. In both my interviews with agents and their interactions with
buyers, "I'm not like other agents" was a common refrain.

Agents so highly value the act of distinguishing themselves from their peers that instructors in real estate licensing classes made references to it throughout the curriculum. At a real estate licensing class titled "Construction Basics," ostensibly about building codes and plumbing, electrical, and heating systems, the instructor told an anecdote about how she once inquired about an apartment building's electrical wiring on behalf of a buyer she represented. She then spoke about how agents need to make similar efforts to build a personal brand and establish a good reputation:

> What you want to do is make yourself unique. So tell your clients what you can do for them that other agents can't or won't. You'll want to tell them how you're special and why you're the best agent around. That's the first thing you should be communicating when you meet with them.

The same instructor, in a class on the different types of multiunit buildings (condo versus co-op), said, "You've got to have your own type in this business, your own personality, and clients can remember who you are, how you do your work." She became more animated, raising her arms and pointing at the class as she said, "Be service oriented! That's how I've been in this business for twenty-five years!" In many licensing classes—regardless of the topic of the particular session—instructors stressed the need for clients to like and appreciate their agents.

In interviews, agents made similar points. One agent, who worked in Manhattan and Brooklyn and had a degree in economics from an Ivy League school, said he often cited his pedigree and work ethic when talking to potential clients:

> I always tell buyers that most agents are bad at their jobs. They're lazy and usually pretty stupid. And I'll say I chose to be an agent when I could have had a Wall Street job. I do it subtly, but I want them to know how hard I work at this, not like a lot of other people, even the other agents at [my firm].

An agent in Buffalo said that she put a lot of effort into establishing herself as hardworking, telling buyers, "This isn't a part-time job for me, I'm not a housewife who does this on the side." Agents broadly affirmed their personal rigor and commitment to their occupation in early meetings with buyers, and they belittled other agents in order to create contrast. This helped individual agents establish a sense of their own honesty and availability in their relationships with buyers.

The first time real estate agent Miguel met Josh, who was looking to buy an apartment in central Brooklyn, the two rushed through the viewing of an apartment for sale. Miguel then invited Josh to lunch. They chatted about Josh's current apartment (a rental in Williamsburg), and Miguel began to talk about his passion for his work. He said he thought most real estate agents did the job because they didn't know what else to do. Miguel, however, had wanted to be a real estate agent since he was in college. "I love helping people find homes," he said, "and I love helping people figure out what their best future living situation will be." He talked about his love for the city and Brooklyn in particular as Josh peppered him with questions about the market. Miguel said that, unlike other agents, he would be in constant contact with Josh throughout the process: "I know a lot of [agents] who sort of shut off after like 6 p.m. That's not me." Miguel told Josh that good agents, like himself, actually slept very little and were always tied to their phones in order to have the most current market information. When they parted, Miguel said he would send Josh some new listings to visit in the coming week. He added that Josh should feel free to call, email, or text him at any time.

These expressions of availability and passion were extremely common in early meetings with clients and throughout the search process. In email correspondence, agents sometimes apologized for delayed responses even though their replies were sent the same day—typically just hours after receiving a message.

At least with Josh, Miguel's declarations of high energy and strong work ethic were convincing. After Josh had purchased an apartment, he explained why he was happy with the process. He told me, "The main thing is that [Miguel] did not disappoint. I'm a very anxious person, or at least I can be, and I don't think he minded my constant text messages." Nor was Josh unique in this sentiment: buyers often cited this kind of attentiveness as a reason they liked or were satisfied with their agents.

In addition to describing themselves as devoted to their clients, agents denigrated the work ethic of other agents. Nancy, a real estate agent working in Manhattan, actively disparaged other agents while showing a listing to prospective buyers Adam and Eli. The three were viewing a one-bedroom apartment and discussing the hardwood floor, which looked worn. Nancy said, "Other agents will tell you [that] you have to settle for this," as she tapped her toe on the floor. "Like they'll just say anything to close, but I know we can do better." To another client she made a similar comment about the location of an apartment they had just viewed. She told the buyer that other agents would try to convince him that the neighborhood they were in was the best location for his price point, but she was not going to let him settle.

Nancy worked hard, and she wanted her clients to know it. At another open house with Adam and Eli, Nancy emphasized the amount of effort she was putting into their search. The open house had been announced just the day before—a Saturday—and when Eli thanked Nancy for bringing it to their attention she smiled, batted her eyes and, feigning embarrassment, said, "You know me, always working the most." Adam and Eli said they would consider making a bid on that apartment, but it sold to another buyer three days later. "They're disappointed," Nancy told me after talking to them, "but there might be something else in the building." Nancy began looking for other apartments to view in the next few weeks, but she also wrote a letter to every current resident in the building where Adam and Eli had considered making an offer. The letter informed residents that her clients wanted to buy an apartment in the building, and that they were preapproved for a mortgage so the transaction should not be difficult. The letter included some personal details about both Eli and Adam—their jobs and how long they had been a couple—as well as background on Nancy's experience as an agent. Close to a month later, after Nancy and Adam and Eli had viewed half a dozen other apartments, Nancy received a call from an agent representing a potential seller in the building where she had sent the letters. After viewing the apartment with Nancy, the couple decided to make an offer on it.

After he and Eli had made an offer, Adam told me that he thought Nancy had been a good agent. "I remember dealing with agents when I was renting and they fucking sucked. Nancy wasn't like that." Unlike other agents, Adam said, Nancy had been responsive and had made a demonstrable effort during the search. According to him, she had "always been super communicative." He reiterated these sentiments five years after the purchase. He said that he and Eli loved Nancy, retold the story of Nancy sending the letters, and described her as "extremely hardworking."

In interviews, agents complained about the particularly bad reputation of their occupation, which they sometimes attributed to bad press. One agent working in Brooklyn said, "You never see a story about good agents just doing their jobs. It's always, look at this agent who committed mortgage fraud, or look at this agent who's telling black people they can only live here or there. I think it's unfair." Another agent working in Syracuse complained of years-long local news coverage of a real estate agent who had set up a front company to accept mortgage payments from vulnerable buyers she represented during the search process.[14] "This woman," she said, "is sucking up all this attention, and it's harder to get clients. A few referrals have talked about [the news story], and who knows about many people have decided we're all bad because of it." Whether or not bad publicity prevented prospective clients from employing real estate agents, agents were broadly concerned with how they were represented in the media and popular culture. Yet in trying to bolster their reputations and dispel notions of agents as greedy or untrustworthy, agents somewhat counterintuitively provided their clients with real evidence of *other* agents' unethical or illegal behavior.

In the competitive world of New York City real estate, agents value their relationships with clients (and potential clients) over their occupation's reputation more broadly. One agent working in Manhattan reported always telling new clients about his old brokerage firm in order to praise his current one:

> [The old firm] was a place where agents would make fun of buyers especially if they weren't that rich. They made racist jokes and talked about parts of the city in this really gross way. They just didn't care about clients like we do here. They didn't even really like their clients.

He went on to describe his current firm's professional workplace atmosphere as well as its concierge service, which any listing or buying client—regardless of their price point—could call at any time to get tickets to events or reservations at popular restaurants. Multiple brokerage firms in New York City provided similar perks, either staffing them in-house or contracting them out to private concierge services. Agents would remind new clients of the concierge services in early interactions and often mentioned their brokerage firm's name when doing so—for example, "Here at [my brokerage firm] we have this great service . . ." When I asked why he would talk up the benefits of his new firm by disparaging his old one, this agent told me: "I tell my new clients about [the old firm] because I want them to know we're not shitty people here."

Some more experienced agents said it hadn't always been this way. One agent who had been working in Westchester County for over twenty years noted that concierge services and this kind of competitive behavior with clients were not always part of the job. She attributed the shift to more client awareness and knowledge of the sales process:

> I think something happened in the last ten years where everyone started talking about being the best, being better than other agents. It's got to be

because buyers now have all the tools to do this on their own, so we all started flexing our muscles and preening so they would still think they needed us. And now everyone is backbiting.

The "backbiting" is real. In drawing contrasts with others, real estate agents drew on available narratives regarding the negative behavior of brokers. These included stereotypes of agents as lazy, uncaring, and racist, or as dishonest.

Don, a real estate agent working in Brooklyn, was with clients at an open house. The listing agent had not followed Don and his clients through the house; she looked at her phone while Don and his clients asked her questions. As they stepped outside and waited for an Uber to take them to another open house, one of Don's clients commented on the listing agent's apparent disinterest. Don furrowed his brow and said,

> You know what, there are a lot of [agents], when they list a house, they don't think they have to do any work. And it's also the same people who lie about counteroffers and try to get you to get your bid up. It's the kind of business where people think they can act like that.

Despite the fact that they knew the public held them in low regard, and despite their complaints about how they were portrayed in media, agents themselves perpetuated the kinds of negative stereotypes associated with their occupation. Comparing themselves favorably to bad agents may have served to foster connection with a particular buyer, but it simultaneously reproduced the negative stereotypes that most agents found frustrating.

REAL ESTATE WEBSITES

While contrasting themselves with other real estate agents helped individual agents rhetorically frame themselves as trustworthy, it did not necessarily overcome the problem presented by online competition. Agents no longer hold a monopoly on housing inventory information. Craigslist.com has become the dominant medium for information on available rental listings in the United States, but multiple websites provide information on available units for purchase.[15] The most popular of these are Realtor.com, Zillow.com, and Trulia.com (purchased by Zillow in 2014). These sites attempt to provide blanket coverage of the United States, though in practice the breadth of their information and accuracy likely varies by location. Others with less traffic or covering more limited geographies include PropertyShark.com, Redfin.com, and Streeteasy.com. Many other websites display listing information for one major metropolitan area.

These websites began to appear in the late 1990s and early 2000s with the explicit goal of making it easier to search for and list a housing unit. These websites gather data directly from brokerages as well as from municipal agencies and private firms about recent housing transactions. Most of the interfaces allow anyone to search by geographic area (city, zip code, neighborhood, scaled map) for houses recently sold or currently on the market; listings typically include information on unit price, square footage, and year built. Some use algorithms to produce estimated prices for units not currently on the market—Zillow has trademarked the name "zestimate" for its estimated prices.[16]

While some major metropolitan areas, like New York City, never had just one MLS, it is fair to say that the availability of *free* information on websites like Zillow and Trulia has challenged real estate agents' authority over housing information. The 2017 American Housing Survey, a biennial survey conducted by the US Census, showed that for the first time, people living in urban areas in the United States cited the internet as the most important source of information for their housing search. This is a major shift for both buyers and sellers in the housing market. One buyer who did not use a real estate agent for his most recent purchase put it succinctly: "There's absolutely no reason you need a real estate agent to buy a house when all they're supposed to do is search for you. Maybe twenty years ago when there was no Zillow you needed one, but not anymore." Agents were acutely aware of how much information buyers could access on their own—most of the buyers I interviewed who used agents reported looking at listings online during their search, and all said they had perused listings online before they had contacted their agent. Some reported that they continued to look at listings online regularly even after their purchase had been completed. And while agents sometimes expressed ambivalence about whether housing websites made their work easier or more difficult, they generally agreed that they needed to justify their worth to potential clients in light of the information available online.

Websites and Prices

Agents often justified their role quite overtly. In interviews and in early meetings with clients, agents would disparage real estate websites, usually critiquing them for inaccurate information that could harm clients' chances of buying or selling houses at the best price. One agent working in New York City said, "I tell my clients to be really suspicious of the prices listed on Zillow. If there's just one wrong number, the algorithm is off and the prices for a neighborhood are going to be off." Another agent working in the Hudson Valley said, "I think [real estate websites] have gotten a lot better, but there's still a huge accuracy problem." Another said:

> Zillow knows it's wrong and they report their average errors every year, but obviously not very prominently on the site. The problem, I think, is that clients trust the first number they hear and so when an agent comes in and tells them something different from Zillow, it's really hard to say, "No, the website is wrong and this person—you know, a human being—is right." There's something about the website that makes it seem even more official.[17]

In his first meeting with buyers Chelsea and Jordan, Luis, an agent working in Manhattan and Brooklyn, was defensive about how he had honed his sense of prices. When Chelsea mentioned that she and Jordan had perused Zillow and Trulia before meeting with him, Luis said, "Oh, that's fine to look at pictures, but don't trust the prices. I've been in this business a while, so talk to me for prices and comps." ("Comps" refers to "comparable properties.") Similarly, when Andrew, a buyer in his late twenties, first met with real estate agent Thomas, he had brought along a list of places for sale he had found online. When Andrew tried to hand Thomas the printed pages, Thomas waved him off, saying, "This is a full-time job for me, and so I know what the comps are like. We're going to have a much easier time getting a good deal because I've already done all the searching there is to do." Agents generally tried to establish their authority in early meetings, and one way they did this was by claiming that information available to clients via other media—particularly websites—was simply wrong.

Buyers sometimes reported similar reasons for why they thought agents were useful. A recently divorced wealthy woman who was looking for a new apartment admitted that she had the time to do a lot of searching on her own, but she doubted the accuracy of free information. She said, "If I had to do this on my own I probably could, but I just find it hard to believe all those prices [online] are right."

Agents told their clients cautionary tales about the dangers of relying on housing websites, and clients tended to believe them. In their initial meeting, Lucy, an agent working in Brooklyn, and John and Steven, a couple looking to buy a house, discussed, among other things, real estate websites.

Lucy told them about a seller represented by another agent at her brokerage firm who, despite the agent's pleas, had refused to reduce the listed price of his house for a year because he believed in the estimate provided by Zillow. Months later, when I interviewed John after he and Steven had made an offer on a house, he recalled Lucy's story about the intransigent seller who believed Zillow over the real estate agent. John said that he was initially skeptical of the need for a real estate agent, but Lucy's claim that real estate websites' pricing could be wrong had helped convince him that using an agent was the right thing to do:

> I was getting ready to do this by ourselves and we started pricing things on-line, not in an organized way but just looking. And our friends kept saying we should use an agent. But I was torn. I felt like I could do it, but I kept hearing these horror stories about the prices being wrong online. After we saw how great [Lucy] was and hearing more about how Zillow is sometimes fucked up, I'm glad we had her. She was so helpful.

While both real estate agents and buyers frequently mentioned the inaccuracy of real estate websites as a reason to use an intermediary, buyers likely sought out agents for multiple reasons. The high amount of uncertainty in the purchase of a house—compared to more rote, repeated, and familiar types of transactions—leads buyers to rely on real estate agents despite agents' decreasing monopoly on listing information.[18] Buyers also seek to make the search and purchasing process more familiar by finding their agents through their existing social networks or by purchasing directly from family members when possible.[19]

While the buyers who did not use real estate agents cited the availability of online listing information as a major factor in their decision not to use agents, they exhibited some key differences from buyers who did use agents. Independent buyers tended to have prior experience purchasing a home or had flexible work schedules that allowed them to commit time to the search. For example, one buyer—an early employee of what was now a large publicly traded technology company—had not used an agent. When asked why, he simply said, "Why would I use a real estate agent? They don't do anything." He had left his work a year before starting his search for a house, and while he consulted occasionally for his previous employer, he had no full-time job. In other words, buyers with little time or experience in the housing market might be more inclined to use agents.

Nevertheless, agents' own work in translating the value of their labor to potential clients should not be discounted. For buyers like John, who reported initially feeling dubious of the work real estate agents did on their behalf, agents' rhetoric about websites was convincing.[20]

Websites versus Lived Experience

While agents professed to be more knowledgeable about local prices than real estate websites were, they also attempted to establish authority by demonstrating their local knowledge about neighborhoods. Agents framed their labor as beneficial to buyers because, unlike websites, agents could talk about what it feels like to live in a certain place. They could provide more in-depth knowledge about local amenities. One agent working in Brooklyn emphasized her ability to explain the meaning of different places to potential buyers:

> What you get from me that you won't on the web is, I can paint a portrait of what it's like to actually live somewhere. I can tell you about what bakeries are good, even how many bakeries there are in Greenpoint [a neighborhood in north Brooklyn]. Or, like, what it's like to walk to the train during a hurricane, because I've done it and I've been doing it for years now.

Another agent working in Manhattan similarly argued that her knowledge of the different place reputations of various neighborhoods, and her ability to discern and communicate these symbolic boundaries to clients, represented the value of her labor. Referencing two different Manhattan neighborhoods, she said, "Living in the Upper East Side means something different than living in Murray Hill, and I think the whole point [of being a real estate agent] is to help buyers understand the difference. You can't get that sense just being online." Another, who worked in a commuter suburb north of New York City, spoke about her local knowledge on an even smaller scale. When asked about real estate websites, she said that there were no sources of information online that could tell her buyers "which neighbors are OK and which ones are trash." She added, "I live here so I know." Another real estate agent told a buyer that he had "walked into 80 percent of the buildings in New York City" and that his time spent in the market was an asset no real estate website could match.

By the time they begin the search process, homeseekers usually have some idea of where, in general, they want to live. The confluence of agent and buyer knowledge about a narrowed set of neighborhoods provided opportunities for agents to demonstrate their expertise in ways that resonated with homeseekers' existing understandings of neighborhoods.[21] It also allowed agents to contrast themselves with real estate websites, which lack the ability to engage clients in the same way. Agents stressed their local knowledge even if the buyers had outlined a limited set of places they wanted to look for a house and even when the buyers currently lived in the neighborhood where they said they wanted to purchase.

This intersection of buyers' and agents' circumscribed knowledge about different places provided another opportunity for real estate agents to establish themselves as authentic, value-added experts. For example, in her first meeting with Claude and Janet, a couple looking to buy close to their current rental in Williamsburg, Liz emphasized her understanding of the neighborhood: "I love Williamsburg, and the changes in the last ten years are really amazing just in terms of what's around." She began to list various amenities, including new gyms and restaurants. Claude interjected, "The Wythe," referring to an upscale hotel that had recently opened. "Yes, The Wythe is a really good example, and I know all the shops that are popping up around it." She added, in a jokingly emphatic tone, "Zillow can't tell you that!" At one showing Liz asked the couple if they had been to a particular restaurant around the corner from the apartment they were viewing. Later at another, she asked if Claude and Janet had "seen that new men's shop on Seventh [Street]." These expressions of local knowledge established Liz as an authority on the neighborhood. After the couple made an offer on an apartment in a new development close to the waterfront in Williamsburg, I spoke to Janet about the experience of searching for a property. She mentioned Liz's demonstrated understanding of the neighborhood as a reason she and Claude thought Liz had done a good job, saying, "[Liz] really knows the vibe here." She added that the experience had been "a lot more personal" than if they had searched online.

Are Websites All Bad?

Agents did not uniformly reject real estate websites as completely useless or frame them as direct competition. Most agents praised them for, most obviously, making their own work easier. Some real estate websites provide the contact information for the listing agent of properties that are currently for sale, relieving listing agents of some of the burden of having to advertise their units and themselves. Others provided, for a subscription fee, personalized analytics about agents' job performance and advertising effectiveness.

Agents who had been working since before the rise of housing websites reported that listing websites save time by consolidating information. One agent who had worked for forty years on Long Island said that despite the efficiency of the old MLS systems, new websites with better user interfaces "centralize everything in a way that makes it easy for me to plug in a few things like price and square feet and basically get all the info plus their open house times." An instructor at a Manhattan real estate licensing school who appeared to be in his seventies told a class:

> When I started you really had to get out there and look for listings. I remember knocking on doors and trying to get friendly with doormen in big buildings so I would know who's moving out. Now, you'll see, your broker will just have you clicking all day in front of a screen.

Most agents reported spending several hours a day looking at listings online. Those who worked for larger brokerage firms reported receiving formalized instruction on how to use and interpret information presented on real estate websites and how to compare it to their firms' proprietary listing information services.

Aside from the obvious ways that easy access to information aided agents, some agents claimed that the proliferation of real estate websites also makes for better clients, especially better buyers. Thomas explained to me how the appearance of Streeteasy.com, a real estate website for listings in New York City (now owned by Zillow), changed his business model. He noticed that his listings business dipped when Streeteasy.com began providing more and more available listings online, as more landlords and sellers felt confident in pricing and advertising their rentals and homes on their own. In response, he decided to become an agent representing only buyers and joined a buyers-only brokerage. "People thought I was crazy," he said. "They asked, 'How are you going to make money without listings? You're never going to get paid.'" He was convinced, though, that the transition made sense because buyers would always want to use an agent; he was not dissuaded by the internet's history of supplanting other intermediaries like travel agents. "There's a big difference between a five-hundred-dollar plane ticket and a million-dollar home. With million-dollar homes, [buyers] will want a seasoned professional." Thomas continued to explain that real estate websites make for more "educated" buyers, which is a boon for business:

> [Buyers] come to us and they have a pretty good idea of the marketplace and a pretty good understanding of what they want. . . . We get a consumer that

understands somewhat the mechanics. We have to know what they're looking for in order to be able to provide it for them.

He was not overly concerned that buyers' improved understanding of the process might obviate the need for agents:

> They still need someone to tell them if [their goals] are realistic and guide them through the process and the nuance. . . . The real estate market is built on relationships, and if you're a buyer and you don't have a relationship with anybody you may make the wrong calls. Agents, when they deal with one another, understand each other's character over time. The web has just created more transparency and made it more real time.

While many agents agreed that real estate websites did indeed facilitate their work by making clients more informed about the available housing stock and the outlines of the local housing market, few were as optimistic as Thomas. Agents broadly appreciated some aspects of real estate websites, but most regarded them as an underlying threat that required them to assert the value of their labor to potential clients.

DEEMPHASIZING ECONOMIC INTERESTS

Agents' ability to turn individual transactions into an ongoing livelihood depends on building relationships with buyers, sellers, and other agents. To that end, in interactions with their clients the real estate agents in this study consistently sought to frame their labor as economically disinterested. By this I mean that agents avoided talking about their fees, did not dwell on the ways they made money or how much they made, and occasionally even obscured their own economic interest in closing deals.

Past research on other kinds of economic transactions has provided numerous explanations for why actors in given markets might want to shift attention away from their own pecuniary benefit.[22] In particular, studies of what might be called morally problematic or taboo markets, like markets for sex, human tissue, or secondary life insurance for terminally ill people, show that actors engage in a great deal of rhetorical reframing of their actions as they try to highlight the good and benevolent aspects of their products.[23] But in the United States, where property has always been a commodity, the housing market would seem to be different. Real property ownership has existed for centuries, and homeownership is widely understood as a defining element of citizenship and status attainment.[24] On the face of it, there would seem to be no need to obfuscate anything about the financial aspects of housing transactions, since housing is neither a new nor a taboo commodity.[25]

If the product and market are widely accepted and understood, agents' tendency to downplay their own interests might be read as an attempt at professionalism. Agents deemphasized their economic interests not because they thought they could fool their clients into thinking agents were completely benevolent, but instead because doing so bolstered their claims to professionalism and honesty.

Gift Giving

Agents demonstrated their attention and dedication to their clients by organizing events for them and giving them gifts. One agent periodically invited his recent clients for cocktails at a restaurant he rented out. He said he did it as "just a little thank you" to his clients and an opportunity for all of them to "schmooze." Another agent similarly organized lunches and cocktail gatherings for his recent clients, complete with musical entertainment. Kim, who worked mostly in the West Village neighborhood in Manhattan, would offer to take her clients out to an expensive popular restaurant on the anniversary of their closing date.[26] In addition to invitations to dinners and events, agents also regularly sent clients, and even individuals who had referred clients, gifts. Gift giving was extremely common and generally occurred both when a client closed and during the winter holidays. For example, multiple agents sent their clients Kiehl's giftboxes filled with various upscale skin products that varied depending on the recipient's gender.

Don, who worked in Brooklyn, sent all of his clients who still had Brooklyn addresses gift baskets from Sahadi's, a well-known local specialty foods store. Other agents gave their clients expensive linens, gift cards to department or electronics stores, bottles of wine or liquor, high-end candles, and upscale baked goods. A *New York Times* story reported agents giving closing gifts as varied as personalized bobbleheads, a hand-crafted dollhouse that cost over $2,000, artwork, and even a pet dog.[27] While the high price tag of some of these gifts may be unique to New York City, agents from across the state reported that gift giving or simply sending notes during the holidays was routine practice.

These gifts and events served multiple purposes. Agents framed these acts as personal touches that helped demonstrate the value of their labor.

As Johnny, who one year gave his clients gift certificates to the department store Barney's for the holidays, said:

> Part of being a good agent is really showing that you care and you're thinking about clients. Remind them how hard you work. I actually think most agents do care, but you've got to show it with gifts and cards. I would tell any new young agent to show your clients gratitude because they didn't have to use you in the first place.

Aside from reminding clients of agent labor and attention, these gifts also embedded clients in webs of obligation. In his study of Canadian real estate agents in the 1970s, the sociologist J. D. House (1977:51) described the need for agents to periodically reactivate their relationships with clients in order to "maintain an imbalance of obligations in the relationship so that the client is continually in his debt."[28] The goal of gift giving was to ensure that former clients would use the same agent again if and when they moved, as well as to generate referrals. As an instructor at a Manhattan real estate licensing school once told the class, "This is a referral-based business so don't screw up your reputation." In every interview, agents who reported regularly giving gifts to current and former clients said they did so because it presumably made clients more likely to refer others in the future.[29]

At times these webs of trust and obligation went beyond recognized business practices, such as gift giving, to more substantive social relationships. One agent working in the Hudson Valley said that she regularly saw multiple former clients, and they had developed "real friendships." One agent working in Manhattan said that his "best friend" was a buyer he had represented. And one agent working in a college town said that she had been trying to find a couple a house for over year; in the meantime, the agent and her husband now regularly had dinner with the buyers. Although she admitted she did not think that by now the couple was still interested in buying a house, she said, laughing, "I have so much time involved with [them], damn it, they're buying a house. I'm not giving up!" A 2019 *New York Times* article reported on agents and their clients entering romantic partnerships, perhaps a natural extension of the agent–buyer relationship since it allows for the sharing of intimate details about finances, taste preferences, and current romantic entanglements.[30] These social relations were, however, not the norm. Most agents did not report developing friendships with clients but instead attempting to remain friendly and helpful.[31]

Agents invoked these referrals and personal relationships as reasons for not requiring buyers to sign exclusive buyer–agency agreements. While almost all agents reported having sellers sign a listing agreement—which gives an agent exclusive rights to represent the seller—not requiring a similar contract with buyers points to a more general sense of trust that agents extended to buyers. Agents considered buyers who contacted them and began to rely on them for listings but then did not use them for the purchase disreputable, but as one agent said, "I think it happens so rarely that no one really cares." Indeed agents reported that this was extremely uncommon, so they generally felt comfortable not requiring any written contracts at the outset of working with buyers.[32] As one agent working in Manhattan said, "Every buyer I've ever had as a client has come through a referral of someone I represented before, so I'm not worried about them screwing me." Agents generally assumed that buyers who had contacted them through referrals were not going to rely on agents to discover listings and then not use them to actually purchase a unit. These clients might need some convincing about the worth of real estate agent labor, but the agents were confident that if these buyers worked with an agent, they would be loyal. Kim, the agent who invited her clients to dinner on the anniversaries of their closings, said that she gave gifts because it made her feel like a "good person" and that "putting out that kind of good karma will mean I'll get good referrals down the line." Gift giving and other social activities with former clients, then, not only distinguished agents' work from that of real estate websites but also ensured the trustworthiness of new buyers who came from referrals.

Inviting past clients to dinners and sending them ecards and physical holiday cards also provided agents with opportunities to reactivate their relationships. Periodic emails with information on new listings and market information performed a similar function. Some who worked at large brokerage firms would send their firms' quarterly or annual reports—which usually resembled glossy magazines—along with handwritten notes. Agents also used social media to keep in constant, if relatively uninvolved, contact with clients. Agents would like and comment on multiple posts by clients on Facebook and Instagram around the anniversaries of their closings.[33]

Some more experienced agents noted that the amount of attention that brokerage firms and agents were giving to clients—particularly in the form of concierge services and elaborate gifts—had increased in response to the rise of real estate websites. One agent, who had been working in Manhattan for close to twenty years, reported, "There's been a big move toward service, and I think that makes sense. All these websites do the other parts of the job anyway." Agents reengaged clients and demonstrated their continued usefulness by recommending contractors, plumbers, electricians, HVAC services, and interior designers to buyers who had recently purchased a house. In addition to concierge services, some of the brokerage firms of agents I observed or interviewed provided in-house lists of recommended vendors for services ranging from architects to accountants, bridge loans for clients transitioning between homes and in need of cash before closing dates, and event planning. An agent whose boutique brokerage firm offered the latter said, "We think that after you buy a house you should have a party in it, and we can do that for you."

People and Places over Profit

In interviews with me—as opposed to in discussions with their clients—agents readily acknowledged that the type of sociability they fostered with their clients was meant to increase the chances that these clients would refer other clients in the future. Agents described building their business as a series of successful service interactions with buyers and sellers, leading to more referrals, with the network of people ever expanding. This focus on ensuring good service manifested in the ways described above, including gift giving. And yet, particularly in the case of gifts, agents rarely mentioned the prospect of clients providing referrals in the future. When agents and clients talked about the gifts given and social events organized by agents, agents would speak about them as simply benevolent acts of someone more akin to a friend than a service worker.

Luis, for example, sent out annual holiday-themed cards and various gifts with photos of himself in or near iconic New York City places, like the Chrysler building and the High Line, to all the clients in his contact list. Right before the holidays he had taken Eddy and Anna, a couple looking to buy in Brooklyn, to view two houses. After the New Year, Luis set up more showings. On a relatively warm Sunday in January the three were viewing a one-bedroom apartment in a new development and discussing the neighborhood when Anna said to Luis, "Oh, I wanted to thank you for the card; it was so cute." Luis laughed and said, "Thanks! It's something I like to do for my friends every year." At the time when the cards had been mailed, Luis had only met Eddy and Anna once, and only in the context of showing them apartments. Yet, given the opportunity, Luis referred to them as friends.

Similarly, when Ben closed on an apartment in the Lower East Side of Manhattan, his agent Liz gave him a bottle of scotch that cost over $100. (At an earlier showing Ben had mentioned that he liked scotch.) Ben thanked

BENEVOLENCE, INTEREST, AND ESTABLISHING AUTHORITY 37

her effusively and they hugged. Liz then remarked, "I like to give presents to everyone, but you get a special gift." A few months before, a couple represented by Liz had closed on an apartment after a relatively drawn-out negotiation with the seller that Liz had described as "arduous." At the closing Liz gave the couple a large crystal bowl, saying, "You two have earned a special gift." In fact, all of the clients that closed with Liz during my fieldwork received personalized gifts at the end of their search process.

Buyers would occasionally reference these gifts when explaining their satisfaction with agents. The husband from the couple who had received the crystal bowl, for instance, said of Liz, "She really took care of us and even gave us presents she really didn't have to. That bowl is really beautiful. We just have to find a place to put it. I would say she went above and beyond." Almost four years later, the buyer still had positive things to say about Liz and mentioned that he and his wife had received other small gifts from her, usually around the holiday season. Agents intended this gift giving to increase the possibility of receiving referrals in the future, but in interactions with buyers would frame them as simply thoughtful offerings from a friend.

Beyond framing their gift giving as benevolent, agents deemphasized their own economic interests by simply avoiding talking about commissions.[34] Listing agents and buyer's agents both have clear and obvious incentives to complete a transaction.[35] Despite the overt economic reward that agents receive when a buyer purchases a house, agents generally did not talk about commissions during the search process. In early conversations, agents assured buyers that their fee came from the seller—that the brokerage firm the listing agent worked for would charge the seller the commission and half of that would go to the buyer's agent. Buyers, according to their agents, therefore need not concern themselves with direct payment. While technically true, sellers (and their agents) generally know they must pay their listing agent a fee out of the sales price and so set their prices and negotiate accordingly. As one agent who worked in Manhattan said, "Buyers who think they aren't paying for any of the agent are wrong." Yet agents representing buyers often framed their fees in this way.

When a prospective buyer asked Chandra, an agent who worked in Queens, how she got paid, she responded, "Oh, don't worry about that. The seller is the one who pays me." Another agent working in Brooklyn described how she avoided talking about commissions with buyers:

Sometimes it's a weird conversation, and I actually don't like having it because I want [buyers] thinking about what they want, not about me. I usually just say something like "All you have to know is that you don't have to pay me anything, I get paid from the sale."

At an open house in the Tribeca neighborhood of Manhattan, a buyer and a real estate agent, Brandon, were handed a listing sheet by a listing agent. Listing sheets display all the major details for an offered property, including the address, the price, building information and amenities, pictures, and the contact information of the listing agent. The buyer already knew the price of the unit, but when she saw the price displayed at the top of the listing sheet, she said lightheartedly to Brandon, "You could make a lot off this one." Brandon laughed and said, "I guess so," and then quickly, "What do you think of it?" He then asked her questions about the lighting and moldings, thus immediately shifting the conversation away from talking about his own economic interests—and the price in general. Neither of them returned to the subject of Brandon's commission for the rest of the search process.

In interactions with buyers, agents deemphasized their own economic interest and framed their labor as both emotionally beneficial for clients and socially beneficial for communities and even the national economy. In most of her initial meetings with prospective buyers, Liz would talk about the joy she received from finding people homes. To one buyer who asked her why she got into the business, she said, "You'll see how exciting it is when we get you the perfect place. I get to have that feeling all the time." When Tim, a buyer in Manhattan, asked his agent Nancy a similar question, she responded, "What could be better than helping people find a home? Not a lot of people can say their job is so happy."

At a showing with buyers Chelsea and Jordan in Prospect Heights in Brooklyn, agent Luis described his work as not for himself but on behalf of the neighborhood. The three were talking about new amenities in the neighborhood, a change they attributed to the development of the Barclays Center—a large indoor professional sports and entertainment arena in central Brooklyn that typified the high-profile, large-scale changes in neighborhoods and real estate markets during Michael Bloomberg's twelve years as mayor. As they discussed the number of upscale restaurants and shops on Flatbush Avenue, which bordered the Barclays Center to the southwest, Luis said that he thought local residents appreciated many of the changes and that a good real estate agent should be attuned to what was going on in a neighborhood in order to improve it. "I think the cool thing about my job is getting to be really in touch with what's going on and really just working to make things around here better." This exchange echoes Liz's interactions with Claude and Janet in Williamsburg, in which she emphasized her local knowledge as a way both to showcase her lived experience in the neighbor-hood and to act as a booster for that place.

Kim, the agent who worked in the West Village of Manhattan, was also a longtime resident of the neighborhood. When I asked her what she enjoyed about her job, she stressed the location of her work: "I live in the best neigh-borhood in the best city in the world, and you're damn right I tell that to my clients." She was similarly enthusiastic about the loveliness of the West Vil-lage in interactions with buyers. One afternoon while visiting some available properties with very wealthy married clients, Kim and the buyers entered a large, recently renovated townhouse. Kim pointed around the gracious entry and gestured with her arms as if to accentuate the high ceilings typical of the townhouses in the neighborhood. She exclaimed, "Now this is why I love my job! Isn't this neighborhood perfect?" Other agents spoke similarly about their intimate relationships with the places where they worked. One agent who worked in Harlem, in Manhattan, said that the neighborhood "had its secrets" and that he took a great deal of pleasure in knowing them. Another agent who worked in the waterfront Brooklyn neighborhood of Cobble Hill said, "I love the charms of the neighborhood, and I want every-one else to know how great [Cobble Hill] is."

In general, agents were eager to describe their work as improving local communities, often through development and higher property values. One agent working in the Hudson Valley said:

> There's some new construction near me right now. I'm supposed to know all about it and when [the new housing units] hit the market make sure the prices are good because it's going to change the prices of everything else around here. I want all my clients who have bought recently to have their property values going up and be able to get sellers really good prices too. It trickles down, you know, to everything like schools and jobs. But you have to start with getting property values up. It's all part of my work.

On occasion when buyers would ask agents about what appealed to them about their work, agents would describe a desire to impact broader economic trends for the better. Lucy told one of her clients that after the Great Recession, she felt that her work could contribute to stabilizing the economy. In a conversation about housing market trends in New York City in the previous few years, including the speedy return to prerecession prices, Lucy told her client, "I thought that if I could do this well and hold myself to high standards then maybe I was doing my part to make sure all the things that made the meltdown wouldn't happen again." In these interactions agents shifted the conversational focus away from their own interests and framed their labor as a benevolent form of service on behalf of their clients, a given neighborhood or town, or even the economy writ large.

Deemphasizing in Interaction, Acknowledging in Interviews

In conversations with me, agents dropped much of the pretense of benevolence. Some began answering questions about why they did their job or what made them happy about their work more generally with the same "love of the neighborhood" and "joy in making people happy" lines that they said to their clients, but they would quickly acknowledge another reason they sold property: commissions. For example, Kim, after telling me that she based her work on love for the West Village, said, "You know, this job can also be very flexible and can make you a lot of money. That's why I first got into it." When asked why she did her work, one agent working in Riverdale—a small, very wealthy neighborhood in the Bronx along the Hudson River—said, "The money, duh! No one would do this job if it wasn't lucrative. Yes, I definitely like it for other reasons, but anyone who says they don't care about money either married right or is a liar."

Almost every agent I interviewed mentioned pay—and often a flexible work schedule—as a reason they enjoyed their job, even as most sought to temper their economic desires with the above-described benevolent aspects of the work.[36] One agent working in Manhattan said, "I know finding people apartments is great and its own reward, but I need to close deals to live." One agent working in Brooklyn said, "The best thing about this work is finding people houses and getting to explore the city. Of course there's the money too." Another working in the Hudson Valley responded, "Well the money is pretty good. But, you know, it's also just a great job because I get to make people happy."

The point is simply that while in one-on-one interviews agents freely acknowledged their economic interest, in interactions with clients they shifted focus away from their direct economic interests. Instead of talking about their commissions, they attempted to frame themselves as benevolent facilitators who worked diligently for buyers in their search for a home. Some of them presented themselves as neighborhood boosters or ethical market actors concerned with the health of the overall economy. The way that agents deemphasized their overt economic interest shows that to appear credible to their clients, market intermediaries must avoid seeming overly avaricious. More broadly, markets rely on interactional demonstrations of sociability and economic disinterest—particularly from market intermediaries. In other words, economic transactions often require participants to perform in ways that deemphasize individual overt economic goals.

ESTABLISHING AUTHORITY AND SELLING PLACES

In a market defined by less and less monopolistic control of information, how does a market intermediary with already weak claims to expertise establish authority? Real estate agents were adept at framing their labor as ethical, disinterested, necessary, and benevolent. While agents' own rhetoric cannot entirely account for the continued proliferation and success of their occupation in the age of Zillow, the ways they talked to clients about the worth of their labor does help explain their clients' satisfaction and agents' ability to gain referrals. After all, the vast majority of buyers and sellers buy or sell houses only once or twice in their lives, so they have few comparisons to make when dealing with agents.[37]

In order to establish authority in their relationships with clients, agents related examples of other agents' bad behavior. Ironically, while this habit of disparaging other agents may help individual agents build trust with particular clients, it undermines the reputation of the entire occupation. A parallel exists in public opinion of elected officials. Americans strongly disapprove of Congress but generally approve of the representatives from their districts.[38] Agents described the shortcomings of real estate websites and played up the services that agents provide during and after the transaction. They warned their clients of the disastrous consequences of trusting the information presented on real estate websites without question. Agents also argued that they brought something unique to the search process since real estate websites could not offer the sorts of information gleaned from spending time in a neighborhood.

Finally, agents sought to frame their work as benevolent. They told clients that they did their work for the satisfaction of matching people to houses, for the civic pride found in boosting the neighborhoods where they worked, and, sometimes, as a contribution to the health of the overall economy. With clients, agents avoided talk of commissions or their desire for future referrals, although they did acknowledge these interests in interviews. This split between deemphasizing economic interest in interactions with buyers and acknowledging them in interviews reveals how authority in economic markets can be derived through performances of benevolence. Avoiding overt references to their own economic interests also fit with broader notions of how agents saw themselves as experts in the search for a home.

Agents acted as salespeople of places, able to convey the lived experience of a particular neighborhood. In doing so they affirmed that the places in which they worked were desirable, tasteful, and therefore worth the cost. Indeed, as the remaining chapters demonstrate, establishing authority—where buyers trusted agents and saw them as helpful sources of information—allowed agents to influence buyers' preferences, upsell buyers, and differentiate neighborhoods.

2

ROMANCING THE HOME

Act happy! Your clients will notice.
INSTRUCTOR AT A MANHATTAN REAL ESTATE LICENSING SCHOOL

They're there to guide you through the emotional journey of buying and selling.
ADVERTISEMENT FOR BERKSHIRE HATHAWAY HOME SERVICES

At any given time, urban residential real estate markets have units for sale that are broadly similar across multiple criteria (neighborhood, size, price, building type, architectural style, etc.). How is it that buyers come to think of one unit or one neighborhood as preferable to others? How do buyers decide that a particular house is *their* house? How are they able to make such consequential decisions based on one or two viewings of an hour or less?

This chapter reveals agents' key roles in shaping buyers' desires. Agents used their authority to link aspects of buyers' identities to places. Agents were also quite adept at getting buyers to feel certain emotions that affected how they judged houses.[1] They elicited these emotions to help narrow the available options, since experiencing emotions like excitement, confidence, or fear could harden buyers' stated preference for a building with a doorman or within three blocks of a subway stop, or convince them that they needn't live in a city-designated historic district after all. By cultivating particular emotional responses to spaces and places, agents repeatedly convinced buyers to change their minds and make purchasing decisions they had previously ruled out.[2]

This chapter shows that market intermediaries play a powerful role in shaping consumers' experiences by making buyers feel like they are making the right choice. Given that buyers' choices affect both what they pay and how others regard them, buyers in a given market must *feel* that they are making informed distinctions between products—and real estate agents help them do that.[3] For most buyers, purchasing a home is a momentous and rare financial decision. Economic actors faced with uncertainty and risk turn to other signals, including their own emotions and intuitions, as proxies for information. They look to their emotions to reassure them of their decisions, shore up claims to knowledgeable action, and instill confidence in their ability to accurately judge market behavior. Sociologists of economic decision-making see emotions not just as a resource for achieving market goals but also as a way that actors create meaning and value in economic transactions.[4] In the case of real estate transactions, agents use buyers' demographic and taste characteristics to ascertain which properties and neighborhoods will be most likely to create a sense of both desire and urgency in their clients. At the scale of a city, these interactions match buyers and neighborhoods in a way that reifies boundaries and distinctions— certain types of residents belong in certain types of neighborhoods.

In what follows, I show how agents drew on housing market conditions in the aftermath of the Great Recession to motivate buyers and ordered the sequence of housing units that buyers viewed to make buyers feel confident they were purchasing the right house at the right time. I show how agents used aspects of buyers' identities to slot them into different parts of the city. Throughout, I demonstrate how important emotions were to the purchasing process. Agents were keen to get buyers to feel excitement about their potential purchases and anxiety over the possibility of missing out on a good deal. These interactions between agents and buyers reveal a highly dynamic search process in which buyers' desires were so loose and undefined that they could easily be shaped by interactions with agents.

BUY! BUY! BUY!

Agents often pointed to the particular conditions of New York's housing market as a way to motivate sales. More specifically, the astounding rebound of prices throughout the New York City metro area in the years immediately following the Great Recession provided the backdrop for buyers' and agents' conversations on the financial benefits of purchasing a home. In 2012, when my ethnographic research began, the Great Recession had officially ended (at least according to the Federal Reserve) and national housing prices had stopped their decline (according to the S&P/CoreLogic/Case-Shiller home price index, which tracks average home prices month to month).

While some parts of the country were still reeling from a collapse in hous-ing prices, particularly exurban communities in Sunbelt states like Florida and Arizona, many of the nation's urban centers were experiencing a steady climb back toward pre-crisis prices. According to the S&P/CoreLogic/Case-Shiller home price index, prices in 2012 increased in all twenty of the nation's largest cities for the first time since 2007. In New York City this marked the beginning of a massive and steady increase in real home prices that continued into 2019.[5]

Rising housing prices sparked endless discussion among New York-ers interested in real estate. In April 2012 an article in the *New York Times* asked if the current level of consumer confidence in the housing market could be sustained.[6] Not long after, apartment prices throughout the city were topping records set just before the Great Recession.[7] In January 2015 and January 2016, with prices in Manhattan now well beyond prerecession records, the *New York Times* published pieces with breathless headlines about the previous years' astronomical prices.[8] Real estate brokerage firms like the Corcoran Group and Douglas Elliman released their own assess-ments of the market showing that prices for housing all over the city were at all-time highs, with the median price for a place in Manhattan reaching the astounding mark of over $1 million. Commentators likened investing in New York City real estate to putting money in a Swiss bank account—with the same safety of return on investment.[9] Financial trend pieces began framing parts of the city that had historically experienced disinvestment as great places to buy apartments since they would undoubtedly provide huge returns.[10] Barely five years out from the largest economic crisis since the Great Depression—a crisis largely driven by a housing bubble—agents and buyers chatted about how housing was clearly a good investment. One agent who worked on Staten Island referred to the Great Recession as "just a little blip." According to these market intermediaries, betting on higher prices in the near future was a smart gamble.

In interviews, real estate agents reflected on how changing market con-ditions affected their work. The crash caught them by surprise, but the post-recession boom restored their faith in real estate as a sure thing. One agent who had worked in Manhattan for ten years (before, during, and after the Great Recession) said in 2013:

> I really am shocked at how much [my work] has changed just in the last few years, up and down, or really down and up. I remember in 2006 telling clients about how nothing was like real estate as a place to put your money. Then it all crashed, and I couldn't say that anymore. Mind you, prices in New York

weren't terrible—they dipped but weren't terrible. But we were all running around with our heads cut off. I have some friends who work on Wall Street, and they wanted to sell everything they owned. No one thought prices could ever be like before. And now it's like nothing ever happened. I'm back to telling people "Buy buy buy," because [prices] are only going to go up.

Another agent working in Brooklyn put it more succinctly: "If the market hadn't bounced back so quickly, I don't think I'd be talking about resale value as much as I do." Even in less expensive housing markets, agents reported talking about resale value and profitability more than they had prior to the Great Recession. One agent in Albany said, "The market has settled, and talking about investment makes more sense now."

Agents, who are paid on commission, have clear incentives to encourage activity in the market. Agents are always telling buyers to make an offer, but market conditions affect the rhetoric available to market intermediaries. Most agents, particularly ones working in New York City, reported that prior to the recession they often encouraged buyers to buy sooner rather than later, based on the premise that prices were only going to keep increasing. During the recession they stressed the potential financial returns of low-interest mortgage loans and low prices—buy low, sell high! Four to six years later, agents had returned to communicating the urgency of buying now to avoid further price increases.

In a postrecession boom environment, real estate agents had plenty of contextual resources to remind buyers of the economic benefits of buying a house, thereby affirming their identities as prudent economic actors. For example, Travis, an investment banker in his late twenties, got in touch with real estate agent Thomas through a coworker. At their first meeting, Travis and Thomas talked mostly about Travis's work and his desire to buy a place close to his office. Travis said that his work was "very important" to him and that proximity to his firm—preferably closer than the rental he currently had in Tribeca—was his highest priority.

At the first open house they went to, Travis said, "I don't care that much about other stuff," referring to building amenities like a twenty-four-hour doorman. "My job is pretty global, and I have to be in the office at all hours." Travis reiterated this when, as they rode the elevator down from the apartment, Thomas mentioned how these building amenities often help with resale value. Travis responded, "That's not super important."

Over the next month Thomas stressed resale value at every open house he visited with Travis. At one, a studio apartment in a new high-rise with views of neighboring buildings and the streets of the financial district below, Thomas said to Travis:

> The prices in this neighborhood are really picking up. We have some negotiating room, I think, because there's still some vacancy [in the building], but it's all upside looking at the trends. I mean, you could sell this place in less than two years, say if you had to move out of the country, and probably make a lot.

Travis nodded but still did not seem particularly interested. At the next showing, however, Travis's first question for Thomas was whether he thought the resale value of the unit they were viewing would be as much as the one they had seen previously. The unit was very much like the last one: a studio in a high-rise building packed with amenities. Thomas responded affirmatively: "I think they're very similar." At a later showing Thomas asked Travis what he thought of the apartment, and Travis said he liked it because of its views and because "depreciation won't be a problem."

While Travis had initially expressed disinterest in resale value, by the end of the search he had incorporated it into his decision-making process. Resale value had become part of the adjudication process and ultimately part of Travis's explanation of his decision to purchase the unit he did. After making an offer on one of the apartments they had seen—not the one closest to his office—Travis said, "I ended up thinking about a lot of things when choosing, and I'm lucky because all the real estate close to my office is booming." When I asked about the possibility that his job might require him to move, he said he was sure he would sell the apartment and get a higher price than what he had paid.

After the sale was complete, Thomas told me he was glad Travis had expressed more interest in resale value, since it dovetailed with an aspect of Travis's identity that he thought was salient: "For a mobile guy like him I think resale is going to very important." Thomas also said he had trusted his intuition in guessing that someone like Travis, who worked in finance, would be amenable to hearing more information about the market, prices, and resale value. "He wasn't into it at first, but I thought he'd want to know these kinds of things."

Resale value was, perhaps unsurprisingly, something agents from across the state said they focused on in interactions with buyers. One agent working in an upstate New York county, where median house prices were essentially unchanged from 2010 to 2015, said in 2013, "I always tell buyers it's a good time to buy. Even when they say they're going to live in a house forever

I say, 'Sure, live in the house forever, but buy now because it's more likely that prices go up than down.'" One agent working in Manhattan said in 2012, "I tell my clients what everyone knows, demand is so high and there's no end. Prices, I think, are just shooting up, and I can't see them stopping." Another working in the Cobble Hill neighborhood in Brooklyn said in 2013, "If I had more money, I'd buy a second and third apartment and sell them in a year or two; they'll be worth 50, maybe 60 percent more." While housing prices were increasing at a rapid clip, incomes in New York and across the country were not keeping pace.[11] The Nobel Prize–winning economist Robert Schiller calls the agents' fervent belief in increasing prices regardless of market fundamentals "irrational exuberance" (2005 and 2015).[12]

Agents also talked up less obvious ways that financial policies rewarded homeowners. One agent working in Westchester County, a suburban community north of New York City, explained in 2013:

> Interests rates are at the lowest I've ever seen, so it really is a great time to take out a mortgage. . . . Also, most people know about the home mortgage interest deduction, but some don't know about writing off your local property taxes on your federal taxes, so [buying] is the smart thing always. And buying now is a sweet deal. If I didn't already own, I'd buy right now, and that's what I tell my clients.

According to the Federal Home Loan Mortgage Corporation (Freddie Mac), a federally sponsored enterprise that buys and bundles mortgages to sell in the secondary market, the average interest rate on a thirty-year fixed-rate mortgage was 3.66 percent in 2012 and 3.98 percent in 2013. Just before the housing bubble burst, the average was closer to 6.4 percent. Banks did tighten their standards for loans in the wake of the housing crisis, including requiring higher credit ratings and larger down payments. But a buyer who could meet these standards would be borrowing money at cheaper rates than before the recession. The real estate agents I observed, who were largely dealing with a relatively affluent client base, told their clients that buying a home at this time was relatively cheap and financially prudent— the smart thing to do.[13]

For example, Miguel, an agent working in central Brooklyn, had a first-time buyer, Martin, as a client. After their initial meeting at an open house in a new development, they went for coffee, and Martin admitted that his decision to buy was tentative. He said he wasn't sure if now was the right time in his life; he mentioned a heavy workload as part of the reason for his ambivalence. He had decided to meet with Miguel partially out of curiosity and partially out of what he described as obligation—he and Miguel had met at a mutual friend's wedding in the Hudson Valley, and Martin had said he would meet with Miguel to discuss the housing market when they were both back in the city. As Martin described the sources of his ambivalence, Miguel nodded understandingly, but he immediately began talking about how buying now was the financially sensible thing to do. "Look at the interest rates right now," he said, "I really think this is the time to make that choice." Martin made an offer on an apartment less than three months later.

About four years after Martin had purchased his house, he believed he made the right decision. The Federal Reserve had begun to raise the benchmark interest rate, and although the increase had been small, Martin was extremely relieved that he had bought when he did. While he did not know how, if at all, the rate on his mortgage would have changed if he had waited four more years to buy, Martin said, "I'm just sure I got the better deal, and I think [Miguel] deserves a lot of credit for knowing the market." In fact there had been relatively little change in average interest rates on thirty-year mortgages in the interim: 3.98 percent in 2016, and 3.99 percent in 2017, though up to 4.54 percent in 2018. But Martin's relief reveals how the ways in which agents drew on market conditions to encourage buyers shaped how buyers interpreted their own purchasing decisions.

Looking back on their choices, buyers like Martin would often reference the descriptions and rationalizations articulated by their agents. More broadly, they came to see themselves as canny purchasers who had bought at the right time.

Other agents, like the one working in Westchester County, reminded their clients of aspects of tax policy that favored homeowners over renters. In the United States, the home mortgage interest deduction has traditionally been a huge boon for homeowning taxpayers—especially wealthy ones—who itemize on their federal income tax returns, allowing them to deduct the interest they pay on their mortgages from their taxable income.[14] The 2017 overhaul of the federal tax structure has somewhat reduced this incentive by raising individual taxpayers' standard deduction and lowering the ceiling for both the home mortgage interest deduction and state and local property taxes, but it remains to be seen how these changes will affect either the housing market or real estate agents' sales pitch. In addition to federal policies and tax incentives favorable to homeownership, New York's extremely uneven and unequal distribution of property taxes favors owners over renters, owners of high-priced properties over lower-priced ones, and owners of single-unit houses over owners of condos.[15] Agents rarely mentioned this aspect of housing policy, however, perhaps because the laws were so byzantine that they themselves did not have a firm grasp of them.

SEQUENCING TO PRODUCE CONFIDENCE

Agents had other ways to make buyers feel confident in their decisions. The order in which a real estate agent shows houses to a buyer is, to a certain extent, beyond their control: units are shown only at certain times, and buyers have their own scheduling limitations. Even so, agents insisted that the order in which buyers viewed houses influenced buyers' opinions of the units and ultimately their purchasing decision.[16] In the same way that agents talked about market conditions to assure buyers that the best time to buy was now, agents sequenced showings to focus buyers' attention and evoke feelings of confidence in them. Agents from across the state, working at various price points, reported sequencing as a useful sales strategy; by varying the types and prices of units early on, agents could capitalize on the urge to end searches quickly that consumers feel when they are presented by a wide range of options.[17]

Simon, a man in his late twenties, wanted to buy an apartment in the Crown Heights neighborhood of Brooklyn for under $400,000. He had been referred to Don, a real estate agent working in the area, by a mutual friend. He seemed very eager to shop for houses. At their first meeting, Simon brought along a printed list of available units he had found online. He insisted on going to visit these units with Don, and he was fairly adamant that he wanted to purchase one of them. When Don asked him why, Simon responded, "I've been looking at what's available for a while, and these were the only ones that looked good."

Don told Simon they could visit the units Simon had selected, but he also added other properties to the list of places to see. When they next met, Don had created a map of units to visit that included four Simon had suggested, plus an additional two that Don had chosen. They took a circuitous route to the properties and viewed Don's picks third and fourth. At these two, Don appeared far more excited and engaged with Simon, specifically regarding the fact that these two units had been recently foreclosed. This, Don argued, made them more attractive to a buyer since negotiations would be short—foreclosed units are sometimes sold at auction, and, more important, the banks or investors who owned Don's two picks would be less inclined to haggle over price than the resident-owners selling Simon's picks. Don and Simon discussed this at one of the foreclosed units:

> DON: If you make an offer on a place like this you close faster. There will be a lot less messiness.
> SIMON: You mean with the bank?
> DON: Yeah, with the whole process in general. I think it makes a lot of sense.

While visiting the fifth apartment, which was owner occupied, Don echoed his earlier remarks regarding the economic rationality of buying a foreclosed unit. He said to Simon, "Owners feel like their houses are worth more because, you know, they've lived in them and whatever. It's smart to avoid all that when doing a deal."

When I later asked Don why he wanted Simon to view the foreclosed units third and fourth, as opposed to just providing Simon with his opinions regarding foreclosed units, he said, "It's kind of a sweet spot for people's attention." This strategy apparently worked. Before he made an offer, Simon told me, "I kind of don't want to be pulled into a long back-and-forth [with a seller]. If I decide I want something, I should be able to get it." After he made an offer on one of the foreclosed units, he added, "I didn't want to waste time. I wanted to make the deal, and I think [making an offer] on an empty place was just the smartest way to do it." Sequencing, and agents' work more broadly, affects buyers' feelings about their purchases. Simon's interactions with Don not only gave him confidence in his economic decision-making but also changed his opinion about which units to consider and ultimately purchase.

One buyer, a client of real estate agent Brandon, reported a similar change in stated preference. Using a refrain common among agents and buyers in New York about spending more to get more, he credited the sequence of showings to explain his and his wife's decision. "Brandon took us to a bunch of places early where we realized if we spent a little more, we could get a lot more. . . . I think we were being timid before we started, and seeing these beautiful apartments gave us a better perspective." Like Simon, whose views changed according to what he saw during the search, this buyer attributed a clearer understanding of the market to seeing a particular kind of unit early on. Sequencing, then, not only draws buyers' attention to specific qualities of a place but can transform buyers' preferences and give them confidence that their decision is based on experience in the market — even if this experience is highly curated by their agents.

Agents also used sequencing to highlight their own knowledge and boost their occupational authority. For example, Andrew, who wanted to buy an apartment in the Lower East Side, approached Thomas with several places he had found online. They visited nine units, including four that Andrew had found. They scheduled these showings during a patch of hot, humid weather, and the units Andrew had chosen were in buildings with no elevators. Thomas, who wore a suit on all three days they went to showings, was sweating visibly and remarked on the number of stairs they were walking up to view Andrew's picks. Thomas made sure to follow up each of Andrew's picks with showings at units in newer buildings. Not only were the lobbies of these buildings air conditioned, but the units themselves were much cooler since they had central air conditioning instead of relying on window units.

After arriving at one of the newer apartments a four-block walk from one of Andrew's picks in a prewar brick building, Thomas engaged Andrew specifically about the temperature:

THOMAS: It's a lot cooler in here, huh?
ANDREW: Yeah. Today's the worst [hottest] day so far this year.
THOMAS: Imagine trying to sleep in [the previous] place on a day like this.
ANDREW: I know, yeah, you're right, this feels a lot better.

Andrew eventually made an offer on one of the units Thomas had chosen. When I asked Thomas why he had shown Andrew units in that order, he explained that he had been annoyed with Andrew's presumption of knowledge about the market. Sequencing, Thomas said, was a way to establish his occupational expertise, which in turn would allow him to influence Andrew's decision. When I asked Andrew about the purchase, he admitted that central air—or, more specifically, Thomas's strategic deployment of central air—had been part of his choice. He said, "It felt like [Thomas] was saying you're stupid if you don't take this. And I'm not stupid." Agents, in other words, shaped buyers' experience of the housing market so that purchasing the agents' preferred units seemed like the intelligent thing to do.

When agents had no control of sequencing, both buyers and agents appeared less focused on the sales process and less sure of their decisions. For example, Antonio and Irene, a couple looking to buy in Brooklyn, had busy work schedules and could rarely see a unit at the same time. Irene's brother referred them to real estate agent Kim to help look in Brooklyn, despite the fact that Kim lived and worked mostly in the West Village. Kim found her inability to coordinate their schedules frustrating: "I can't get into a rhythm with them because one sees a place and has to talk to the other, but then it's like two months before they can look again. It's too long of a lag." About five months into the search, Antonio said, "It's been scattered because we haven't seen many places together. The apartments I've seen with [Kim] have been great, and that's exactly what [Irene] says about the ones she has seen. But I just can't get a good sense without comparison . . . maybe now isn't the right time [to buy]." After another four months in which the couple was rarely available, Kim made less of an effort to send them listings. "I'd love to see them again when they have more time, but for this to work you really have to be available to see lots of places quickly. Otherwise I just can't judge what's right for you." Antonio also lamented the lack of sequencing, saying the search process had been "difficult" and that "it would have been better if we had looked at apartments closer together." Without sequencing, Antonio felt unable to distinguish between units and lacked certainty about any decision. Kim, for her part, was irritated at her inability to present units in an order that she saw as necessary to making the sale. Fewer interactions also meant Kim had less opportunity to cultivate a sense of urgency among her buyers—a common practice described further below.

Sequencing allowed agents to draw on the various tools at their disposal, from a unit's location, the seller's finances, or even the weather, to narrow buyers' vision of available units, exercise their superior knowledge of the market, and instill buyers with a sense of confidence. A respondent working in the Hudson Valley related a recent sale where sequencing had fostered a connection between her clients and a particular house:

This couple is super twee or whatever. They were moving from Brooklyn to start some kind of health products line, and the guy had a beard and she didn't wear any makeup. Get the idea? They had come up a few times and I got to know them. So I put together a list of places to see on that Sunday they were coming up. . . . I had four places that were near their price but one that was *them*. I mean, it was what we call a real fixer-upper, old, creaky, but with inlay and old wood everywhere. The other three were all standard suburban houses, so I wanted to show this one last. Like, I wanted them to ride the train down remembering it, thinking about cooking up their homemade whatever in that old kitchen. And I was so right. They were crazy for it, talking about how they loved it compared to the boring stuff. And they called me from the train saying we should put in an offer. So yeah, I think the order is a big deal. For them it was like I was able to say, "Look at how you'll be so much happier in a place like this."

This agent believed that showing the house that she felt best matched the couple's identity last increased the buyers' connection with the house. Sequencing helps close deals because it creates comparisons and contrasts and amplifies buyers' attraction to a particular place.

IDENTITY AND SELECTION IN INTERACTION

Like the agent in the Hudson Valley, most of the agents in this study described their work with buyers as a process of matching neighborhoods or individual units with a buyer's identity. This act of narrowing buyers' choice sets allowed buyers to envision themselves living in a specific house. Agents generally spoke about their labor as a form of identity work, in that they helped buyers see aspects of themselves. One agent working in Brooklyn explained that she communicated a lot more to prospective home buyers than simply information on available units:

> What I do, it's really a whole lot of things. I'm a mother, a therapist, a cheer-leader, an interior decorator, a financial adviser. And you know, it's a tough job because it's stressful for everyone involved, but the most important thing I do is help buyers understand just how important a home is. When I think about it, I've owned my apartment for almost twenty years, and it's where I raised my kids and it's where I spend the most time. So I want to get buyers to think that what they're looking at is not just a place where they're going to sleep, but it's a whole life.

Another working in Suffolk County on Long Island said:

> I think this job is really complicated. People don't just need me to tell them buy low or sell high—that's the easy part. The deeper part is explaining to them which houses are right and which are wrong, and that depends a lot on who they are. Who they are and also who they want to be down the line.

Buyers, too, thought of their agents as more than simply sources of information on available units. One who had purchased in Brooklyn said, "I loved going through [the search process] with [my agent]. [She] had a good sense of the kind of life I want to have." Agents construct a future for buyers, prompting them to think about what they want their lives to look like once they've moved into a townhouse with a garden or a studio in a building with a roof deck. Agents are asking their buyers, either implicitly or explicitly, to think about their plans for having children and raising families, how long they'll be at a given job, or their long-term financial goals. All of these conversations are taking place in the context of differentiated neighborhoods. Neighborhoods not only are culturally, symbolically, and demographically distinct from each other, in that we associate different types of places with certain kinds of people, but also have the power to shape our identities.[18] In the process of matching buyers to particular neighborhoods, agents established their professional authority and also reified the reputations of places.

Matching Consumers to Neighborhoods

One agent, Brandon, had clients who were moving to New York City from London. While the couple had spent time in New York before, the husband mentioned that he and his wife were open to experiencing the city anew. He said, "I know a little here and there, but I wouldn't say my sense of [the city] is total." Brandon took them on a series of showings of units in trendy buildings in Soho and Tribeca and along the West Side Highway. SoHo and Tribeca are small, wealthy adjacent neighborhoods in Lower Manhattan that were once home to light manufacturing. By mid-twentieth century the industry was gone, and SoHo in particular became known as a part of Manhattan friendly to artists who could use the lofted floor plans as living and studio spaces. Martin Scorsese's 1985 film *After Hours* portrays SoHo as a comically harrowing place filled with intense artists, angry punks, and retro weirdos. Over the next few decades the neighborhoods further transformed into an elite residential and commercial space while retaining its industrial-chic look—many buildings have cast-iron facades constructed in the late 1800s.[19] Today SoHo and Tribeca are some of the wealthiest parts of the city, home to celebrities like Mariah Carey, Robert DeNiro, Iman (and the late David Bowie), and Beyoncé and Jay-Z. Apartments regularly sell for $5 to $10 million.

At one open house Brandon was describing the neighborhood and told the buyers, "Living here means a lot—it's going to signal that you have taste." At another he said, "Moving here can be your last move because nothing can really compare." Brandon made these statements with an awed enthusiasm. He excitedly talked about the history of the neighborhoods, the celebrities that lived there, and their cultural cachet. Over the weeks that Brandon showed these buyers different apartments, the neighborhoods became synonymous with refined sensibilities, good taste, and high status— place reputations built up over these multiple interactions.

After the buyers purchased a sleek apartment in Tribeca, just blocks away from famous and expensive restaurants like Nobu, Bouley, and Locanda Verde, the husband reflected on their decision.[20] "Let's put it this way," he said. "Walk around where [the new apartment] is and I wonder if you'll ever find another neighborhood so classic and so identifiably New York." These interactions between buyers and real estate agents create an identity—a vision of what life either will continue to be like or will become for residents of a particular place. "Nowhere else is going to match this kind of living," said the buyer; "just think about all the restaurants. I doubt we'll have any need to move in the future." Nearly five years after the purchase, the buyer still referred to the neighborhood in the same terms he had used right after he and his wife bought their apartment. They remained very satisfied with the apartment as well as the surrounding neighborhood, noting that it was "incredibly central," "close to everything," and that "the architecture in the neighborhood [was] so unique." "I'm really happy with the apartment these past few years, and I remember [Brandon] was so good at explaining all the details and all the amenities." The couple has no plans to move.

In general, market intermediaries do work that imbues products with various meanings specific to particular kinds of consumers.[21] In the housing market, real estate agents construct a vision of the future that help buyers imagine what their lives would be like if they purchased in a given neighborhood. The agents continually exposed buyers to a range of ideas about houses that framed purchases as cultural accomplishments that would transform buyers' lives. As one agent put it, buyers "can't just think about houses as money or money pits; they also have to believe that what they're buying is an ambitious project where they're accomplishing something." This inclination to make sure buyers felt bonded to neighborhoods through emotional connections and common identifications played out during showings.

One buyer, Sam, an engineer for a large internet company in his mid-thirties, was very focused not only on the prices of different units but also on the potential for rising property values across different neighborhoods. In early meetings with Liz, his real estate agent, Sam expressed concern that buying in the Williamsburg neighborhood of Brooklyn would not be as economically savvy as buying in Greenpoint, a bordering neighborhood to the north that had lower prices but seemed poised for more development, construction, and potential price increases. Early on, Sam often wondered aloud about rates of appreciation and changes in housing prices; he was clearly focused on the economics of the market in this one part of Brooklyn. At the first showing he and Liz visited in Williamsburg, he referred to the listing price and asked, "I could pay this much for something farther north and have it be worth more in five years, right?"—essentially asking Liz if she thought prices in Williamsburg had or were close to peaking while those in Greenpoint still had room to grow. Liz answered, "Sure, that's probably true of a lot of other places." She added, "It's also important to think about where you actually want to have a life."

Liz did not want Sam to forget about money entirely, but she did want him to develop an emotional attachment to a potential home. Sam's home would not only be an investment; it would be where Sam was going spend his free time, linking him to amenities like public transportation, restaurants and bars, local stores, and potentially other anchoring institutions like schools and places of worship. At other open houses Liz spoke with authority about the amenities in Williamsburg, explaining, for example, how quickly one could reach other parts of the city on public transit. As they visited more open houses, Sam voiced less concern about prices and resale value as Liz peppered her commentary with more and more information and opinion about differences across neighborhoods in northern Brooklyn.

Different neighborhoods have different symbolic meanings, signaling to others who know the city not only a resident's socioeconomic status but also their cultural tastes. On multiple occasions Liz mentioned to Sam that Williamsburg had far more amenities than supposedly up-and-coming neighborhoods like Greenpoint and Bushwick and that as a single man of means, Sam should find these desirable. At one showing Liz said to Sam, "I think I'd rather be close to the L than the G," referring to particular subway lines. (The L is an east-west train that runs through Williamsburg and connects it to Manhattan, while the G, the only subway running through Greenpoint, is a north-south train that does not go to Manhattan.) She added, "Being off the L, it's going to have a lot more to offer."[22] At the end of one afternoon they found themselves in Greenpoint, having seen one apartment there and two earlier in the day in Williamsburg. Liz asked if Sam was hungry. When he said yes, Liz replied, "I don't know too many good places around here; let's drive back down [to Williamsburg]." Greenpoint has hundreds of restaurants and cafes, but Liz's comments communicated to Sam that none of them were worth her time when Williamsburg offered more satisfying options. These interactions also communicated to Sam that he ought to be the type of person that eats at restaurants in Williamsburg, not Greenpoint.

These bits of information and opinion, sprinkled throughout Sam and Liz's interactions, eventually won Sam over. He made an offer on an apartment in Williamsburg and explained how it was "just so much easier to get to." He went on to say that Williamsburg was "where all my stuff is. Everybody knows it, and it's not like I'm worried people won't come over cause it's too far away or whatever." Sam had come to consider local amenities and geographic proximity to Manhattan as important factors in his decision and eventually agreed with Liz that someone like him should live in Williamsburg.

Michael had been renting in the East Village neighborhood in Manhattan and was now looking to buy an apartment. He came to his first meeting with agent Luis wearing a stylish button-down white shirt and well-fitted slacks with a neon pattern. Michael mentioned that he was employed in fashion and wanted to stay below Fourteenth Street, but he did not specify a location beyond that. When I later asked Luis for his assessment, he replied that Michael looked like a "fashion gay" and that "fashion gays were are all in the Lower East Side." Accordingly, Luis communicated to Michael that the Lower East Side might be a good place to look for units "that would best fit" him.[23] In their second meeting Luis and Michael were walking from one showing to another when Michael pointed and said, "I know a guy who lives in this building." "Yeah," responded Luis, "I've worked with a lot of guys in your industry who've ended up here."

Over the next seven weeks of visiting open houses, Luis interspersed his and Michael's conversations about units with examples of prior clients who worked in fashion and lived in the neighborhood. At a newly constructed glass-and-steel condo building nestled between the more typical brick tenements, Luis told Michael that another client who worked in marketing at an international fashion label had viewed an apartment in the building about nine months earlier. At an open house for an apartment in a large housing complex deep in the Lower East Side by the East River, Luis and Michael talked about how the unit had clearly not been renovated since the late 1970s, but they also discussed the great view. Michael asked the listing agent, "What are the neighbors like? It doesn't seem to be a lot of young people." The listing agent said, "I think that's changing. There's a new generation moving in." Luis added, "That's true. Not in this building but just around the corner I had a guy just buy a place. He's your age. He's a fashion photographer." Luis also made frequent reference to the neighborhood's many boutique clothing stores. At one open house he jokingly warned Michael that the apartment was very close to Assembly—a small clothing store where T-shirts cost over $80 and sunglasses regularly went for $500—and that Michael might not be able to control his shopping habits. Eventually Michael made an offer on a unit in the Lower East Side.

When I spoke to him about the search process and his final decision,

Michael admitted that he was buoyed by the prospect of living in a fashionable neighborhood. "I thought I was going to stay in the East Village, but I think the scene down here is a little cooler." He went on to describe the connection to the neighborhood he had experienced as a result of Luis's matching work, explaining that there was so much "stuff" for him in the Lower East Side. Michael then listed a number of bars, stores (including Assembly), and restaurants in the neighborhood that he liked. Luis's ability to select aspects of Michael's identity and match them to a particular place created Michael's neighborhood preference.

There are, of course, risks associated with using demographic characteristics to match clients with particular places. One agent noted:

> You have to spend time with [a buyer] and get to know them a little. You might assume that because they're rich/poor, old/young, black/white, whatever, they'll want a particular kind of place. You're not supposed to do this legally, but it's also bad business, because rich people can want low-key places and old people can want to live in Bushwick.[24]

Agents must be sure that the identities they seek to highlight during the sales process resonate with a buyer's sense of self. In other words, if agents are hoping to generate a buyer's excitement and arousal about a place through matching, the agent must select an identity that makes the buyer feel good. Buyers must feel that agents are providing places that fit with their broader understandings of who they are.

The "Why Questions"

When I first met Sarah, a real estate agent in her early forties, at her office for our initial interview, she greeted me in her brokerage's conference room. After we exchanged pleasantries, I began to explain my research when she interrupted me.

"Where do you live?" she said.

"I live in the Lower East Side," I said.

"Why?" she said. "I would've guessed Brooklyn."

For Sarah, something about my presentation of self marked me as a Brooklyn resident, and there must have been a particular reason someone who looked like me lived in the Lower East Side instead of Brooklyn. The fact that I didn't live in a place that matched the way I looked required an explanation.

For agents in general, part of matching a buyer with a given neighborhood or house is *excluding* other places as inappropriate choices. Agents sometimes worked to incite negative feelings against places they felt did not fit the buyer. This often happened in interactions with buyers where agents would ask "why questions" clearly meant to communicate confusion or even downright disgust at the idea of a particular buyer searching in a neighborhood the agent did not believe was a match.

For example, on one of their visits to open houses, Luis and Michael were discussing what kinds of furniture could fit into an apartment they had just seen in the Lower East Side. Michael said, "I have this one friend who lives on the Upper East Side, and she has this massive dining table that can seat like twelve people." Luis stuck out his tongue, feigning disgust, and said, "Why does she live on the Upper East Side?" The Upper East Side is an elite, expensive neighborhood—home to Madison Avenue and many of the city's largest and most famous museums, including the Met and the Guggenheim—but it certainly has a reputation for being fusty, old, and snobbish. It didn't make sense that Michael, who was young and stylish, would know anyone who lived on the Upper East Side. When I asked Luis later about the Upper East Side comment, he said, "Would you ever live there? It's just for old white ladies. I mean, when was the last time you were even there?" Before I could answer, he said, "And I don't mean to go to the Met or whatever. There's nowhere to eat or drink or have fun."

Sarah was occasionally as pointed with her assessments of clients as she had been with me. She had buyers, a couple looking for a two-bedroom, who had been searching for close to three months and had viewed apartments only in the Murray Hill neighborhood of Manhattan. Murray Hill is on the East River, near multiple hospitals where both of the buyers—health care professionals—were employed. At one open house one of the buyers asked if they should look in Chelsea, a cross-town neighborhood on the West Side. Sarah raised her eyebrows and her voice went up as she said, "What? Why? Are you going to take the 7 to the 6 every day? Why would you want to be around all that construction at Hudson Yards?" Sarah was referring to the trains the buyers would have to take to get from Chelsea to their work (she did not mention cross-town buses) and to a massive new residential and commercial development on the West Side. The buyers did not look at any apartments in Chelsea; they eventually bought in Murray Hill. Sarah's dismissal of Chelsea in interactions with the buyers foreclosed it as a possible neighborhood in which to search.

Asking "why questions"—as in, why would you live there?—established symbolic boundaries between different types of neighborhoods.[25] Agents used buyers' consumption habits and demographics to slot them into particular places and exclude them from others. Miguel, who worked largely in central Brooklyn, was showing clients—a couple with children—houses in a neighborhood called Prospect Heights. The neighborhood has a reputation for attracting professionals with young children—a *New York Times* article from 2016 highlighted the neighborhood's schools and its proximity to Prospect Park and the Brooklyn Museum.[26] At the first open house they visited, a two-bedroom condo in a newly constructed building amid the area's more traditional brownstones, Miguel named some restaurants along Washington Avenue, one of the neighborhood's main thoroughfares. Then he said, "I know some people are moving farther east now, but I don't know why. Like why would you want fewer trees and more homeless and less restaurants? Why would you want a longer commute?" These why questions circumscribed the areas in which particular buyers should look; they shaped place reputations and created or maintained the symbolic meanings of different neighborhoods.

Agents expressed shock or antipathy at the idea of certain clients possibly considering neighborhoods that didn't match the agent's conception of the client. This heightened buyers' connection to specific places and helped shape their preferences for the neighborhoods they eventually chose. As one of Miguel's clients said after making a purchase in Prospect Heights, "This neighborhood is perfect. I'm not sure I would have liked anything in Crown Heights." Crown Heights is the neighborhood just east of Prospect Heights.

Particular Kinds of People in Particular Kinds of Homes

Matching clients with neighborhoods is only the first step for real estate agents who are attempting to establish a sense of connection between buyers and properties. Agents use the same sorts of occupational, demographic, and cultural characteristics they use for neighborhood matching to cultivate buyers' attachment to individual units.

Charlie and Alexa were a wealthy couple with two children looking to buy in the Park Slope neighborhood of Brooklyn. At a showing of a recently renovated brownstone, Alexa wondered out loud about resale value. Johnny, their real estate agent, reminded the couple that "no one can tell the future." He turned to look around the house, opening his arms up as if to embrace the space, and said, "Places like this are pretty special. You get the old exterior and this newer inside that's a lot more comfortable for you and your kids." The listing agent (who joined them for the showing) immediately piggybacked on Johnny's comments about children, reporting that the couple selling the house had a large family and "liked to cook a lot and used the kitchen all the time," adding that "they also raised their kids here." Throughout the search process, Johnny repeatedly invoked domesticity and childrearing. At one open house he pointed to a working fireplace (an uncommon amenity in New York City) and evoked images of Charlie, Alexa, and their kids enjoying the holidays: "You know this is perfect for Christmas or Chanukah, I mean everyone sitting around the fire opening presents."

When Charlie and Alexa eventually did make an offer on a house, Alexa mentioned that she was excited because she knew her kids were "going to love the new place." She said she hoped her family could move in before Halloween, in time to carve pumpkins and set them out on the front steps. Four years after Charlie and Alexa had completed the purchase, Alexa echoed the ideas of domesticity that Johnny had evoked throughout their search. "We've had such a great time here with the kids," she said. "They have a really, I guess, deep connection to [the house]. It's where I've raised them so it's special." She added, "Birthdays, holidays, you know, it means a lot to have them all in the same place every year." Buyers clearly found agents' rhetoric linking houses to domesticity and childrearing potent and durable.

These interactions with real estate agents affected buyers' stated preferences. Will and Katie, first-time buyers who both worked in design, made an offer on an apartment in the Lower East Side of Manhattan after a five-month search. After the deal had been completed, they said that their agent, Thomas, had made them rethink what to value in their purchase. Initially the couple had wanted, as Will put it, "the cheapest smallest thing, as long as it was new." Intent on being the first occupants in their purchased apartment, they sent Thomas a list of tiny apartments they had found online. These apartments were small even by the standards of the Lower East Side—a neighborhood full of former tenement buildings. Early in their search Thomas showed them larger units slightly above their stated price ceiling. At these showings he talked about how having more room would give them more flexibility in decorating the apartment. Eventually the couple decided to buy a larger unit that they could renovate to match their personal needs and style. Will said, "What ended up becoming the most important thing for us was 'Is this the place that we can make comfortable?'" For Will and Katie, working with a real estate agent reoriented how they thought about their purchase and changed their stated preferences. They began to deemphasize some aspects of a unit, like its newness, and stress others, like its potential for personalization.

Gender During the Search for Housing

Real estate agent Liz spoke about individual units in differing ways depending on the gender of the buyer. One of Liz's clients, Erica, an advertising executive in her mid-thirties, was buying for the first time. After renting in Williamsburg for nearly ten years, Erica said she had had enough of "throwing money away" when she could be building equity. She wanted to invest in real property. Since her industry was based in New York City, Erica said she could not see herself ever moving out of the city.

At her initial meetings with Liz, Erica talked a lot about her job and her love for it. She liked working long hours and said that she wanted an apartment on the smaller side that would be easy to maintain. Liz took Erica to four showings of spacious (by New York standards) apartments in newer developments with large windows and high ceilings. At each of these units Liz mentioned something about the new kitchens, which had stainless steel fixtures, new appliances, and large amounts of countertop space. At one Liz mentioned the size of the refrigerator and said she wished she had one that large. At another she said, "If I lived here I would be in this kitchen all the time." While it certainly behooves an agent to talk about the aspects of units they think are attractive, Erica had not expressed any interest in kitchens or cooking during their interactions; her penchant for working long hours and desire for a manageable unit suggested anything but such interest.

In contrast, Liz used very different language in her showings with Jack. Jack was similar to Erica in many ways. He was single and a long-time renter in Brooklyn who had decided to buy. He was searching for a one-bedroom apartment a few months before Erica, at around the same price point. And like Erica, Jack worked long hours at his consulting job in Manhattan and expressed a desire for an apartment that would be easy to manage. The units that Liz showed Jack were like the ones she had shown Erica: condos in newer buildings with large windows and new finishes; they had comparable kitchens with shiny stainless steel faucets, large gas range stoves and other new appliances, and lots of countertop space. In her interactions with Jack, however, Liz did not dwell on these aspects of the units. She even cut off conversation about the kitchen at one unit when, at an open house, the listing agent mentioned the generous countertop space, saying to Jack, "I know you don't care so much about cooking."

The divergent ways that Liz expected Jack and Erica to evaluate similar units tapped into stereotypes about gendered behaviors at home. Liz assumed that despite no apparent interest, Erica would like hearing about the apartments' kitchens while Jack would not. Agents generally tended to focus more on kitchens and other aspects of houses associated with domesticity when showing units to female buyers. One female agent working in Rochester said, "In my experience it's a common understanding that men and women care about different stuff in the house."

When agents were working with young heterosexual couples (both married and unmarried) who did not have children, I observed several of them commenting directly to the female buyer about housing units being big enough for children. When going on showings with men and women from heterosexual couples individually, agents mentioned having children to the women but not to the men. I observed agents mentioning children to heterosexual women buyers eight times when looking at units without their male partners, but I never once heard agents mention children to men who were looking at units without their female partners. These comments, often delivered excitedly or with a wink, included phrases like "This place is great if there's a third on the way" and "You know this room could always be a nursery."

In one meeting with a woman in her early thirties, Liz asked the buyer if she liked to have people over. The buyer responded that she had a long-term boyfriend. Liz raised her head, widened her eyes, and then asked if the buyer and her boyfriend were discussing cohabitation. "I don't mean to pry, but I just want to get a sense of what we're looking for here." After the meeting, Liz explained that given the buyer's age and relationship status, she thought the buyer seemed likely to "settle down" soon, so she would try to find units that could accommodate two people. This was despite the fact that the buyer had stated that her decision about purchasing a home would not include her boyfriend. During the next three months Liz would bring the boyfriend into the sales process both implicitly and explicitly, saying that a particular unit was "too small for two people," and asking, "Are we ever going to meet this man of yours?" This went on until the buyer did bring her boyfriend along for showings.

While the buyer may have brought her boyfriend along simply to appease Liz, the effect was that once the boyfriend was introduced, Liz essentially treated them as a couple purchasing a home, asking for both of their opinions. Moreover, Liz's early categorization of the buyer as a person "ready to settle down" dictated what units Liz thought were appropriate to show; she ruled out units that could not accommodate two people. The process had consequences for the purchase: of the nine units Liz selected for the buyer, none were studios, one was a small one-bedroom, six were large one-bedrooms, and two were two-bedrooms.[27] The buyer eventually made an offer on of the two-bedroom apartments Liz had shown her, saying:

> Looking at apartments made me realize how small everything is in this city. I should probably get the biggest thing I can afford. If things change, I could sell the place, but I could also just have someone move in with me and it wouldn't feel cramped.

She added, "I think I'll be happier with bigger in the long run." Liz had used her own criteria in deciding which units to show and, in effect, matched the buyer's gender and relationship status to a particular kind of apartment—a bigger one. Despite the buyer's early statement that she was buying for herself, she eventually expressed satisfaction with Liz's matching work; she pointed to the size of the unit she purchased as a quality she valued for both emotional and practical reasons that changed her initially expressed preference.

While agents' responses to buyers' stated preferences and their attempts to shift how buyers evaluated houses could be seen as unnecessary, irrelevant, or, as in the cases just described, sexist, the point is that agents mobilize stereotypes about how different types of people use their homes and neighborhoods to move transactions forward.

PRODUCING EXCITEMENT

Both agents and buyers spoke of the "excitement" they felt when finding a unit or neighborhood that matched buyers' senses of self. In interviews and in interactions with buyers, agents used other words and phrases describing how the buyer should experience the right unit and what feelings should be elicited when buyers saw them: "wow factor," "breathtaking," "giddy," "gleeful." Importantly, these strong feelings of excitement involved more than just simply liking a particular housing unit.[28] As one agent explained:

> There are a lot of nice apartments out there and you'd like plenty of them. I mean, anyone would, they're so nice. But nice is not what you're looking for.

> If you like something, great, but do you *love* it? Does it make you light up?
> Does it make you want to write a check immediately? That's the kind of feeling
> [buyers] are supposed to have.

This excitement described by agents was an actionable emotion, a positive
feeling of arousal and interest, that buyers often pointed to as a reason for
selecting the unit they did.

When real estate agent Brandon met with a recently divorced woman
looking to buy a smaller apartment than the one she had shared with her
husband, he asked specifically about what she liked and disliked about the
unit she currently lived in. When he asked the buyer her least favorite thing
about her current apartment, she responded, "Well, I really don't like how
musty it is. It feels old. The only good light in the whole place is from the
windows in the bedroom. . . . Those windows face south, and it just lights
up every morning."

After the meeting, I asked Brandon if he would search for units with
south-facing windows. He replied:

> Probably yeah, but it's more than that. There's something about a new place
> being refreshing; I see it with a lot of recently divorced people, where they
> just feel like they need something bright and new. It's not just the windows,
> it's about newer things.

Brandon found six apartments for the buyer that had all been constructed
within the last ten years. These units did indeed have large windows with
lots of light, and during the open houses Brandon described the units as
"bright," "airy," "luminous," and "fresh." Their conversations, however,
went beyond lighting. He asked the buyer if she thought they had "that
new quality" they had talked about. At the third unit they visited, Brandon
pointed to the large windows and said, "Isn't this great?" The buyer nodded
her head, smiled, and excitedly said, "Wow, oh yes."

Over the next two weeks, Brandon and the buyer visited more open
houses, where they talked about a range of other aspects of the apartments,
including architectural styles, appliances, and building fees. At no point,
however, did the buyer's interest come close to what she had displayed at
the third unit. When leaving one open house, Brandon suggested returning
to the third unit he had shown her at a different time of day. He told her,
"You'll really be able to see all the different tones [of light] if we go in the
evening." After the second visit, the buyer decided to make an offer. She
later said the unit had "a kind of intangible quality" that made it feel "really

special." "It's what I need right now," she added, "something a little more open." Here the interactions between Brandon and the buyer had generated not only a desirable physical characteristic of a unit—large windows—but also the excitement that accompanied it. Brandon focused the buyer's attention on a particular physical aspect of potential apartments that the buyer then used in decision-making.

Another of Brandon's clients described how positive affect or expressed excitement during the transaction shaped her future experiences of a house:

> When we bought our last apartment, we had an agent we didn't really like, he was always so glum. We started calling him Eeyore [the donkey character in the Winnie-the-Pooh books and films who is pessimistic and anhedonic and talks with a deep voice very, very slowly]. He was never excited about anything, and I think that mattered. We never really felt great about our last place. [Brandon] made us feel a lot better about buying our new place because it was clear that it was just what we wanted.

Excitement as an expressed emotion flowed from agents to buyers. Buyers generally took their emotional cues from agents, and many agents described their own performance of excitement as a key part of making successful matches between clients and houses. In this sense—and in contrast to a simple broker who simply acts as a conduit for information or resources—the work of market intermediaries is not simply to bring a buyer to a product. Rather, market intermediaries create arousal in the buyer by highlighting how a product matches them in some way.

When Steven and John, a white couple looking to spend millions of dollars on a house, first met with Lucy, they said they knew what they wanted. They told Lucy they wanted to live in Brooklyn Heights, Cobble Hill, or Carroll Gardens: three affluent and largely white Brooklyn neighborhoods on the East River known for their picturesque brownstones and tree-lined streets.[29] After Lucy and the couple spent their first day visiting open houses, Lucy told me she had a good handle on the type of unit they wanted: "I think they're looking for something with a really classic exterior that looks historical, so I want to look at Brooklyn Heights." A few weeks later Steven and John found three units in Cobble Hill online that they wanted to view. Lucy added two more, both Federal-style brownstones in Brooklyn Heights with red-brick exteriors and arched doorways. Both properties were emblematic of the neighborhood's architecture, but both were also priced at least half a million dollars higher than the couple's initially stated price ceiling of $3 million. At the two units she had picked out, Lucy took a few minutes to describe the exteriors. At the first one she mentioned that Brooklyn Heights was the first neighborhood to be declared a historic district by the city's preservation board. John took off his sunglasses and, looking around, said, "I can understand why—this is so handsome!" At the second unit Lucy said, "Isn't that brick beautiful? I mean it's so classic, right?" Steven agreed, "Yeah, it's gorgeous." Lucy continued, "I actually really love this location too. It's funny, it's right in between these few blocks where all these writers used to live, Walt Whitman and Arthur Miller, some others I think," as she pointed southwest.

Over the next two months Lucy and the couple viewed twelve more units, ten of which were not in Brooklyn Heights. John and Steve were more subdued in their assessments of these properties. For example, John described one unit as "nice," shrugging his shoulders when he said it— nothing, it seemed, had excited the couple as much as the houses in Brooklyn Heights they had viewed earlier. When Lucy informed me that John and Steven were going to make on offer on one of the first units that Lucy had selected and praised in Brooklyn Heights, I asked her why she thought the couple had chosen that one. She said:

> I think it's about the history of the neighborhood. They were really into how old all of the houses are and what famous people lived there and when. It's not that it's about glamour, but they definitely wanted a place that had a history and image, like a specific look.

John echoed Lucy's assessment:

> The beauty of the neighborhood is unbeatable. It's like the West Village, but without Sixth and Seventh Avenue running through it. I really liked how stately it looked, and I think [Steven] really liked the history. Not just Walt Whitman and Auden and all that but like, [chuckling] they just renamed one of the parks after the Beastie Boy who died because he lived there too. So I think it was a lot of things. It's the kind of place where we could look at beautiful houses and be tickled by all the fun facts that come with [them]. Who could pass up a brownstone in Brooklyn Heights? I mean, we've all seen *Moonstruck*, right?

Moonstruck is a 1987 romantic comedy starring Cher and Nicholas Cage that takes place in Brooklyn Heights. In the film, tellingly, characters remark on the large size of the protagonists' Brooklyn Heights townhouse.

It is revealing that John's and Lucy's accounts highlight similar aspects of the neighborhood as reasons for the couple's choice. While the buyers came into the transaction knowing they wanted to live in a certain part of the city, Lucy was able to parse the reasons behind their stated preference and further draw them out during the search process. As a result, the agent and the buyer gave similar explanations for why a particular unit resonated with the buyer and was ultimately the right match. John's explanation, moreover, shows how agents used this matching process to spark a specific, actionable kind of excitement. John's interest in the cultural history of the neighborhood was fostered by his early interactions with Lucy, and he subsequently expressed increased excitement about Brooklyn Heights. John stated that the unit he and Steven were buying was "just what we were looking for. . . . It feels good to know we're in a place that really suits us."

Over four years after they purchased their home, the couple still recounted the feelings of excitement they had experienced during the search. Recalling *Moonstruck*, where Cher falls in love with a passionate Nicholas Cage even though she's engaged to his drab brother, John said, "I remember being so in love with this house when we first saw it," adding that others they had viewed had been "lackluster" by comparison.

This analogy of "falling in love" was common among buyers as well as agents, and buyers often attributed their decisions to these amorous feelings for neighborhoods and houses. For example, agent Nancy was visiting open houses with buyers Adam and Eli. They had already viewed an apartment in a building where the couple had wanted to buy, but the unit sold to someone else before they made an offer. At a subsequent open house, Adam and Eli reacted indifferently to the apartment they were viewing—they had blank expressions as they moved through the place, and they did not ask many questions or stay particularly long. As they were leaving, Nancy said, "That was a bit of a letdown, huh?" Referring to the building Adam and Eli had wanted to buy in, she said, "I know you were really in love with that other place." Eli sighed and lamented, "Yeah we really did love it." Five years after they had purchased a different apartment in that same building where they had initially fallen in love, Adam still used metaphor. He said of Nancy, "She understood how much we loved this place."

When agents fail to generate an emotional connection between buyers and neighborhoods, it's all the more difficult to close a sale. Isaac, a buyer in his late twenties, had just graduated from a prestigious business school and worked in the financial district (FiDi) in downtown Manhattan—a neighborhood that included Wall Street and is filled with high-rise residential buildings. The neighborhood is not known for many cultural attractions or amenities; as one agent said, "The only reason I'd ever live there is if I worked there." At Isaac's initial meeting with his agent, Thomas, Isaac expressed ambivalence about living close to his office, saying, "I don't really *need* to live that close," and "I'm not opposed to [living in the financial district], but I'm open to other places too." Despite these signals, Thomas began compiling a list of apartments to visit in FiDi.

Thomas kept faith through three months of showings in which Isaac displayed little interest in the apartments he was seeing. At every showing Thomas brought up how close Isaac would be to his job and how most people who worked in finance downtown also lived downtown. At a showing in the fourth month, Thomas mentioned that the unit was on a particularly peaceful block, if Isaac ever wanted to work at home. Isaac responded, "But what if I want to go out? This is so dead." After another two months Isaac gave up, telling Thomas that for now he would continue to rent his current apartment.

Thomas had expanded the search beyond FiDi in those last two months, but it was too late. The failure to appropriately match Isaac to the right neighborhood early in the sales process meant the transaction lacked excitement and arousal. As Isaac put it, "I didn't see anything that wowed me." He disparaged FiDi as uncool and said, "I just got tired of looking." In short, mismatching a buyer blocks the development of excitement and arousal, dampening the chance of completing the transaction.

PRODUCING ANXIETY

Real estate agents also moved transactions forward by describing market scarcity, or the need for buyers to act quickly to purchase a particular unit.[30] Agents highlighted scarcity by quoting statistics regarding the lack of available inventory, the rise in the average number of bidders on units, and the extreme shortening of the time units were on the market.[31] They intended these scarcity statistics to alert buyers to the necessity of acting quickly since units could be lost to other bidders. These statistics made buyers feel anxious, fearful, and worried, which would make them more likely to complete a purchase.

One agent who worked in Manhattan reported:

> I've been a broker for about fifteen years, and I don't think I've ever seen things moving so fast. It's pretty amazing what sellers are asking for and even more amazing what buyers are willing to pay. I think they're more and more

afraid that if they don't jump on something, they'll lose out and have to keep looking forever.

Another agent working in Brooklyn said:

> The real thing I'm focusing on right now is trying to get [buyers] to understand turnover. It's just unbelievable how short units are on the market right now since demand is so high, and so everyone is scared that if they don't make that one bid they'll miss out.

Agents highlighted scarcity even in locations where units lingered on the market. An agent working in central New York State explained:

> We don't have the kind of demand you have in the city, but that doesn't mean people don't want to jump on something when they like it. I had a house, a really beautiful four-bedroom that we listed at $224,900. We got interest early on from one couple, but I kept telling the sellers to put them off because someone with a better offer would come. And we waited three or four months, and this other couple came along and offered a ton more. So we went to the first ones and told them the offer, and we ended up selling to them for $269,000, which is crazy. . . . I think we got it up because I said to [the buyers], "Look, this is the only original Victorian on the market right now, and it's the only one that predates 1890," or something like that. And boom! They just went for it.[32]

No matter the specifics of any given housing market, listing agents singularize houses to create scarcity. Agents believed buyers would enact "naive economic theory"—in this case, the belief that if a product is scarce within a given market, it is presumed to be more desirable and worthy of a higher price.[33]

Agents' emphasis on scarcity impacted buyers' feelings and, in turn, their stated preferences. For example, Tim was looking to buy his first apartment in Manhattan. At their initial meeting, Tim told his agent Nancy that he felt no immediate pressure to make an offer. Instead he said that since he planned to live in New York the rest of his life, he wanted his apartment to be "very special." He went on to say, "I want to take it slow and look at everything." Over the first two days as they viewed apartments, Nancy brought up the low inventory in Manhattan as well as the declining average time units were spending on the market. Nancy also reinforced her point with outside information: "I emailed him a copy of this report from last year about how time on the market is at its lowest since even before 2008."

Tim seemed to be affected by the information, especially after a unit he said he liked—but didn't love—sold one week after he had viewed it. When this happened, Nancy reminded him of her earlier warnings about scarcity. She reported: "I said to him, 'See, I told you we were going to have move very fast.'" Only five weeks after their initial meeting, Tim decided to make an offer on a unit.

After the sale, I asked Tim about the decision. Sighing and shaking his head, he said, "I'm actually kind of dazed. I just didn't think it would be this fast. It was like all of sudden I needed to say yes, and I was worried that if I didn't say yes I would miss out on a good place." The exposure to scarcity affected Tim in a way he did not anticipate, and it altered his perspective on the purchasing process. Several years later he was still in the same apartment. He recalled the feelings he experienced going through the search process and how Nancy had helped him deal with them: "What I remember is feeling knocked around, you know, like thrown into a boxing ring. Nancy was my trainer in the corner yelling, 'Do it! Do it! Or you're going to get knocked out.'"

At a showing in a new development in Queens, the listing agent said directly to a wincing buyer, "You know how they say global warming will cause all these water wars? That's like apartment hunting right now. It's like you better get everything you can now." Buyers used words like *tense*, *scared*, and *worried* to describe their experiences. Even when buyers suspected agents of overemphasizing low inventory or rising prices, the stress of scarcity was still effective. One buyer said:

> I think [my real estate agent] was trying hard with the numbers. She kept saying how we needed to look fast and buy fast and I think it was a bit of a sales hoax. But she really was right and we made an offer quickly when we found our place. . . . It was a good offer because we were afraid we'd miss out.

Another buyer explained that even though he wanted to take his time with the search, the amount of information his agent provided him about the rapidity of the market had been "daunting," so when the agent recommended making an offer after only four weeks of searching, he agreed.

One buyer offered a particularly vivid description of her search process four years earlier:

> I just remember being so freaked out because it was literally one apartment after another [that] I looked at selling the next day. I remember getting used to that news from [the real estate agent] like picking up the phone and just

holding my breath and every time it was, "Oh, that place we looked at yesterday has an offer," "Oh, remember that apartment you said you liked, well they have ten offers!" I'm not joking, it was scary.

Agents exposed buyers to the scarcity and intensity of the market, and this exposure clearly evoked feelings of fear and anxiety about the market. As a result, buyers reported feeling pressured to make deals quickly, even when they assumed agents were overstating the necessity to do so.

One agent working in Manhattan expressed reservations about highlighting scarcity:

> My job is to get the best outcome for my client, so I'm often encouraging them to wait . . . even in this market. I see some [listing] agents trying to bullshit about the multiple offers they're getting, but that's just a sales tactic and I'm telling my guys to hold off. . . . Yes, [buyers] get nervous but I try to explain that, you know, patience is a virtue.

A few agents from across the state reported similar sentiments, saying that techniques that pressure buyers were "sleazy" or contributed to their occupation's poor reputation. However, most agents reported invoking scarcity because they thought it increased the chances of a sale, reflected actual market conditions, or, in most cases, did both. As one agent said, "I feel like the best way I can help [a buyer] is by being honest about the market. Right now that means telling them to move as fast as they can."

AGENTS AND CHANGING PREFERENCES

Market intermediaries—in this case, real estate agents—play an important role in shaping consumers' choices. They link identities to products and evoke emotions from consumers, which can make consumers understand some purchasing options as more appropriate than others. In some cases, market intermediaries can even alter buyers' preferences.[34]

Market intermediaries' ability to infuse products with meaning illuminates both the instability of individual preferences and the power of market intermediaries in shaping economic outcomes. The interactions I observed between agents and buyers made clear that agents often had the power to change buyers' stated preferences in the housing market. As a result of interacting with agents, buyers changed their minds about where they wanted to live and what kinds of houses they wanted to buy. Once they entered the search in earnest with agents, buyers' ideas about how the purchase should unfold, which houses were right for them, how much they wanted to pay (further examined in the next chapter), and even the neighborhood where they should live were deeply dependent on interactions with agents. The next two chapters explore how these interactions between agents and buyers not only altered buyers' preferences but did so in ways that create inequality across neighborhoods.

3

MALLEABLE PRICES

[Buyers] always spend more than they think they will, they just don't know it yet.
AGENT WORKING IN BROOKLYN

With people who have enough money, it's never going to be about price. It's going to be about how a place makes them feel. With everyone else, you kind of have to stay within budget.
AGENT WORKING IN MANHATTAN

Every one of the forty-nine buyers who purchased a home with the help of a real estate agent in this study paid more than his or her originally stated price ceiling. They were upsold.[1] Buyers' offers exceeded the amount they initially said they wanted to spend by anywhere from $2,500 to $3.4 million. Over and over again, I heard agents tell buyers that spending just a small amount more would get them a studio in a newer building or closer to a subway station. And I saw agents convince other buyers that purchasing a townhouse was better than buying an apartment—even though the former would cost hundreds of thousands of dollars more.

Real estate agents play an undeniable role in shaping homeseekers' preferences and decision-making, even when it comes to the seemingly sticky issue of how much a buyer is going to spend. Buyers and agents are necessarily interacting with each other throughout the sales process as they visit open houses, constantly discussing how a given housing unit might change a buyer's life. In this chapter I explore how these interactions affected the dollar amounts buyers were willing to pay for homes.

The evidence presented below reveals an intriguing trend: wealthier buyers were upsold at dramatically higher levels than less wealthy buyers. Interactions between agents and very wealthy buyers lacked overt discussions of prices and instead focused on aesthetic and geographic preferences—what kind of house did these wealthier buyers want, and where did they want to live? With less wealthy buyers, in contrast, agents were more willing to intervene and instruct on what buyers could expect to receive within a given price range. Agents' deference toward wealthier buyers, especially regarding financial issues, produced situations that allowed agents to more easily reorient them toward vastly more expensive housing units. Conversely, because interactions between agents and the less wealthy focused more explicitly on price, the margin of upselling tended to be smaller. Different styles of interaction between buyers and agents, in other words, contributed not only to buyers' preferences when it came to where to live and what kind of housing unit they wanted, but also to the prices they were willing to pay.

Previous work in the sociology of markets has demonstrated that prices are subject to various social factors like a seller's status and a buyer's adherence to local norms. But to fully understand how buyers come to pay the prices they do, we must study the sales process itself. In other words, markets—and the inequalities they produce—are constituted on the ground in interactions between market actors.

WHERE DO PRICES COME FROM?

Capitalist markets need prices. Market actors require some sort of rubric to determine how much they should ask for an item they wish to sell, and how they should pay for an item they wish to buy.[2] Models from classical economics treat price as an objective product of certain market conditions: prices reflect some aggregate form of value, created by how much of something there is and how badly people want it. However, as many economists and sociologists have pointed out, this theory of prices cannot account for the reality of pricing. Price is not so easily predicted as a function of supply and demand. This is especially true in the housing market.[3]

Some sociologists have argued that prices are an artifact of relationships that create trust and obligation within networks. Consumers and suppliers establish various types of relationships, including relationships with market intermediaries, that influence their agreed-upon prices.[4] When individuals or firms have a wide range of ties in a market they increase their access to information which can lower the prices they pay.[5] Close network ties also reduce transaction costs between consumers and suppliers because participants trust each other; they deem the more formal and time-consuming aspects of exchange unnecessary.[6] Put another way, I can have faith in a handshake deal with a close friend, though I might feel more secure with a written contract when doing a deal with someone I barely know. Prices in a particular market also reflect status differences across sellers.[7] Higher-status sellers can charge higher prices for their goods, even if such goods are of comparable quality to those made by lower-status producers.[8]

While the network approach can help us understand what happens *within* a market, it struggles to account for the ways that markets are connected to the rest of social life.[9] Markets are fundamentally spaces of meaning-making.[10] Given this, prices are not produced simply by variations in network ties; rather, market actors' collective beliefs dictate value and acceptable forms of payment.[11] Prices, then, are the result of culture—the shared understandings market actors have about different products.[12] And as shown in the previous chapter, market intermediaries play an important role in shaping buyers' understandings of and feelings toward particular products in a given market.[13]

An illustrative example comes from the world of modeling. The sociologist Ashley Mears (2011) spent years studying pricing in the market for fashion models. What she found is that a fashion model who takes a job being photographed for a catalog will diminish her chances of obtaining more sought-after editorial jobs—being photographed for fashion magazines—in the future. These editorial jobs are highly coveted even though they pay little because they sometimes, though extremely rarely, lead to what Mears calls an "editorial jackpot," or a contract with a high-end fashion label that can pay millions. Buyers, sellers, and intermediaries in the modeling industry—scouts, photographers, agents, labels, editors, and the models themselves—are socialized into thinking catalog and editorial work are distinct. As distinct forms of work within the local culture of the modeling world, they are rewarded with different levels and forms of compensation. Catalog models generally command higher prices but much lower prestige.[14] Understanding cultural classifications is, then, at the heart of understanding value and prices.[15]

These approaches provide powerful explanations for why certain products are valued more than others and how prices come to be.[16] But in the case of real estate, it is clear that consumer preferences are highly malleable and contextually dependent. How is it that consumers decide to pay a particular amount in the moment? Or, more to the point in the case of upselling, how do consumers' attitudes about the appropriate price for housing change as transactions progress? Observing the interactions that constitute economic exchanges, particularly between buyers and real estate agents, gives us a window into this process.

The prices consumers pay are not static or even just the result of cultural orientations; they are produced through interactions that reciprocally condition subsequent action.[17] Once actors understand the process of transacting, they come to expect similar situations to play out in similar ways.[18] But most buyers only interact with real estate agents one or two times over the course of their lives, while agents, as skilled market intermediaries, reenact sales transactions every day at work. Because agents have more experience with the market, they are better able to control the script and how action unfolds, which means they have an opportunity to shape buyers' understanding of pricing and the housing market.

WHO KNOWS ABOUT MONEY?

Real estate agents, as skilled market intermediaries, managed buyers' experiences in ways that convinced buyers to spend more than they initially thought they would. However, the content and quality of the discussions between agents and buyers were not consistent across buyers. Real estate agents spoke differently about money with clients they perceived to be wealthier. While there is no one definitive marker between wealthier buyers and less wealthy buyers—the distinction was born through observation— agents broadly agreed that in a market like New York City, buyers who could afford above the median price for an apartment in Manhattan (between $800,000 and $1 million during my fieldwork) were wealthy.[19] Everyone else was not.[20]

Agents interacted with clients searching for houses at higher prices as if these wealthier buyers, by virtue of their wealth, were better investors and had a deeper understanding of economic purchasing. As real estate agent Liz put it after her first meeting with Claude and Janet, who wanted to spend $2.7 million on an apartment, wealthier buyers "are very smart, and if they can spend that much on a house, I know I don't have to spend too much time going over the details of financing and all that." Claude and Janet were first-time buyers and were younger than Liz, so Liz's assessment of their knowledge was not based on some prior experience they might have had in the market. Instead it emerged from Liz's belief that wealthier buyers either knew about money or, because they had a lot of it, didn't need or want to talk about money. This conceptualization of wealthier buyers as innately good with money parallels the treatment of privileged people in various other settings, including elite schools, universities, and firms, where they are often credited with inherent talent and a strong work ethic regardless of their actual performance.[21] And this presumption of knowledge about or indifference to money meant that, generally, wealthier buyers and agents talked about price points only at the very beginning of the sales process, when agents were gathering initial information on the buyer, and at the very end, when they were constructing and negotiating an offer on a unit.

Real estate agent Brandon rarely discussed prices during showings with wealthier buyers. When the issue did come up, usually because the buyer prompted it, the conversations were characterized by a great deal of deference.[22] For instance, Brandon had buyers, a couple from South Florida searching for a New York City apartment, who were looking to spend $6.75 million. At the open houses they visited, Brandon and the buyers discussed various aspects of different units including building amenities, architectural and interior design styles, and the qualities of different neighborhoods in downtown Manhattan. These conversations lacked discussion of the prices of the apartments under consideration, some of which were as high as $9 million. When looking at the fourth unit in their search, which was in the Tribeca neighborhood of Manhattan, one of the buyers asked Brandon how much more the apartment could be worth in the near future. This was the first overt mention of price I had witnessed during my trips to open houses with Brandon and this couple. Brandon's response was coy. He said he wasn't sure he could tell the buyers anything they didn't already know. "All I can tell you is that property values here have always been high and have only gone up and up since the dip," he said. "But you know that." The buyers seemed to agree. They did not press Brandon on the point and did not bring up prices again when they were visiting other open houses.

Brandon acted similarly in his interactions with the couple moving from London discussed in chapter 2. With them Brandon also avoided talking about the specifics of resale value; he instead focused on the cultural status and accessibility of the neighborhood. Though they initially stated a price ceiling of $2.5 million, the couple from London eventually offered $2.96 million. The South Florida couple made an offer on an apartment for $8.25 million — $1.5 million more than their initially stated price ceiling.

I found it surprising that an experienced and ambitious agent like Brandon would forgo opportunities to demonstrate his knowledge of the local market. Agents are, after all, steeped in the market in a way most buyers, regardless of their wealth, are not. In contrast to the ways that agents freely demonstrated how their knowledge was superior to websites and that they were more ethical than their colleagues, or sought to establish themselves as authorities on neighborhoods and amenities, their interactions with very wealthy buyers were almost entirely devoid of any sort of didactic character when it came to prices.[23] For example, Kim, an agent working in the pricey West Village neighborhood of Manhattan once told a couple—first-time buyers who worked in tech whose stated price ceiling was $8 million—to simply go with their gut on questions of price and value. When they asked her if she thought a particular townhouse listed at over $9 million was a good deal, she said, "Whatever you think is best is best. We'll look at comps later, but if you think it's worth it, then it is."

Interactions between the elite and their service providers are often patterned so that elites are continually reassured that they are entitled to their specific desires and opinions when it comes to consumption practices.[24] However, agents were not simply validating wealthy prospective homebuyers' desires; they were also crediting them with a type of economic authority and knowledge regardless of whether or not they actually displayed it. Put another way, agents seemed to think very wealthy people deserved deference simply because they were wealthy.

It could be that agents treated wealthy buyers with deference not because they thought wealthier buyers were indeed more knowledgeable economic actors but simply because agents thought wealthier buyers didn't care to talk about money. In other words, agents may have wanted to spare wealthier buyers the embarrassment of discussing their astounding economic resources.[25] Either way, agents believed that extreme affluence brought flexibility to wealthier buyers' price preferences. Indeed, wealthier buyers, agents believed, lacked constraints on the prices they could offer for houses. Agents assumed wealthier buyers did not need help securing mortgages—if they needed mortgages at all—and did not require information about how the sales process worked. Nonrepresentative industry data on home sales in Manhattan from a time not long after my fieldwork do indeed indicate that the higher-priced properties tend to be purchased by buyers who are less dependent on financing and can make all-cash offers, meaning that agents' assumptions about wealthier buyers' price point flexibility may be accurate—wealthier buyers have vast amounts of capital and don't need mortgages.[26]

Yet in interviews, agents did consistently say that wealthier people were uniquely knowledgeable about markets. Miguel was elated when he met with a couple in their twenties looking to spend $950,000 for an apartment in the Brooklyn neighborhood of Prospect Heights. They were going to be Miguel's highest-paying client to date, and I assumed—incorrectly—that his excitement stemmed solely from the fact that he stood to make a great deal of money on the commission. When I asked about the buyers, he said he was excited for a different reason: "It's a relief because they don't need financing. I can focus on doing my job instead of holding their hands all the time. . . . I won't have to explain every little financial detail." By treating wealthier buyers as if they were knowledgeable and financially able, agents lend wealthier buyers a type of interactional credit that minimizes the appearance of informational asymmetries. Indeed, wealthy buyers, like individuals or organizations who are deemed worthy of risk and receive a loan, got the benefit of the doubt in judgments regarding their economic knowledge.[27] This belief—that wealthier clients were economically knowledgeable and capable—meant agents felt that discussing prices and economic decision-making more generally was unnecessary.

Interactions between agents and less wealthy buyers unfolded very differently. Agents were broadly more instructive and authoritative with less wealthy clients. "They want to be sure you know what you're doing," said one agent working in Brooklyn about why agents needed to demonstrate authority with less wealthy buyers. He continued, "This a huge deal for them. This is the biggest thing they'll ever buy, and that makes them really anxious." A less wealthy buyer echoed these sentiments: "I've never done this before. It's the most stressful decision I've ever made, and I definitely needed a lot of calming down throughout the whole thing." Agents often used the term *hand-holding* to describe their relationships with less wealthy buyers. They assumed that the less wealthy lacked a base knowledge about how to use their capital and required more guidance and instruction than their more affluent counterparts. Even if less wealthy buyers did not express initial anxieties about price, agents sought to establish their superior knowledge about the process.

For example, recall the interaction between Thomas and Andrew: Andrew the buyer who had brought a list of units to visit he had found online, and Thomas the agent who literally waved away that information as inferior to his own market knowledge. In that interaction Thomas was disparaging the information Andrew had provided. He was instructive—occasionally to the point of being rude—during the search process.

Andrew had said he wanted to spend less than $625,000 on an apartment. As their search continued, Thomas did not hide his exasperation with Andrew; he frequently corrected or disagreed with the buyer about the value of different units. One Sunday Andrew met Thomas at an open house where the listing agent handed them a listing sheet. Andrew and Thomas peered at it together, and after quickly scanning the apartment, Andrew pointed to the price on the listing sheet and said, "I'm not sure this place is worth that." Thomas gave what looked like a forced smile and said, "Don't worry, you should leave those kinds of things to me." A few minutes later they had gone through the apartment and Thomas said, "I think it's a fine price." After Andrew left a showing, Thomas turned to me and said, with some agitation, "I'm a professional. I'm useful for *him*, not the other way around."

Generally in interactions between agents and less wealthy buyers, agent authority was overt, agents openly disagreed with buyers' statements about valuation and pricing in particular, and they did not conceal their frustrations with what they considered to be less wealthy buyers questioning agents' expertise. In short, the less wealthy were not afforded the kind of interactional credit that wealthy buyers received.

Agents who worked with a range of buyers not only considered less wealthy buyers less financially savvy but also tended to be more judgmental of their behavior, often spoke of them in belittling ways, and broadly said that less wealthy buyers required more attention. One agent working in Brooklyn said of her work, "With buyers who are looking for small, cheap deals it's no fun. They take a lot of time going over the process like getting loans and everything." Agents were also concerned that buyers who needed financing might fail to secure a mortgage. Furthermore, when purchases are financed with a mortgage, they are subject to more scrutiny. Banks making loans require homes to be appraised, opening up the possibility that the bank might decide the unit is not worth the price the buyer offered. Buyers who do not require financing do not necessarily have to have units appraised before they close a deal, so they are free to offer any amount for a particular unit. Agents certainly know this, and it dovetailed with their understanding of wealthier buyers as more willing and able to go far above their price ceilings.

While narrating his professional history, one agent working in Manhattan said that as his career progressed and his client base became more affluent, he was able to spend more time on the aspects of his work that he enjoyed. This included providing his clients with in-depth architectural histories of potential houses and spending more time following the churn of restaurants, bars, shops, and other amenities in the neighborhoods where he worked—in short, steeping himself in the lived experience of the neighborhood in order to sell it. He explained that while less wealthy buyers required attention from him regarding "how to actually buy a house," working with wealthier buyers liberated him from the more mundane aspects of his job. Agents liked participating in the production of neighborhood reputations a lot more than working through the financial and legal minutiae of housing transactions.

The distinct ways agents treated wealthy and less wealthy buyers is further illustrated by the different reactions Lucy had to two different clients who were hesitant to share the details of their financial lives. The first, a buyer who was looking for houses listed at less than $700,000 in the Boerum Hill neighborhood of Brooklyn, did not email Lucy any financial documents confirming he was precertified for a mortgage loan after their first meeting. A wealthier buyer looking to purchase a townhouse for over $3 million in the neighboring Cobble Hill section of Brooklyn also did not follow up with any financials. When I spoke to Lucy a week after meeting with the first client, she complained that he might not be a "real buyer . . . just wasting my time." Conversely, when I asked Lucy about the wealthier buyer who had not provided her with any bank statements or any other proof of ability to pay, she brushed it off: "I'm not worried about it, it's just one step of many." The buyers' initially stated price ceilings were a strong signal to Lucy in determining which clients were worthy of deference.

Wealth was not the only display of status that earned potential buyers interactional credit. Agents sometimes offered deference to clients who were making all cash offers, regardless of their price ceiling (i.e., they did not require a mortgage), who worked in certain occupations (e.g., finance), and, occasionally, who were older or who had experience in the market. For example, one agent working in Manhattan said, "You can assume older buyers or the ones that have lived [in New York City] awhile are a little more seasoned." Note, however, that in the examples of Lucy's treatment of buyers above, the first buyer, who wanted to spend $700,000, was clearly older than Lucy, while the second, who wanted to spend $3 million, was around her age. Indeed, experience alone rarely earned buyers much credit. One couple, whose stated price ceiling was $650,000, had purchased their last apartment in New York City three years prior to beginning their new search. But interactions with their agent, Miguel, were not marked by deference. The three of them constantly discussed prices. At their first open house he told the couple, "Don't worry, I'll walk you through everything." After a Sunday of visiting multiple open houses, he said, "I know this is a lot [of information] to take in, so let me think about these prices," adding that he would contact the buyers soon. Age, occupation, or whether or not a buyer had previously purchased a house all mattered less than buyers' initially stated price ceiling.

UPSELLING THE VERY WEALTHY

On her first outing with Bill, an executive at a financial services firm whose stated price ceiling was an all-cash offer of $900,000, real estate agent Liz took him to three units listed above $1 million. Showing clients housing units listed at prices higher than the buyers' stated price ceilings was very common across price points, but the interactions played out differently with very wealthy buyers. Luis, for example, told me that he sometimes takes clients to see properties he knew they can't afford simply to see what sparks their interest. In the case of Chelsea and Jordan, whose stating price ceiling was $680,000, he said he was showing them a listing at $750,000 because "I want them to know what's possible, what's out there. . . . I want to see what they'll respond to." Liz was up to something else. In keeping with the patterns of interaction I witnessed between other agents and wealthier buyers, Liz never mentioned price to Bill, and Bill did not bring it up.

Agents widely assumed that wealthier buyers had much softer limits on their price points. As one agent who worked in a very wealthy town on the Long Island Sound put it, "In my experience, there's not a big difference between one or two or five million [dollars]." One agent who specialized in high-end brownstones in the Fort Greene neighborhood of Brooklyn said that buyers "always spend more than they think they will; they just don't know it yet." Another agent working in Manhattan said of his buyers, all of whom were very wealthy, "They always spend more than what their budget is, always."

After about three months of searching, Bill made an offer on a unit for $1.2 million. There had been no discussion of price while Bill and Liz were visiting open houses; it was only once Bill agreed to make an offer that any particular dollar amount was mentioned. Certainly buyers, even very wealthy ones, are limited in what they can spend by their actual capital (i.e. income, savings, current assets, ability to secure loans or financial support). Agents nevertheless assumed the structural limitations on individual buyers' abilities to pay were far less constraining for buyers at the higher end of the market.

Given that agents rarely discussed price with wealthier buyers, how did upselling actually happen? In their interactions with these wealthier clients, agents encouraged them to form preferences for building and architectural styles, neighborhoods, and amenities that were above their stated price point—but they did this without mentioning price. For example, Brandon had a client, a single middle-aged man, who initially said he wanted to spend $2.9 million somewhere in Manhattan. The buyer complained that his recent divorce settlement had left him with a budget of only $2.9 million; this was the most he was willing to spend. Brandon began showing him units around that price. At these showings, however, Brandon and the buyer spent a great deal of time talking about the distasteful aspects of units.

At one Brandon brought up the narrow windows, which were "especially small for a new building." At another, older building he commented, "It's surprising to see a prewar [building] with such low ceilings," later adding that the unit was "kind of blah." The buyer also focused on things he did not like, complaining about the distance of certain apartments from subway stations or the ugliness of particular building exteriors.

After visiting seven listings and not being excited about—let alone liking—any of them, the buyer seemed resigned. As they left an open house, Brandon offered to take the buyer out for coffee to talk about the search so far. As they discussed the units they had seen together, the buyer glumly said, "I don't think we've seen anything unique." Brandon agreed and apologized. "It's my fault," he said. "I'm going to do a lot this week to find you some things that are really special." The next three apartments they visited were priced between $700,000 and $1.4 million more than the buyer's initial price ceiling. Brandon told me that he had not asked the buyer if looking at higher priced units was acceptable; instead he simply sent the listings to the buyer and set up showings.

The mood of these showings was markedly different from that of their previous outings. This time around, Brandon and the buyer focused on the positive aspects of these more expensive units. "This place," Brandon said to the buyer at a unit priced at $4.05 million, "is more your style." Brandon praised the look of particular moldings, remarked on "gorgeous" views, and often used the word *special* to describe these pricier apartments. Eventually the buyer made an offer on an apartment for $3.9 million, over a third more than his stated ceiling.

While agents avoided directly discussing prices with very wealthy buyers, this did not mean they entirely avoided talking about market conditions. The remarkable ways the New York City housing market had changed since the Great Recession were common knowledge, and agents sometimes drew on the historically low levels of inventory to induce anxiety and, in effect, upsell wealthy buyers. For example, one respondent working in Manhattan said of wealthy buyers, "I have to show them how the market is crazy right now. Even with these big deals I've been doing lately, I have to remind them about how there's no inventory, and if I keep reminding them, they'll start to understand they have to reevaluate how much they want to spend." Exposing clients to the market gave agents a way to upsell wealthy clients while still maintaining a deferential demeanor regarding price.

Agents' commentary on scarcity could drive clients to act quickly and spend significantly more than they originally anticipated. A couple looking for a house in Brooklyn with a stated ceiling of $1 million made a $1.65 million offer only three weeks into their search after their agent continually invoked the scarcity of townhouses in the neighborhoods where they wanted to live. Despite the fact that the couple had indicated they were looking for a condo or co-op, their agent Lucy took them to four showings at townhouses in central Brooklyn, all listed between $1.495 million and $2 million. Instead of mentioning price, she talked about how much more space they would have in a townhouse, as opposed to a condo or co-op apartment in a multiunit building. Additionally, Lucy continually brought up the city's low level of available houses, quoting statistics about the lack of available housing and the "incredibly short closing times" for townhouses in particular. At one house Lucy said, "These are really amazing pieces of property, but they're going like hotcakes. There are 50 percent fewer units for sale here than there were last year. It's the lowest inventory in the last seven years." The buyers turned to each other, and the husband remarked, "Well, we better get on top of it, right?" (When I later asked Lucy where this statistic came from, she said she could not remember exactly but that it was probably from "some industry report.") By the time Lucy had shown the buyers two more houses the following week, the buyers had decided to make an offer.

This was the shortest time from initial meeting to offering that I witnessed. The buyers, however, were satisfied at the time with their decision to spend over 50 percent over their stated price ceiling. I spoke to the wife the week after they made the offer, and she seemed to agree with Lucy's framing of the market: "I don't think [the search] was fast at all. I think that with the market being what it is, we ended up doing great." Years after they had made their purchase, however, her attitude had changed. She said that the process had "probably been rushed," and there were a few things she wished they had considered more carefully about the purchase. In particular, the townhouse was a longer walk to the subway than it had initially seemed, especially in bad weather, and they had spent more than expected replacing much of the house's plumbing. She blamed the market—not Lucy—for the speed at which they had made a decision: "Maybe we should have been a little more thoughtful and taken our time, but the market around here was just so crazy." However, she described the price they had paid as the "correct" amount.

The consequence of avoiding price talk—and the deferential ways agents and buyers interacted more broadly—was surprising: wealthier buyers were upsold at much higher rates than wealthy clients. Agents' deference meant that the amount a buyer was going to offer was less overtly codified than in conversations with less wealthy buyers. Instead by eliciting buyers' preferences on nonprice aspects of houses, including location, building amenities, building type, or architectural styles, agents created situations that allowed wealthy buyers to be upsold at a very high rate. Agents and buyers discussed what buyers liked but not whether they had any constraints on their ability to spend. The broader point is that the prices buyers are willing to offer emerge through interactions between buyers and agents. While agents and less wealthy buyers engaged in similar discussions of preferences, they also explicitly discussed price. As a result, less wealthy buyers were not upsold to the same extent as wealthy ones.

UPSELLING THE LESS WEALTHY

Less wealthy buyers also paid more for their housing than they had originally anticipated, but at lower rates than their wealthier counterparts. Agents and less wealthy buyers spoke about prices constantly. For example, Liz was trying to convince her buyers, a couple looking to buy in Brooklyn, to raise their suggested bid on an apartment by $10,000. She said this was necessary to engage the seller in negotiation instead of being rejected outright. The buyers were apprehensive and agreed to raise their offer, somewhat begrudgingly, only after an extensive conversation in Liz's office. During the conversation Liz kept referring to $10,000 as a small amount to pay to become "homeowners." "Isn't this exciting, to get to own a home?" she said. She added that she thought the $10,000 rise seemed "worth it."

After the deal had been completed, I asked one of the buyers about his experience with the purchase:

> We knew we were paying a bit more than we should. . . . But we really wanted this place and so didn't want to risk low-balling and have [the seller] have another open house and go through [with] another offer. . . . We really wanted to own.

The buyer glossed over his previous discomfort with paying more specifically because ownership was so important to them. He and his wife had agreed to offer $685,000 instead of their initially stated ceiling of $675,000. As this example shows, agents actively and openly discussed prices—actual dollar amounts—with less wealthy buyers. Many agents, like Liz, framed paying slightly more as a way to attain some kind of status related to home-ownership.

Sarah talked openly about prices with a couple who had made an offer on an apartment for $710,000, $20,000 higher than their initially stated price ceiling. When the couple met with Sarah and asked about dropping out of the negotiation process, she responded by connecting the price to other symbolic values of the house: "I know it's a little more than you wanted to spend, but it's really got that warm kind of feeling you were looking for . . . plenty of room for your kids too." In contrast, four months earlier Sarah had a very wealthy couple with children, with an initially stated price ceiling of $1.25 million, offer $1.75 million on an apartment. When the seller countered with a higher price, the buyers asked Sarah about dropping out of negotiations. In their case, however, she did not try to persuade the buyers to continue. Instead she informed the listing agent that the buyers had decided to keep looking.

Recall the single female buyer whom Liz pressured into bringing her boyfriend to showings and who ultimately bought a two-bedroom apartment. That buyer's initially stated price ceiling was $660,000. All of the listings that Liz forwarded her—ostensibly because they could accommodate her *and* her boyfriend—were listed between $665,000 and $730,000. At one showing of an apartment listed at $715,000, with both the buyer and her boyfriend present, Liz said, "OK, let's talk money. I know this is over $700,000, but it's perfect for the two of you. I think we can get them down a little too." The buyer ultimately made an offer on a two-bedroom apartment for $689,000, about 4 percent higher than her initially stated price ceiling. With less wealthy buyers, the direct and open talk of prices lead to small margins of upselling, and the difference between their initial ceiling and what agents thought they should offer was typically described as a necessary investment to secure the kinds of domesticity and status often associated with homeownership.

When I asked them about these practices, agents often said that less wealthy buyers did not have the ability to go much beyond their initially stated price ceilings. They contrasted these buyers' situations with the flexibility associated with wealthier buyers. One agent said, "People who are spending $500,000 or $600,000 probably don't have a lot of wiggle room." Another agent who worked with a range of clients in Brooklyn said, "It's no use pushing people who are buying in Bushwick. If they could afford more, they'd buy in Williamsburg."[28] And one agent working in Manhattan said, "With people who have enough money it's never going to be about price. It's going to be about how a place makes them feel. With everyone else, you kind of have to stay within budget." Buyers with lower initially stated price ceilings usually required a mortgage, and agents regarded prequalification amounts as a relatively hard limit. Mortgage underwriters also require units to be appraised, which limited upselling because a less wealthy buyer could not freely make higher and higher offers on a particular unit if that home was unlikely to be deemed worth the offered price by the mortgage lender's appraiser.

Buyers were not, however, total doormats when it came to discussing prices. Some less wealthy buyers I observed occasionally bristled at the lack of deference from agents. For example, over a span of thirteen weeks Liz visited several units with a buyer searching for an apartment in North Brooklyn for under $750,000. In early visits the buyer, a marketing executive in his late twenties, was generally animated when talking about prices. He mentioned that he had spent the last few months searching real estate websites to get a sense of what he could expect to purchase at his price point. Liz was generally affable in their discussions but also firm in insisting that her knowledge of the market was likely more comprehensive. She sometimes seemed annoyed with the buyer's eagerness to display what he had learned online—she once rolled her eyes when the buyer began listing prices of recently sold units on a particular block.

On what turned out to be their last day viewing open houses together, Liz and the buyer visited a condo that the buyer had asked to see, listed at $749,000. After briefly looking around the unit, the buyer commented, "There's no way this place is worth that." Liz sharply disagreed, responding that she thought it was actually quite a good price. Liz then admonished the buyer for spending too much time on Zillow, which she said provided an "unrealistic snapshot" of the market. Afterward I asked Liz about the exchange. She was exasperated: "All [buyers] think about is, 'Oh, she showed us around the house, just like doing a Vanna White with a house.' There's a lot more to it than just opening the door and go ahead, go in." Liz's buyer did not return her next email, which contained new listings, and the relationship seemed to have ended. In this case Liz's lack of deference resulted in a failed deal.

"THE VIEW I'LL HAVE NOW"

Agents' different styles of interacting with buyers, depending on their perceived wealth, produced dramatically different levels of upselling. Buyers whose initially stated price ceiling was $1 million or over made offers on average 23 percent higher than what they had said they wanted to spend. Buyers whose price ceilings were under $1 million offered an average of only 5 percent above their initially desired price points. In dollars, the twenty buyers who began the search for housing wanting to spend $1 million or more ended up paying on average a little over $900,000 more than their stated price ceilings. For all the other buyers, the increase was about $34,000. Across all transactions, home buyers' initial price ceiling was positively and strongly correlated with the difference between the initial price ceiling and the actual price offered by 0.79 (p<.001).[29] In other words, buyers' initially stated price preference is highly correlated with the margin at which they were upsold.

One possible explanation for agents' varying treatment of buyers is simply that wealthier buyers have more money: they have more cash on hand and can secure more financing—if they need it at all—compared to less wealthy buyers.[30] Put another way, wealthier buyers are upsold more because they can afford to spend more. Real estate agents are perhaps correct when they assume wealthy buyers' stated price ceilings are softer. As a result, the gap between wealthy buyers' stated price ceilings and the actual price they intend to offer—the "reservation price," in real estate parlance— tends to be greater than that of less wealthy buyers.

Ability to pay is certainly *a* factor in explaining this outcome. But reports from both buyers who used agents and buyers who did not, as well as from buyers who had bought before and buyers who were purchasing a house for the first time, indicate that buyers primarily raised their reservation price because their interactions with real estate agents altered their price preferences. For example, Brandon's buyer, the recently divorced man who had a stated ceiling of $2.9 million and offered $3.9 million, had bought property in New York City before. Echoing another one of Brandon's buyers quoted in chapter 2, he told me that at least initially he really did not want to spend more than $2.9 million: "$2.9 million really was what I wanted to spend. But I'm very happy with how things turned out, because I realized if I spent more I'd get more. I'd get a much better place." Other wealthy buyers expressed this sentiment, saying that while they spent a lot more than they thought they would, it was worth it. One buyer, who had an initially stated price ceiling of $2.1 million but made an offer for almost $2.9 million, said, "Was it more than I wanted? Yes. But I couldn't have spent [$2.1 million] and gotten the view I'll have now."

Interviews with buyers who did not use agents showed an awareness of how agents attempted to shape preferences. Buyers who did not use agents reported spending very close to or even significantly under their desired price cap. One couple who had initially stated a price ceiling of $4.5 million went with Brandon to view five apartments. The first two were priced at $4.7 and $4.9 million, while the next three were all priced over $5.3 million.

After the five showings, the couple told Brandon that they had changed their minds and decided not to buy at that time. When I spoke to the one of them a little over a month later, however, he told me that he and his wife had actually continued to search on their own.[31] When I asked why he had not continued to use Brandon's services, the buyer said, "I stopped using him because he was always trying to make me see more expensive places." Unlike most buyers, they were obdurate in their price preference and put off by Brandon's attempts at upselling. By not interacting with an agent and performing the search themselves, they avoided being upsold.

Agents, of course, have a financial motivation to upsell their clients. Past research suggests that by and large, it is not worth agents' time to try to get their buyers to pay higher prices, or to wait very long for a higher bid to come in if they are representing sellers.[32] This calculation may change, however, if an agent is representing buyers with higher price points. Brandon's commission on a $3.9 million sale was over $15,000 more than it would have been on a $2.9 million one. Yet even if agents were purposefully upselling wealthier buyers to create higher commissions—and none admitted to this—they still had to convince buyers to raise their ceilings. Agents must demonstrate to buyers the need to spend an extra million dollars, and they do this by controlling the search process. Put another way, the work of getting buyers to a higher price point, even if it is for the purposes of raising agent commissions, happens through interaction.

The malleability of buyers' price preferences is further illustrated by one case of a less wealthy buyer who *did* spend far more than her initially stated price ceiling. The buyer, Kathy, worked as an architect. In her first meeting with her agent, Thomas, she stated that her price ceiling was $500,000. After the meeting Thomas excitedly told me that he was a fan of the architecture firm where Kathy worked and appreciated its designs. When they next met to view units, they did not talk about price but rather about the designs of the units and about architectural history in general. Over the course of the search, they critiqued building layouts, construction materials, and designs more generally. As the search progressed, Thomas sent Kathy more and more expensive listings that he thought would interest her because of their designs or building histories. At showings they continually focused on the architectural aspects of units, with no discussion of price. Eventually Kathy made an offer of $609,999, more than 20 percent above her initially stated price ceiling. This was by far the largest margin for any buyer whose initially stated price ceiling was less than $900,000. Factors other than wealth could make agents avoid talking about prices, but avoidance of price talk produced the same outcome: larger margins of upselling.

Buyers' price preferences were created during the search, with agents generally exercising a great amount of influence over the process.

GETTING TO A PRICE

This chapter has shown how the price offerings that individuals are willing to make are contingent on their interactions with other market actors. Interactions between market intermediaries and buyers affected the prices buyers were willing to offer. And upselling, as this account reveals, is dependent on appropriate displays of affect that are made possible by particular power relations between market actors.[33]

In the specific case of New York City real estate, the quality of interactions between real estate agents and home buyers varied with buyers' price points. Wealthier buyers—like privileged people in a host of other settings—were credited with existing knowledge about money and treated with deference throughout the purchasing process, an approach that ultimately led them to spend more. Compared to interactions between agents and less wealthy buyers, where interactions focused on prices, the interactions between agents and wealthier buyers systematically avoided prices and focused on other aspects of particular housing units. Agents upsold less wealthy buyers to a lesser extent because agents assumed these buyers had more practical constraints (e.g., a buyer who needs a mortgage to finance the purchase of a house is limited to an amount determined by the bank granting the loan). Moreover, the constant talk of prices quickly narrowed the range of acceptable prices for less wealthy buyers. The case of real estate shows the utility of an interactionist perspective and illuminates *how* purchasers come to offer the prices they do.[34]

The interactional patterns described here are likely to be at work in other housing markets. This is an empirical question; it is of course possible that the particulars of the New York City housing market (e.g., low inventory, rising prices) make it uniquely suitable for upselling. In a local real estate market with an oversupply of similar-quality housing stock, for example, agents cannot draw on market scarcity in their interactions with buyers. That being said, agents across New York State reported that they can almost always highlight some aspects of a neighborhood or even a particular unit to make a house seem uniquely desirable and worthy of a higher price. And despite the seemingly unique conditions of New York City's housing market, at the time of my fieldwork it was broadly similar in terms of affordability to several other metropolitan areas in the United States. This is to say that if local market conditions affect upselling, the pattern described above likely exists in many other housing markets.

Beyond housing markets, the mechanics of upselling may play out differently when the economic stakes are lower and the cultural discourses surrounding the commodity are less stable. Moreover, as market intermediaries compensated by commission, real estate agents have a strong financial stake in upselling.[35] We know, however, that upselling does occur in many different kinds of markets. For example, the sociologist Robin Leidner (1993) describes how organizations can structure their employees' labor in such a way as to encourage upselling. Fast food workers are given scripts punctuated with phrases like "Would you like to supersize that?" meant to induce the customer to spend more money. While the upselling described here was the outcome of interaction, others have documented it as a result of more conscious (and nefarious) efforts by intermediaries in both the housing market and other contexts.[36]

What are the consequences of unevenly distributed upselling on the housing market in general? Put another way, if elite buyers are being pushed to spend more and more in a competitive housing market, what does this mean for the geography of opportunity in places like New York? In the next chapter I examine how upselling affects broader trends in the housing market. We already know that the housing market stratifies individuals in space by wealth and race and ethnicity, and that real estate agents have historically played a part in producing these unequal outcomes. Chapter 4 connects interactional mechanisms like upselling to geographic inequality and variation across neighborhood housing prices.

4

REAL ESTATE AGENTS AND NEIGHBORHOOD INEQUALITIES

It's the law. You can't really mess around with that stuff though a lot of agents do.
AGENT WORKING IN BROOKLYN ON FAIR HOUSING LAWS

There's a lot of segregation in this city and a lot of it is self-segregation . . . so different neighborhoods are still thought of certain ways. I'm not imposing my opinion about neighborhoods, but if someone tells me what they want, I think I can help them make a selection about where to look.
AGENT WORKING IN BUFFALO

In early 2017 I received an email from one of the real estate licensing schools where I had taken classes. The email advertised a seven-and-a-half-hour course the next Saturday that could count toward the hours needed to maintain a real estate salesperson license. In New York State, aspiring real estate agents must take seventy-five hours of coursework from a school approved by the New York Secretary of State and then pass a state licensing exam. Licenses are valid for three years. To renew their license, agents must demonstrate that they have completed twenty-two and a half hours of approved continuing education. The email advertised a continuing education course in the form of a "bus tour" of the South Bronx. "Don't just learn the art of real estate investing, **see it in-action!**" read the email. During the day-long tour, agents would also "learn the foreclosure process" and how to "prepare and negotiate a short sale."

For longtime residents of New York City, the idea of investing in real estate in the South Bronx—a historically disadvantaged part of the city—might seem less prudent than buying in Manhattan or Brooklyn. Throughout my fieldwork, median house prices in the Bronx were the lowest of those in any borough. Some agents talked about the Bronx only as a blighted area, the crime-ridden setting of police film dramas like *Fort Apache, The Bronx*, or as a dystopic gangland as portrayed in *The Warriors*.[1] And yet the Bronx was not immune to the kinds of changes happening in the posher parts of New York City's real estate market. Local real estate blogs and newspapers reported on the transformation of the South Bronx in particular and predicted a coming spike in prices. As the *New York Times* put it, "the South Bronx beckons."[2]

In the previous chapters I showed how the work real estate agents do affects prospective home buyers' preferences in the market. That is, the ways buyers and agents interact shapes how much buyers are willing to pay in the housing market. The email from the real estate licensing school illustrates how agents can view these effects as intentional; the course being advertised was designed to teach agents how to profit from rising prices and even push them higher by taking advantage of low-priced houses in foreclosure and boosting prices in the short term. In this chapter I leverage multiple types of data to examine how the interactional work agents do, reproduced at scale, reifies the symbolic boundaries of neighborhoods and increases the inequality between them.[3]

REAL ESTATE AGENTS AND INEQUALITY
IN THE HOUSING MARKET

Residential segregation by race and ethnicity and by income are facts of American life. Segregation structures unequal access to goods and services.[4] Differences in housing type, location, tenure, and equity contribute to negative outcomes for poorer, black, and Latino households across a host of short-term and long-term measures in the United States. Differential access to homeownership is a crucial aspect of racial inequality in wealth—the so-called wealth gap. Even those black and Latino households that own their homes are at a disadvantage, since their homes are more likely to be in majority-nonwhite neighborhoods, and homes located in majority-white neighborhoods appreciate more quickly than those in black and Latino communities.[5]

These differences are the result of sociohistorical and legal processes like redlining and blockbusting that were not only common among real estate agents, banks, and developers for most of the twentieth century but also facilitated, if not demanded, by the federal government, which sets rules for mortgage lending.[6] Apart from these structural and institutional factors, individuals bring race-based biases to their decisions about housing.[7] Residential sorting, in other words, must be understood as a complex process that combines racial bias with institutional and structural racism.[8]

Agents are a key part of how people find houses; as such, they exercise a great deal of influence over and discretion on behalf of their clients. A good deal of scholarship has focused on one particular aspect of real estate agent behavior: racial steering. Since the Civil Rights Act of 1968—also known as the Fair Housing Act—made discrimination by race in the housing market illegal, multiple studies have sought to test whether agents and other housing market intermediaries, like mortgage lenders, treat potential buyers of different races and ethnicities differently. This work generally employs what are called matched-pair audits, where people who are alike in as many respects as possible except for their race or ethnicity approach the same agents or lenders. These studies seek to determine whether there are any systematic differences in how much information agents give these buyers on available houses, where agents choose to show them houses for sale, or the likelihood of receiving a loan.[9] Since 2000, audit studies have shown that while agents are less overtly hostile to racial and ethnic minorities than in the 1970s and 1980s, they still tend to share more information on available housing with whites.[10] As a result, blacks are less likely than whites to obtain their first choices when searching for housing.[11] Steering by real estate agents both reifies racialized neighborhood preferences and inflates demand for homes in certain white neighborhoods.[12] Increased demand increases prices in these neighborhoods and decreases prices in other (i.e., black/Latino/poor) neighborhoods, undermining wealth accumulation for minorities and the less wealthy. In other words, when deployed in aggregate, these biases help make some neighborhoods hot and others not.[13] While multiple factors play a role in determining segregation and distributing prices across neighborhoods, the practices of real estate agents are undoubtedly part of the process.

Because they are paid on commission, agents have a powerful motive to increase the price and speed of any individual transaction.[14] This interest manifests in multiple ways. As we have seen, agents engage in upselling, primarily by shifting buyers' preferences to amenities associated with higher-priced units—particularly when these buyers are extremely wealthy. Agents can also convince a buyer that a particular unit is worth more than the sale price, so that the current market value of the home is updated and increased when it passes to a new owner.[15] Agents also shorten the search process for buyers, shorten the time houses are on the market for sellers, and increase buyer demand for larger, generally more expensive homes.[16] The commission model also provides a financial incentive for agents to migrate to local markets with high and/or increasing home prices. As we saw in chapter 1, real estate agents typically specialize in particular local markets and even specific neighborhoods. Performing transactions in one small geographic area not only allows agents to develop deep reserves of expertise but also yields shorter transaction times due to "operating efficiencies," or knowing a local market well. This is especially true in areas with higher real estate prices.[17]

Agents' preference for specializing in specific geographic areas takes on additional meaning in the context of residential segregation by income, which is increasing in the United States.[18] That is, the uneven distribution of income groups across neighborhoods has gone up since the 1970s— poor households are more likely to live near other poor households, and high-income households are more likely to live near other high-income households. And not coincidentally, the cities and neighborhoods that have seen the steepest increases in housing prices are places that had the highest housing costs to begin with.[19] In short, as income inequality rises, the most economically well-off places are getting more expensive. The trend is strongest for those at the highest income levels as well as for families with children.[20] Put another way, the households with the highest incomes are more likely than in previous decades to have neighbors who also fall into the highest income brackets, especially if they are white.[21]

Multiple processes in the housing market, from racial steering to growing income inequality, sort high-income buyers (who are more likely to be white) into higher-priced houses, which are, in turn, likely to be within higher-priced neighborhoods. The agents I observed worked mostly in high-priced neighborhoods or neighborhoods that were experiencing massive increases in prices—see figure A.1 in the appendix. They worked with mostly white, relatively affluent, and in some cases extraordinarily wealthy buyers seeking to purchase housing costing a minimum of $399,000. And what I found is that interactions between these agents and the buyers they represented consistently yielded upsells.

Upselling creates positive feedback loops within local housing markets. The process pushes up prices at the higher ends of the market as those more capable of spending more, do. As agents concentrate in already high-priced neighborhoods and then upsell wealthier buyers at higher rates compared to the rates of upselling in lower-priced markets, they contribute to rising prices and concentrate wealthy people who can afford more expensive housing in areas with high pricing. In the aggregate, interactions between agents and buyers affect demand for houses, which in turn affects housing

costs, asset inequality, and residential segregation. Upselling has consequences. And it highlights how micro-level processes affect markets more
broadly.[22]

WHERE DO AGENTS ACTUALLY WORK?

If agents' work has effects on the housing market, in particular on prices,
and agents are not distributed evenly across neighborhoods, then there
should be measurable differences in agent effects across neighborhoods. To
examine where agents actually locate, I obtained the business address of every licensed real estate salesperson in New York State in 2012.[23] Agents have
historically worked within small geographical areas close to their offices
since expertise in one area yields higher commissions, there are costs to
traveling far, and multiple listing systems are organized at local geographic
levels. In other words, various pressures tend to narrow the geographies
in which agents work.[24] Of course agents cross neighborhood boundaries
to do deals all the time; this is perhaps particularly true in New York City,
where neighborhoods of wildly disparate income and housing costs might
be separated by mere blocks. The agents I observed, for example, sometimes worked in various adjacent neighborhoods. A few had done deals
during their careers in multiple boroughs (see table A.1), so the neighborhood in which an agent's office is located is not a perfect indicator of the
neighborhoods in which she or he works. In the analyses described below,
I therefore also measured the "extralocal" effects of agent location on various outcomes, meaning that I looked at the possible effects of agents not
just on the neighborhoods in which their offices are located but on nearby
neighborhoods as well. (See appendix B for further details.)

The sociologist Jacob Faber and I examined the agent business address
data to see where agents do their work. Looking across census tracts—
geographic units that contain an average of 4,000 residents and are often
used in social science research as proxies for neighborhoods—there are
fewer agents in rural census tracts (8.08 agents on average) than there are
within tracts in cities (11.05). New York City neighborhoods have an average
of 11.94 agents per census tract. The census tracts with the highest average number of agents are in the suburbs, defined as places within metropolitan areas but outside of primary cities. These suburban areas average
12.10 licenses per census tracts. Long Island has a particularly high agent
concentration (19.9), while Upstate tracts (i.e., those not in New York City

or Long Island) have fewer (8.2). The census tracts in the top 1 percent of agent distribution—those with over 167 licensees—are largely contained in New York City (mostly in Midtown Manhattan with a few in Queens), but they are also located in several other urban and suburban locations across the state, including Long Island and suburbs north of New York City. So far these descriptive statistics make sense; suburban neighborhoods, where homeownership rates tend to be higher than those in central cities, tend to have more real estate agents per capita even though some neighborhoods in New York City have the highest concentration of real estate agents.

Agents are far more concentrated in tracts with either a white or Asian majority population. Predominantly Asian neighborhoods have an average of 19.9 agents—perhaps reflective of this group's higher rates of homeownership.[25] White neighborhoods have an average of 12.4 agents. Primarily Latino (3.3) and black (2.8) neighborhoods have substantially fewer real estate agents.[26] Agents are also less concentrated in areas with lower home values. Neighborhoods that are in the top quintile of home values have on average 18.6 real estate agents, while neighborhoods in the bottom quintile have on average just 3.6.[27] In other words, the difference in average number of real estate agents in the lowest-valued neighborhoods and the highest-valued is quite dramatic: neighborhoods in the top quintile of owner-occupied home values have an average of over five times as many agents as those in the bottom quintile. This dovetails with the low concentration of agents in black and Latino tracts, since black and Latino neighborhoods also tend to have lower home values.

In the same study, we identified a relationship between house prices and the number of real estate agents in a given neighborhood across New York State.[28] We used the data on real estate agent licenses as well as data from the American Community Survey (ACS)—an ongoing survey administered by the US Census Bureau that collects various kinds of demographic data, including data on home prices. Using data aggregated from surveys collected between 2010 and 2014, we found broadly that the number of agents within and surrounding a census tract correlates positively with home values, even after demographic, economic, geographic, and housing characteristics are controlled for. While this relationship is consistent in neighborhoods across New York State, it is particularly pronounced in areas that are majority white. We also measured the relationship between agent concentration and racial and ethnic segregation and found that places with more real estate agents have higher levels of racial and ethnic residential segregation.[29] These earlier analyses are not causal, meaning that they are not proof that agents drive up prices or increase racial or ethnic segregation, but they do indicate that there is indeed a relationship between where agents are located and the composition of neighborhoods.

Since this earlier research, new data have become available. The ACS releases new data every year, calculated on the basis of surveys from the previous five years. This data series allows researchers to observe change over time.[30] The sociologist Gerard Torrats-Espinosa and I used this updated data to examine the relationship between agent concentration and *change* in median home price in the neighborhood over time. The ACS data from the five-year period 2013–2017 shows an even stronger relationship between agent concentration and home prices compared to earlier research. Indeed, an additional ten real estate agents in a given neighborhood is associated with a 7 percent higher median home price in that neighborhood (in dollar terms, approximately $25,000 on a home worth $356,400—the median home value in New York State in 2017). Using home price data aggregated from 2009 to 2012 and comparing it to data aggregated from 2013 to 2017, we find that more real estate agents in a neighborhood is associated with higher *increases* in house prices in that neighborhood. Agent concentration, then, is positively associated not only with higher neighborhood house prices but also with higher *changes* in house prices over a five-year period.[31] (See appendix B for further details.) More agents means more upselling, and more upselling means neighborhoods with already high prices experience increasing prices at a higher rate.

Agents can certainly anticipate which neighborhoods will have higher price increases in the future, and they may choose to locate in neighborhoods accordingly. Once there, they interact with clients in ways that drive prices up. The work of real estate agents, by pushing prices at the higher ends of the market even higher, expands existing disparities and reifies the class, ethnoracial, and culture-based distinctions between neighborhoods.

LEARNING ABOUT PRICE AND FAIR HOUSING

"If you were to invest in Harlem twenty years ago, would it be risky?" asks Gina, a middle-aged woman leading a real estate salesperson licensing class titled "The Valuation Process and Pricing Properties." Many in the class shout back yes to her question. She goes on to say, "When we're dealing with risk, we're always speculating. But also high risk means higher—what?" "Return," some students respond, while others say "reward." In a classroom filled with about fifty people, most say nothing. Gina nods and says, "Don't be scared about risk. Whatever you do in life, tackle it! There are two kinds of people in this world, those who go towards life and those who run away. Which kind are you?" Such broad affirmations of real estate agents as risk-takers were common in the classes I attended, regardless of the actual topic of the class.

As part of the research for this book, I took the seventy-five hours of courses required to become a real estate salesperson in New York (though I never took the licensing exam).[32] I enrolled at the Manhattan licensing school attended by most of the agents I observed interacting with buyers and over half of the agents I interviewed who worked in New York City. I also attended classes at two other licensing schools—one in Manhattan and one in Brooklyn—but because the curriculum is designed and mandated by the state, the course offerings, at least on paper, were the same. Given my interests in housing inequality, I attended multiple versions of the courses on fair housing to see how different instructors handled the topic and how different groups of agents-in-training responded.

The pedagogy in these courses might be described as casual at best. In most, instructors would page through whatever section in the school-issued textbook was being covered in that particular class. In between reading phrases and sometimes whole paragraphs verbatim from the text, they would intersperse anecdotes from their own experience. Classes that were supposed to last four hours were sometimes dismissed early or, more often, were cut short in order for representatives of brokerage firms to give presentations encouraging students to apply for jobs once they became licensed. One licensing school in Manhattan advertised visits from firms and job placement as a key selling point. The school's webpage read, "Guaranteed Job: Over 95 Salesperson job placements every week at NY's top brokerage firms."

Most instructors favored a style similar to Gina's, asking the class questions and expecting answers that were either commonplace clichés and bromides—"high risk means high return"—or direct quotes from the provided textbook. This gave many classes a grade-school feel. Class time frequently veered wildly off topic. For example, in a "Real Estate Mathematics" class at a school in Manhattan, the instructor and a few students spent the first twenty minutes trading tips on where to get the best sandwich near Madison Square Park. All of which is to say, the seventy-five-hour training required to become a licensed real estate salesperson in New York State is neither onerous nor particularly focused.

Instructors generally talked about prices in terms of location. As in Gina's comment about Harlem, or the course about foreclosure and short sales in the South Bronx mentioned at the beginning of the chapter, instructors told students that they would do well to begin working in neighborhoods that were likely to experience near-term price increases. One instructor at a Manhattan school who appeared to be in his sixties, told the class that when he became an agent he was intent on working in the Upper West Side of Manhattan because he knew prices were going to "shoot up." Another instructor, in a class on real estate taxes and assessment, said, "Everybody knows which parts of the city have the prices and which don't. But the trick is to get in right as prices are going up." He went on to describe admiringly the practice of flipping—buying a house and then selling it quickly for a higher price.

Broadly, real estate licensing instructors framed agents as not mere brokers but as active participants in the market who had the power to increase prices. In another class on valuation, this same instructor first explained that high real estate prices were good for neighborhoods and that it made sense to take out loans to buy real property. "Investment improves everything, and leveraging is great because it allows people to invest in an area and make it better." He went on to say that real estate agents should be encouraging investment: "It's your job to get these things going. Get them moving up." In other words, while instructors told agents to locate in neighborhoods where prices might increase, they also framed agent labor as potentially *causing* price increases.

Upselling and its feedback effects rarely came up explicitly. Instructors did, however, sometimes hint at it during class time. During a "Law of Agency" class, which outlined agents' relationships to buyers, sellers, and brokers, one instructor said that agents are supposed to represent their clients' best interests, but followed this statement with a reminder that agents know a lot more about the housing market than their clients do. "Your clients might not know what they can actually afford or what their house might be worth. It's your job to get them there. Show them what's possible with their given situation."

Talk of prices was constant in real estate licensing classes. In contrast, instructors avoided discussing issues of race and ethnicity except from the exceedingly narrow framing of fair housing laws. In a class called "Fair Housing Laws and Human Rights," instructors would often repeat directives like "Don't discriminate" and "Don't you take them to where *you* think they should be."

The real estate salesperson licensing curriculum in New York State does devote four hours, or roughly 5 percent of the required training, to fair housing laws. In my experience, however, these courses lacked substance and nuance. Generally, students were told they needed to memorize the year the federal Fair Housing Act passed, the classes of individuals protected from discrimination under the law, and the additional classes protected under the Human Rights Law of New York. They learned that steering, redlining, and blockbusting were illegal and that it is illegal for agents to answer clients' questions about protected classes. For example, it is illegal to answer questions about a building's, neighborhood's, or city's racial makeup. Much of this instruction focuses on enforcement rather than conveying the desirability of a more equitable housing market. In the textbook provided by a Manhattan licensing school, the first page of the chapter on fair housing warns aspiring real estate agents about testers working for the state or federal government who pretend to be buyers asking questions that agents legally cannot answer.

The classroom time for the fair housing courses were consistently eaten up by discussions that were at best irrelevant and at worst filled with stereotypes about neighborhoods and their demographics. For example, the agents-in-training at a fair housing class at a Manhattan licensing school spent nearly twenty-five minutes debating whether or not Jews were a race. The discussion was sparked by a comment from the instructor, a woman, who said that male Hasidic Jews would not shake her hand during real estate transactions "because they don't know when I'm on my period." At another, the instructor spent the first fifteen minutes reading the names and describing the content of all of the classes required for licensure. He then spent the rest of the class reading from the textbook chapter on fair housing laws.

At a class in Manhattan on fair housing, Gina began by writing a list of protected classes on the board. She then addressed the class:

This is a disclaimer: we're going to talk about fair housing and we're going to talk about race. I'm going to use examples that aren't me discriminating. Discrimination is happening out there. Right? So what's going to happen is you're going to go to your broker and he's going to say, "If you want to make money, listen to me, forget everything you learned in class, in this building you can't sell to Jews, in this building no Puerto Ricans." This is what you're going to hear. But listen to me. This is when you need to talk about these things. You need to say the stuff here because you're going to operate on your thoughts. So let's get it all out here. Let me tell you something. We all discriminate. We live a life of judgment, looking at someone and coming to a conclusion by just looking at them. There are lesbians and gays. We can say that here. And you know what, they discriminate against each other. I've been in this business long enough. Gays say no lesbians. Lesbians say no gays. Don't think I'm trying to discriminate. I'm trying to help.

Later in the class she said:

Your buyer must form their own opinion about a neighborhood. However, there's no law against the buyers' making their own decisions. So they can do it, but you cannot do it. If they prefer a particular neighborhood that's their choice, and they can share that with you.

She then asked, "If I were Dominican, where would you put me?" Some in the class answered "The Bronx," and a few said "East Harlem." She then asked, "If I were Jewish, where would you put me?" Some answered "The Lower East Side," and one person said "Williamsburg." She asked again if she were Chinese, and many answered "Chinatown."

If any students were offended by this exchange, they did not let on. Most of the class seemed placid, if not disinterested. In her opening Gina had acknowledged that implicit bias exists—"we all discriminate"—but in the rest of the class she argued that if agents had any biases, all they had to do was not talk about them out loud with clients. Furthermore, she encouraged agents to facilitate any of their clients' ethnoracial preferences.

A student in this course asked how agents are supposed to respond to prohibited questions from buyers about neighborhood demographics. Gina said,

You tell them go look it up themselves. You can't do it. Tell them to google, or to go to the census. See, we have to be aware of what we say and how we say it. [She tells a joke about Polish people.] Because this is offensive. It's how people perceive. Are they offended? It's about how people perceive what you're saying.

As the class went on, Gina described steering as "just showing people of a race a place that's their race," and did not elaborate. She then read the passages in the textbook on redlining and blockbusting and recommended that students memorize the definitions.

This particular session was the least substantive of any of the classes on fair housing I attended. Overall, instructors were often meandering and did not effectively communicate the letter, let alone spirit, of fair housing laws or the potential impacts that agents' decisions could have on the distribution of people in the city. Such a lack of preparation meant that agents might be unaware of the laws that are supposed to govern their behavior, or might even feel comfortable bending or actively ignoring them. With this training, perhaps it is not surprising that agents reported that while they avoided overtly mentioning race and ethnicity with their clients, they often ascribed racial and ethnic preferences or biases to their clients and then worked accordingly. This contrasts with earlier decades where agents freely expressed their own racist beliefs about neighborhoods and the housing market.[33] In other words, agents engaged in steering by anticipating what they assumed would be their clients' racism.

AGENTS, NEIGHBORHOOD VALUE, AND RACE AND ETHNICITY

Across the state, almost all the agents I spoke with limited their work to relatively confined geographic areas. Outside the city, that might be a single city within a county; in New York City, that might mean concentrating on a specific neighborhood. Their choice of neighborhoods wasn't random: agents generally reported avoiding poor neighborhoods because working in poor neighborhoods meant lower commissions. One white agent explained, "I really am selling to people like me. I just don't have experience in other neighborhoods, and it's not like I'm going to get it since I'm looking to make more money on fewer deals." Another agent, who had recently started his career in Manhattan, said, "I wasn't going to start in Queens or the Bronx, because the prices just aren't there."

This sentiment was common; the white agents I spoke with did not express interest in working in lower-income neighborhoods associated with low house prices and higher shares of blacks and Latinos.[34] In contrast, the black and Latino agents I interviewed did report working in predominantly black and Latino areas. Past research shown that deals brokered by nonwhite agents are overwhelmingly concentrated in nonwhite neighborhoods—which have lower prices—and that nonwhite agents' networks are largely more diverse than white agents'.[35] But even these nonwhite agents expressed a desire to work in other areas because black and Latino neighborhoods tended to have lower property values and therefore produced smaller commissions. As one black agent who had worked in the Harlem neighborhood of Manhattan for fifteen years said, "I've finally been here enough time that prices are going up, and it's really because of all the white people moving in." Broadly, agents recognized that higher shares of whites and higher prices were correlated.

In interviews, agents readily acknowledged both buyers' racial and ethnic preferences and their willingness to facilitate a racialized housing search. Echoing Gina's instructions on how to deal with clients when they express racial or ethnic preferences, one agent working in Buffalo said:

> There's a lot of segregation in this city and a lot of it is self-segregation . . . so different neighborhoods are still thought of in certain ways. I'm not imposing my opinion about neighborhoods, but if someone tells me what they want, I think I can help them make a selection about where to look.

Many respondents confirmed that racial biases existed broadly. One agent referred to his brokerage firm as a place where race and ethnicity played a large part in agents' decisions. He said:

> My boss talks about race all the time but never actually says it. But I know what he's referring to. He'll say [of clients], "Are they good people?" Are they good people?! And for the first few months my response to that is "What do you mean?" I would get angry about that. But then he just kept asking, and other people I worked with kind of clued me in about what that means. I have unfortunately had to let that cloud my judgments a little bit.

When asked to elaborate on what aspects of work were affected, he said, "Disclosure, fair housing, honestly these things don't help me right now." He later added, "Race definitely plays a part in how we show homes."

Another respondent, who worked in Brooklyn, indicated that he actively discriminated against black homeseekers. He admitted that he engaged in steering because of his assumptions about certain neighborhoods and certain sellers. "I see racism in the market. The Hasids in Williamsburg and the Russians in Brighton Beach and even little old Italian women in Cobble Hill, they don't want to sell to them [blacks]. They're open about it, so it's not really worth it to push." Such comments reveal how agents typically frame their ethnoracial-based practices as a response to client racism and bigotry. No agent expressed the belief that certain ethnoracial groups belonged in certain neighborhoods, but agents readily claimed that their clients did.[36]

Like this agent who pointed to Hasidic, Russian, and Italian sellers' supposed unwillingness to sell to black buyers, agents used their embeddedness in communities as a reason to maintain white neighborhoods in their current form. One agent in a suburban town in the Hudson Valley said:

I've been working here a long time. There's one block where I've sold four houses in the last six years. If I sell to a person who ends up not taking care of the property or whatever, it looks really bad for me, and when those listings come up around that block they're going to go to someone else.

Another agent who worked in New York City explained, "Co-op boards are the worst. And they really remember the broker who sold to the bad guy who all the neighbors hate. So the next time that broker tries to do a deal in that building, forget it." While neither of these agents explicitly mentioned race in their comments, the examples remind us that agents have incentives to work with clients whom they deem similar to the current residents of the buildings and neighborhoods where they do business.

In the four instances that I witnessed where buyers asked agents directly about neighborhood demographics, agents followed the law by refusing to discuss specifics. At an open house in Crown Heights, a neighborhood with a large West Indian population in Brooklyn, a white buyer said to Don, a white real estate agent, "It seems like there are less and less Caribbeans because of gentrification, right?"

"I don't know," Don said, "and I'm really not supposed to talk about it. It's illegal for me to talk about it."

"Really?" said the buyer.

"Yeah, it's against the law. But you can look all of it up yourself."

One agent working in Brooklyn said in reference to responding to questions about race/ethnicity from buyers, "I can tell for some people what was in the neighborhood before weirds them out. It's too Puerto Rican or too Polish.... I could say something like that, but I still feel like it's probably illegal." Another agent said in reference to fair housing requirements, "It's the law. You can't really mess around with that stuff, though a lot of agents do."

Despite their professed concern for following the law, agents readily shared opinions with their clients related to aesthetics and amenities associated with ethnoracial groups—for example, certain architectural preferences or the quality of "hipness."[37] One white agent, who worked at a buyer's-only brokerage in Brooklyn and whose buyers were mostly white, explained his role in the rapidly changing neighborhood of Crown Heights.[38] He described the upward trend in house prices, noting its geographic spread eastward as well as his clients' apparent appreciation for the neighborhood itself:

I really love working here in Crown Heights. I really think it's like the next big thing. It's just literally going [east] block by block. You have Flatbush;

Vanderbilt is so hot—oh, my god. And then Washington is great now. Franklin is OK, maybe Rogers. . . . [Buyers] like to walk out of their apartment and feel like they're on a Spike Lee set. They like the real Brooklyn.

This agent invokes Spike Lee's films, some of which portray black life in Brooklyn, as a reference of authenticity for homeseekers, but he makes clear that he believes there is a geographic limit to white homeseekers' preferences.[39] As a result, he reported not showing his white clients homes in the eastern part of the neighborhood, which was poorer and more black.

Agents working in neighborhoods undergoing upscaling and related demographic changes reported making presumptions about their white clients' willingness to buy or rent in parts of those neighborhoods that remained poor and nonwhite.[40] Lucy was working with a white couple interested in purchasing a brownstone in Brooklyn. At their first open house in the Fort Greene neighborhood, they said they were willing to look in Clinton Hill and Bed-Stuy, two more diverse though gentrifying neighborhoods farther east.[41] The coupled liked the traditional Brooklyn aesthetic, and Bed-Stuy has multiple blocks designated as a historic district because of the brownstone architecture. But Lucy told the couple they would absolutely be able to find something in Fort Greene; she said housing stock in the neighborhoods farther east was not well maintained.

Real estate agent Thomas, who worked mostly in the Lower East Side neighborhood of Manhattan, told me his largely white client base had no interests in looking for housing in neighboring Chinatown because they didn't like "the smell or the grit."[42] Recall the example of Miguel and his clients, a couple who purchased in the Prospect Heights neighborhood of Brooklyn, in chapter 2. At the outset of the search, Miguel told the buyers that the adjoining neighborhood of Crown Heights had fewer trees and a larger homeless population. This closed off the buyers' interest in searching in this more diverse and less affluent neighborhood. Agents' interactions with their clients, in other words, influence their neighborhood preferences. If agents share information meant to dissuade their white and/or wealthy clients from choosing to live in areas with higher rates of nonwhites and less affluent neighbors, these actions can impact rates of segregation and neighborhood change.

Some agents reported being stricter about revealing their own opinions about "good" and "bad" neighborhoods, or the desirability of particular neighborhood amenities, with black buyers. One agent told a story of desperately wanting to suggest to a black couple seeking a home to avoid the neighborhood of Howard Beach entirely. Howard Beach, a neighborhood in Queens, is infamous for its history of racial violence, with notorious cases of white mobs beating and murdering black men in the 1980s and 2000s. However, the agent said, "But I didn't say anything to them—I couldn't. As good as my intentions were, I can't say things like that."

Buyers, for their part, generally assumed some racist practices were intrinsic to the housing market but that their own agents and brokerage firms did not do anything inappropriate or illegal. This is in keeping with agents' tendency to frame their own behavior, and only their own behavior, as upstanding (see chapter 1). Some buyers assumed that agents working in larger, more prominent firms were less likely to discriminate, while others thought that wealth—both their own and the wealth/whiteness of the neighborhoods in which they were searching—reduced the likelihood that agents were acting in racist ways. One wealthy white buyer, who currently lived in and was searching for a house in Manhattan, contrasted the brokerage firm where her agent worked with what she presumed were problematic practices at other brokerages:

BUYER: I know that there's racist stuff happening. It's very American in that way that everything is racist. But if you look at [name of her brokerage firm], they're all educated and professional.
MB: You don't think they'd do anything wrong?
BUYER [shaking her head]: I don't think so. I'm sure there are sleazier agents in other parts of the city.
MB: Like where?
BUYER [shrugging]: Oh, I don't know. You know, like those storefront [brokerages] in Brooklyn. Places where there are actually black people.

The buyer equates professionalism—her firm was one of the most prominent the city with sleek offices and advertisements all over the city, working at almost all segments of the market, including direct contracting with luxury developers—with nonracist behavior. She also makes the astute observation that the agents that represent her likely have less opportunity to discriminate against nonwhite clients since they work in mostly white areas with mostly white clients—New York City neighborhoods are highly segregated by race, ethnicity, and income.[43] Indeed the fact that I observed little overt race talk between buyers and agents may itself be attributable to segregation. That is, there is little need for overt race talk between buyers and agents when buyers, agents, and the neighborhoods in which they are searching are all the same race or ethnicity.[44]

For example, Steven and John, Lucy's clients who bought in Brooklyn

Heights, had come into the search process with a defined choice set, wanting to look at homes in Brooklyn Heights, Cobble Hill, and Carroll Gardens. These three neighborhoods all matched them demographically—they were whiter and wealthier than the city overall. At one point during the search Lucy met the couple and mentioned that she had just visited another open house with different clients in a more racially and socioeconomically mixed neighborhood, Clinton Hill. Steven said, "I don't think I've ever been that far east." John rolled his eyes said, "I'm sure *you* haven't," emphasizing his partner's limited (and racialized) experience in and knowledge about different parts of the city.[45]

During my fieldwork, popular media accounts of racial steering in New York tended to portray it as a problem among independent housing market actors like landlords and agents in diverse neighborhoods in the outer boroughs, rather than a systemic issue that shapes the city's housing market.[46] However, in 2006 the National Fair Housing Alliance (NFHA) accused Corcoran, one of most prominent brokerages in the city, of racial steering in a high-priced neighborhood in Brooklyn. In an encounter reminiscent of the systemic racial boundary drawing that had been part of both federal policy and private practices among brokerages and mortgage lenders for so long, one Corcoran agent actually drew a red line around the neighborhoods he recommended to white audit testers sent by the NFHA. He further broke the law by talking about school quality.[47]

When I asked a wealthy black buyer about racist practices by real estate agents, he said, "I haven't had those experiences myself, but I bet my money has a lot to do with that." I asked if he knew of anyone who had been treated in a discriminatory way during the housing search process. He laughed, pointed to his face, and said,

> Of course! Not getting apartments because they're this color. But you don't often put yourself in that kind of situation. You get your agents through your friends, you know they're not bad. You don't work with people you don't know, because you don't know what they're up to behind your back. You don't apply to this or that building because you know people have been rejected before.[48]

Other research has shown that nonwhite buyers anticipate discrimination in white neighborhoods and have strategies—usually relying on networks—for avoiding situations in which they might be discriminated against.[49]

Broadly speaking, real estate agents' decisions perpetuate the continued segregation of heavily white and heavily minority neighborhoods while simultaneously increasing gentrification in mixed ones.[50] Agents presumed that white clients do not want to live in predominantly black or Latino neighborhoods, or that current residents would blame them for introducing nonwhite homeseekers in white neighborhoods. This racialization of the market is connected to differential prices. Neighborhood boundaries, which were salient for agents, mark home value as well as ethnoracial composition.[51] To the extent that agents are involved in steering, they not only are perpetuating (or exacerbating) ethnoracial segregation but are also manipulating demand for units based on a neighborhood's ethnoracial makeup. In doing so, agents may push up the prices of units in white neighborhoods and decrease the prices of homes in nonwhite neighborhoods.

When combined with the data on upselling, these findings on agent concentration, agent education, and steering illustrate how real estate agents contribute to price differentials across neighborhoods with different ethnoracial makeups. Their interactions with buyers are key to explaining the continued connection of race, ethnicity, and price in the housing market. Areas with black and Latino residents are systematically devalued relative to white neighborhoods. If agents are geographically concentrated in already white and wealthy areas and their presence is associated with higher rises in housing prices, their steering and upselling of buyers accounts in part for variation in house prices across neighborhoods differentiated by race and ethnicity. In other words, when agents are incentivized to concentrate in already white and wealthy areas and upsell buyers within those areas, they play a role in producing both prices and segregation in those areas.

REAL ESTATE AGENTS AND THE FUTURE OF INEQUALITY IN THE HOUSING MARKET

This chapter drew on multiple forms of data in an effort to describe real estate agents' role in neighborhood sorting processes. These findings, combined with those presented earlier in the book, indicate that the work agents do contributes to continued stratification across geographies by house price and ethnoracial composition. Even if real estate agent concentration is driven primarily by "hot" markets—that is, agents are attracted to neighborhoods where the prices are high—there are likely second-order effects on prices for homes in nearby neighborhoods through a demand increase caused by the local concentration of agents and their focus on selling locally. House prices, in other words, experience positive feedback.[52] Regardless of what ultimately drives agent distribution, their concentration in certain places impacts differential pricing—neighborhoods with more agents see higher increases in prices.[53]

To the extent that steering and upselling drive segregation and ethnoracial disparities in prices, one clear implication is that antidiscrimination policies must be strongly enforced—agents should be subject to more testing—and likely expanded to include more training for real estate agents about what types of behaviors violate fair housing laws.[54] Perhaps the state should not accredit classes like the ones I attended; perhaps aspiring agents should instead be required to learn more about the potential impacts of their work in propagating ethnoracial and socioeconomic inequality in the housing market. Real estate agents clearly need more education in both the letter and the intent of fair housing law. Agents—and their instructors—need to understand that any decisions they make that are based on the ethnoracial composition of a neighborhood or identity of a client, regardless of whether they stem from real estate agent or client preferences, are illegal.

That being said, education alone can do only so much in a housing market in which neighborhoods, demographics, and real estate prices remain highly correlated. Real estate agents face intense market incentives to steer. If the mere presence of agents in an area inflates local prices, if agents' networks are segregated by race and ethnicity, and if their avoidance of communities of color increases housing inequality, it is more difficult to suggest a straightforward policy solution. Racial and ethnic inequality and segregation are firmly embedded in market dynamics, and even actors who claim be race neutral still face strong incentives to sustain or even exacerbate disparities. Any effort to ameliorate inequality across neighborhoods will struggle to resolve these issues, since there will always be incentives to create hierarchies of place given housing's role in wealth accumulation.[55] Indeed, the most potent efforts to reduce inequality in the housing market will be ones that decouple individuals' financial interests from where they live.

MAKING PREFERENCES, MAKING PRICES, AND MAKING NEIGHBORHOODS

The vast majority of home buyers in the United States use real estate agents to guide them through the purchasing process. When they do so, they experience the market in a particular way curated by their agents. Their interactions with agents specify, change, and create new preferences about appropriate designs, materials, appliances, buildings, neighbors, neighborhoods, transaction partners, and even prices. Agents instruct their clients on how to value houses, they exercise a great deal of discretion in matching buyers with houses and neighborhoods, and they draw on buyers' various identity characteristics to close deals. While agents risk transactional failure if they emphasize characteristics that do not resonate with buyers' sense of themselves or otherwise fail to generate excitement, their tactics often succeed at getting their clients to bid on a more expensive unit than they had originally intended. Agents' work in shaping buyers' choices leads to upselling. Repeated in aggregate, these practices create positive feedback loops that drive up prices in more expensive neighborhoods. The particular ways that agents perform their role as market intermediaries reify the symbolic, class, and ethnoracial boundaries of different places.

The interactional approach to understanding economic transactions shows that consumers' preferences are mutable, unstable, and dependent on market context. In the housing market, homeseekers' preferences spring from the interactions they experience while searching for a home. Market intermediaries (in the form of agents) play a central role in the real estate market, but many markets feature actors who mediate consumers' experiences by helping them find and narrow search options, negotiate on their behalf, and give advice about valuation and decision-making more generally. And when market intermediaries perform these roles in patterned ways, their work reproduces existing inequalities.

The interactional approach I advocate here builds on a rich and varied scholarly conversation about the nature of economic transactions. I argue that the locus of preferences, decision-making, and ultimately valuation is not in networks or even cultural belief systems but in market transactions themselves. That is, understanding why people buy the things do, and how much they are willing to pay for them, requires analysis of the interactions that market actors have and the contexts in which these interactions take place. In the remainder of this conclusion, I outline some theoretical extensions of these insights and suggest some ways to further empirically test the claims. I then elaborate on why examining prices in the housing market is so important for studying and ameliorating inequality across neighborhoods.

INTERACTION, DECISION MAKING, AND PREFERENCES

Interactions are key to understanding how we form preferences and make decisions. Put more plainly, preferences—and the decisions that flow from them—are products of interaction. They are formed, re-formed, and acted upon during interaction. To fully comprehend how interaction conditions decisions in economic markets, we should abandon (or at least be extremely suspicious of) accounts that describe individuals as having defined and distinct goals that are transsituational.[1] More radically, we might do away with the notion of a preference, or at least any definition that elides the situation and context in which the preference is formed and negotiated.

On the one hand, the many examples recounted in this book of buyers' changing their stated preferences could reflect shifts in the criteria by which they judge houses after learning more about the market. To put this in more formal language, the utility functions of a house changes for buyers when they learn more about their available choice set. Buyers decide to buy more expensive houses because they learn they can; they decide that doing so is an optimal choice. On the other, the myriad changes in preferences described here could be evidence that preferences do not really exist. In other words, preferences are created in the moment they are elicited; they are not immutable sets of inclinations that buyers have before, during, or after the purchase. In light of the robust evidence that preferences are broadly unstable, the latter interpretation seems more plausible, especially given the power agents had in shaping buyers' decisions. What is certainly clear is that consumers, even of products as meaningful, expensive, and consequential as homes, rarely have definitive and set criteria that must be met for them to make a purchase. More generally, economic decisions made rarely—for which consumers have little experience or knowledge—are likely to be deliberated practically instead of in rote ways.[2] This means that when consumers are presented with new or complex purchases, they cannot rely on the types of heuristics they have for more mundane purchases. Instead they will want to work through the situation, seeking to do so smoothly and with the belief that they will benefit in some way from the outcome.[3]

An approach that focuses on interaction between consumers and intermediaries recognizes that consumers are not necessarily equal in their capacity to make choices. Time and material resource constraints, as well as varying expectations about others' behavior, affect how people make decisions like where to live and how much to spend. Relatedly, a focus on interaction brings the effect of expertise—or presumed expertise—to the fore. Decisions within economic markets are often mediated by others who are specifically tasked with guiding us through the market. These market intermediaries appear to us as experts, and they do their work in particular ways to reaffirm this status. Moreover, their presumed expertise creates power imbalances that yield different experiences of the market situation. In other words, the more obscure an economic process, the more power market intermediaries have in determining a particular outcome.

Indeed the broad concerns of economists like George Akerlof and Robert Shiller and sociologists like Pierre Bourdieu—that real estate agents have the potential to deeply affect buyers' housing decisions—are largely borne out empirically. For consumers, transactions like buying a house are rare and potentially daunting, with few direct parallels to more rote or prosaic decisions. Buyers in this study sometimes entered the process overwhelmed, and agents assumed buyers had little knowledge (though they exhibited more deference toward the wealthiest clients). For market intermediaries, however, matching a consumer to a product is rote and familiar; agents had various heuristics and showing techniques for completing transactions quickly.[4] Future research on economic decision-making should be attuned to this particular dynamic in which intermediaries do their work in scripted, quick, or habitual ways, while consumers rely on the intermediary to make the best choice on their behalf and may have more or less reasonable expectations that intermediaries are performing their role in deliberate and thoughtful ways. The different experiences of the same transaction, as well as how consumers and intermediaries manage these differences, helps explain various meso- and macro-level aspects of economic markets like market stability and the reproduction of inequalities in markets.[5]

Statements from buyers years after they had completed their housing searches reveal a marked consistency in how buyers felt about their purchases over time. Almost every buyer who had completed a purchase with an agent expressed broad satisfaction. The only exception was the couple described in chapter 3 who made an offer very quickly, that is, within three weeks of beginning their search. The couple, however, did not blame their agent Lucy for their decision—they blamed the conditions of the market.

The continued climb of prices was the reason buyers gave most frequently for their rosy assessment of their purchase. Looking back, the vast majority of buyers said their agents had judged the market accurately and they would use the same agent if they were to purchase a new house. Like Alexa, the buyer in chapter 2 who used the same language as her agent about childrearing and forming collective family memories to describe her home four years after purchasing, most buyers explained the reasons for purchasing their specific units in terms that reiterated their agents' terms. Their assessments were clearly influenced by their interactions with agents, which provided them with the scripts they used to describe their decisions years after their purchases. Taking an interactional approach to examining economic action, in other words, helps scholars understand why consumers feel more or less satisfied with their past behavior and decisions in economic markets.

To return to the example that opened the book: Ben told Liz to make an offer on an apartment in the Lower East Side of Manhattan rather than Brooklyn, where he initially said he wanted to live. His offer was $50,000 above what he said he wanted to spend. Liz had assessed Ben when they first met and curated the search—the types of apartments she took him to view and the neighborhoods where they looked—based on this assessment. As they visited open houses over the course of several weeks, Liz talked about many things, and these interactions shifted Ben's preferences for a neighborhood and a price. The power of market intermediaries is not simply in translating value to consumers but doing it in such a tailored and distinct way that reifies categories of products and of purchasers. Individuals' preferences are malleable, and intermediaries influence and change them through the course of interactions.[6]

UNDERSTANDING NEIGHBORHOODS, HOUSE PRICES, AND INEQUALITY

In the United States, where you live shapes your life. Different places provide different qualities of life and affect residents across a multitude of outcomes, including their health, wealth, well-being, education, safety, and chances for economic mobility.[7] Price underlies this uneven geography of opportunity. It costs more to live in certain neighborhoods, and their high cost is deeply intertwined with their higher quality of life. There are, of course, plenty of interested parties—residents, landlords, local politicians, community groups—working to valorize the places where they live, but their capacity to do so is highly limited by market forces. Places that have a head start, that is, the ones that are already wealthy, have an advantage in attracting development and increasing prices.[8] Inequality across places is therefore the result of both sociohistoric forces and contemporary efforts by on-the-ground market actors to keep prices rising.

Throughout this book I have argued that real estate agents conceptualize different places in different ways and that these conceptions affect the work they do on behalf of clients. Agents translate the value of different neighborhoods to buyers, and they do this translation differently depending on the buyer's personal, demographic, and cultural identity. What does this mean for understanding neighborhoods? First, it is helpful to remember that most people's residential context is remarkably consistent over their life course.[9] That is, when individuals move, they tend to move to similar neighborhoods in terms of demographic composition, available amenities, and symbolic meanings. This consistency has previously been explained as the outcome of both individual biases and social and economic resources. More recently attention has shifted to the ways in which individuals make their housing decisions, noting that individuals do not have comprehensive knowledge of their options. Real estate agents, as we have seen, further curate homeseekers' experiences of the market, and buyers' selection of a real estate agent is itself a product of geographic and network factors. Homeseekers' social networks not only shape their knowledge about available and appropriate places to live but also lead them to particular agents who have geographically narrowed knowledge of a local housing market. Agents have their own, often hierarchical assumptions about places; the ways they take homeseekers through the market reflect their own stereotypes of both neighborhoods and their clients. Other housing market intermediaries, like mortgage loan officers and appraisers, do the same.[10]

While I have shown how agents categorize neighborhoods depending on their demographics, their amenities, and their housing prices, more research is needed on both the sources and the effects of place reputations.[11] What aspects of neighborhoods are most salient for how agents conceptualize and define them? Do certain specific aspects of neighborhoods—like architectural styles or particular kinds of amenities (e.g., parks, restaurants, schools)—have more potent effects on how agents form their views of places and symbolic boundaries? Are these key signals simply proxies for the class and ethnoracial composition of different places, or do they have independent effects?

Answering such questions will also aid in explaining neighborhood change. Real estate agents are at the forefront of neighborhood branding, rebranding, boosting, and development. Place reputations do not necessarily emerge from the characteristics of neighborhoods themselves; rather, they are constantly being created by actors who have interests in sustaining or changing their meaning. When a white real estate agent decides that certain blocks that were previously inappropriate for white clients are now good matches, this shifts symbolic boundaries and can affect prices and neighborhood residential demographics.[12]

More work is also needed on how homeseekers interpret and act on the information they glean from their experiences with agents, particularly in comparison to the information they may get from friends and family. The findings presented in chapters 1 and 2 indicate that agents have multiple ways to maintain their authority, but it is unclear how long they will be able to do so. As the availability of information on the internet continues to grow and the types of housing market services offered online become more varied, how will homeseekers construe potentially conflicting information?

The findings presented in chapters 3 and 4 point to new empirical questions about how place inequality is maintained. With rising housing costs becoming a major public concern and political cause in cities across the United States, and as housing costs drive up the cost of living in already expensive cities, understanding how and why the wealthiest homeseekers make their housing decisions is key. Why do elite and expensive neighborhoods remain so? Why, in the aftermath of the Great Recession, has high-end real estate seen such a massive boom in price? I have shown how buyers' willingness to pay higher and higher prices stems from interactions with agents. The exuberance agents expressed about rising prices and buyers' inclinations to spend more reveal the reciprocal nature of real estate prices and investment—higher prices convinced buyers and agents that prices would continue to rise, which in turn encouraged buyers to offer higher and higher amounts.[13] This, of course, does not mean prices will rise forever. As the Great Recession showed, when exuberance takes hold and few actors have an interest in declining prices, prices can easily become untethered from important related economic conditions.[14] Already some broad market indicators in cities with expensive real estate markets point to a slowdown in investment as fewer and fewer people can afford to purchase property.[15]

According to the S&P/CoreLogic/Case-Shiller home price index, home prices were up by nearly half from 2011 to 2018, but per capita income rose by only a quarter over the same period. The disparity is larger in cities like New York, Los Angeles, Seattle, Boston, and San Francisco, where housing prices have nearly doubled.[16] Prices may ultimately change as a result of this gap, but agents and current owners clearly have an interest in keeping them as high as possible.

As Friedrich Engels noted over a century ago, a sustained focus on price is key for analyses of housing. When a thing that is so fundamental to human activity and reproduction—houses are where we eat, make love, raise children, and perform many tasks necessary for our well-being—is commodified, there are necessarily going to be conflicts, frictions, and contradictions. An interactional perspective deepens our understanding of where prices come from, since it brings into relief the myriad ways assessments of value are constantly mediated. As I have argued, knowing how buyers come to pay a particular price for housing is an essential step in the fight against growing inequality across people and places.

ACKNOWLEDGMENTS

I should first and foremost acknowledge the individuals who, in sharing their time and insights, made this book possible. While I cannot name them individually here, I am grateful to the real estate agents and prospective home buyers who allowed me to tag along while they viewed homes and took the time to be interviewed.

I am lucky that I am able to thank many of the individuals who supported me throughout the writing of this book. I say "many" because there were innumerable instances of aid—as varied as connecting me to real estate agents whom I eventually interviewed, to texting me an enjoyable gif that provided a necessary, if momentary, distraction from work—that I cannot list here. The point is that many people provided support or advice and so what follows is an incomplete list.

For their help, guidance, patience, and healthy criticism of the project, I thank Eric Klinenberg, Harvey Molotch, Jeff Manza, Gabriel Abend, and Paul DiMaggio. Eric Klinenberg has been a mentor and friend since I first arrived at NYU. His insightful and sometimes skeptical questions at every stage of the process have enriched my research and made me a better and more confident scholar. He has championed my work and pushed me to think about why my research is worthwhile. I am indebted to him for the myriad resources he made available to me and for his continued support. I cannot fully express my gratitude. Anyone who has ever met Harvey Molotch knows that there is no other sociologist quite like him. He encouraged me to follow my instincts when asking questions and helped me carefully construct answers when I was ready to articulate them. He always told me to think critically about the literature on housing markets, including his own incredibly perspicacious work. Harvey is both a personal and an academic lodestar; I can only aspire to his intellectual rigor, charming disposition, and penchant for wisecracking. What a role model! Jeff Manza has been a reliable source of support. From early on, his advice shaped the scope of the project and his vision of the field guided me to locate myself within the discipline. Gabi Abend interrogated deep assumptions I didn't even realize I was making. I thank him for his interest and the time he took to address the project's strengths and weaknesses. Paul DiMaggio came to NYU while the project was already under way, yet conversations with him about his own scholarship and the state of economic sociology proved invaluable to establishing the themes of *Upsold*. I found myself rereading his handwritten notes on an earlier draft up until submission of the manuscript.

One of the pleasures of my time at NYU was the large and helpful faculty who provided comments and suggestions on this project at various points. I thank Delia Baldassarri, Craig Calhoun, Sarah Cowan, Ingrid Gould Ellen, Paula England, David Garland, Mike Hout, Jen Jennings, Steven Lukes, and Caitlin Zaloom for conversations and suggestions about, comments on, and general intellectual influence over the project. Pat Sharkey, as mentor and collaborator, helped me think through some early motivating questions. I am deeply grateful for his continued compassionate support. Colin Jerolmack took the time to thoroughly read anything I sent him—and to take a moment to chat with me whenever I posted up in his office doorway. I don't think I've said, "Hey, got a second?" to anyone else as much, and I don't think anyone else would have responded with an enthusiastic "Of course!" every time. I thank him for his encouragement and advice and for introducing me to Fred Davis. Iddo Tavory's own research and insights infuse my work, and he helped me better position my arguments. I am grateful to many graduate students from my time at NYU for providing various kinds of support, including Hillary Angelo, Daniel Aldana Cohen, John Halushka, Max Holleran, Jeannie Kim, Issa Kohler-Hausmann, Liz Koslov, Brian McCabe, Shelly Ronen, Anna Skarpelis, Adaner Usmani, and Abigail Weitzman. Jen Heerwig taught me statistics! More importantly, she's the hardest-working person I know and yet still finds the time to encourage me. I'm so glad she, Keith, and Sebastian are in my life. Jacob William Faber and Peter Rich have been model colleagues, collaborators, and friends. Our conversations, emails, and texts (mostly *Simpsons*-related) sustained me through writing this book. In Caitlin Petre I found a simpatica scholar, writing partner, and lovely person whose friendship means the world to me.

I am grateful to scholars who have taken the time to read and comment on my work. In particular, conversations with Nina Bandelj, Debbie Becher, Brielle Bryan, Dani Fridman, Adam Goldstein, Dave Grazian, Elizabeth

Korver-Glenn, Ashley Mears, Josh Pacewicz, Anna Rhodes, Elizabeth Roberto, Harel Shapira, Rachel Sherman, Lyn Spillman, Diane Vaughan, and Fred Wherry have shaped my thinking in various ways. Viviana Zelizer allowed me to travel to Princeton once a week to attend her economic sociology class. Her brilliant scholarship has influenced my own, and I am grateful for her encouragement. Marion Fourcade, Jerry Karabel, and Loïc Wacquant, three people I met when I was an undergraduate student at Berkeley, have continued to lend advice and support.

Shamus Khan gets his own paragraph. Shamus's friendship and mentorship proved to be priceless during my time in New York. His depth of knowledge about elites and about sociology broadened my research. His generosity of time and spirit made me feel less isolated and allowed me to enjoy New York City. Everyone should have a friend like Shamus.

Bridget Gorman, Shirley Tapscott, and Sharan Mehta all helped me organize a workshop at Rice University that turned out to be a key inflection point in the development of the book. Chapters were cut, passages were moved, and arguments were relitigated. Kimberly Kay Hoang's constructive criticism made me work harder in many ways, particularly to sharpen the themes of consumption and taste in the book. Adam Reich offered important suggestions on finding a narrative arc and better utilizing existing theory. Mary Pattillo's trenchant read of the manuscript broadened its scope and allowed me to better articulate why my findings mattered. I took every piece of advice she gave since they were all gems.

Two reviewers for the University of Chicago Press were extremely helpful and mercifully very positive. Their feedback improved the book immeasurably. At the press, the legendary Doug Mitchell was incredibly enthusiastic about the project, and I am so grateful for his initial fervent support. I will miss our shared meals and our arguments about Terrence Malick. When Doug died I lost a friend and sociology lost a titan. Elizabeth Branch Dyson has been an amazing editor, pushing the project forward intellectually and practically. *Upsold* is better because of her—better written, better organized, and better titled. I thank her in particular for her encouragement to keep working when I thought I was done. I thank Kyle Wagner and Mollie McFee for taking care of the book at various stages and Ruth Goring for reading it closely.

I am indebted to Jacob William Faber, Peter Rich, and Gerard Torrats-Espinosa for their help with some analyses and for reading various parts of the book. Brian McCabe also gets a special second mention. He read the whole thing, and his thoughts about housing, cities, academia, and life made both me and the book better. He's the best! Audra Wolfe also read a full draft, more than once, and I could not be more thankful for her incisive (and funny and empathetic) comments on substance and style.

I thank Jean Aroom for GIS support and the National Science Foundation's Graduate Research Fellowship, the NYU Graduate School of Arts and Sciences Dean's Dissertation Fellowship, and Rice University's Sociology Department for financial support. Thanks to various audiences where parts of this work have been presented, including annual meetings of the American Sociological Association, the Society for the Advancement of Socio-Economics, and the Urban Affairs Association, the Center for Cultural Sociology at Yale, the Ethnography Working Group at UCLA, the NYU Furman Center, the Population Research Center at UT Austin, the Score International Conference on Organizing Markets at the Stockholm School of Economics, and the sociology departments at Dartmouth College, UCLA, the University of Pennsylvania, and Tulane University. Some of the data in chapter 2 appeared originally in *Socio-economic Review* 14, no. 3 (2016): 461–82. Some of the data in chapter 4 appeared originally in *Sociological Forum* 32, no. 4 (2017): 850–73.

Countless friends and family members have provided wisdom, support, encouragement, and distractions when I most needed them. In particular, Ben Sussman and Corey Ziemba were there for all of it. I am especially grateful to my parents, David and Nina, and my sister, Elena, whose unwavering love made and continue to make my accomplishments possible. Finally, I am still amazed at my luck to have found Bobby Langdon. His passion and intelligence have helped me through my best and worst moments. I love him dearly.

ETHNOGRAPHIC AND INTERVIEW DATA

Before I describe my approach to gathering and analyzing data in more depth, I'd like to address the issue of causality. The project was initially motivated by both empirical and theoretical concerns. Empirically, the lack of observational data on real estate agents—aside from audit studies on their racial practices—meant that their effects on some aspects of individual housing decisions (e.g., price, duration of search) could be measured but not explained. That is, the mechanisms by which agents affected housing outcomes remained opaque. Moreover, the more developed theoretical perspectives on economic action could not account for certain outcomes in markets, like short-term changes in individual preferences. Existing theories presumed a great deal of habit and stability in how economic action unfolds. But to me the ways that decisions like where to live and how much to spend were shaped during interaction were open questions. Markets are undoubtedly spaces of interaction, but we know little about interaction's effects. Put another way, if "people must continually accomplish the definition of the market situation" (Wherry 2012:204), it seemed prudent to pay attention to the moments when these accomplishments—the inherently reciprocal work involved in moving transactions forward—take place. A closer look at interactional processes helps us understand how and why buyers come to feel comfortable paying the prices they do, and better explains why some transactions succeed and others do not.

While there seems to be a growing consensus that ethnographic research can indeed produce causal explanations of social phenomena, questions remain as to best practices for doing so.[1] In *Upsold* I have drawn heavily on perspectives that see interactions as arenas of meaning making—individuals derive a sense of the world and a sense of their place in it through interaction. Ethnography is well positioned to follow and compare meaning making through multiple interactions over time. Doing so yields observable mechanisms that can be generalized when put into conversation with existing theories of the same or similar phenomena.[2] Accordingly, the ethnographer's task is to observe the same type of interaction or situation multiple times to see if and how any variation arises.[3] When there is variation, the ethnographer may begin to theorize the causes by referring to any changing circumstances.[4] More generally, social scientific researchers construct and test theories by shedding as much light as possible on a particular process and identifying the factors that make the process more likely to occur.[5]

Perhaps the best example of how this process of discovering variation unfolded during my data collection and analysis occurs in chapter 3. As I conducted my fieldwork, I began to see dramatic variation across transactions in terms of the rate of upselling. More abstractly, I was seeing variation in one aspect of prospective buyers' housing market decisions. What accounted for this variation? In other words, why were buyers deciding to offer the amounts they did? The answer, as I have argued throughout the book, was in the content of their interactions with real estate agents. As I began to compare cases of minimal and massive upselling, a pattern emerged. In cases where agents showed buyers more deference in interactions and broadly avoided talking about prices in favor of discussing other aspects of houses like location, architectural style, building materials, or symbolic neighborhood meanings, upselling tended to be much higher. Simply put, more deference and lack of price talk led to higher rates of upselling, whereas interactions that heavily featured talk of prices produced lower rates of upselling. I also came to see that these different patterns of interaction that yielded different rates of upselling were determined, in large part, by the buyers' initially stated price ceiling. Buyers with very high initially stated price ceilings—and presumably a great deal of wealth—got deference while buyers with relatively lower ones were in constant conversation with their agents about prices.

How could I be sure that this explanation, and not one of the seemingly obvious alternatives—for example, that individuals with more money simply had more resources they were willing to throw at the deal or were psychologically predisposed to be upsold—was correct? One way was to look for outlier cases, that is, data points that did not adhere to the normal pattern. Recall the example of real estate agent Thomas and his client, an architect, with a stated price ceiling of $500,000. They rarely discussed price and instead focused on design throughout the search process—their interactions were devoid of the sort of disciplining and instruction that Thomas had shown with other buyers around the same stated price preference. In other words, their interactions looked much more like the way Thomas and other real estate agents interacted with wealthier buyers than with less wealthy buyers. As a result, the buyer ended making an offer of $609,999, a relatively large difference from her initially stated price ceiling in comparison to the upselling experienced by other buyers in her price range. This case was the exception—a relatively low stated price ceiling with a high rate of upselling—that proved the rule: the content of the interactions between agents and buyers affected price outcomes.[6] Moreover, the explanation that different patterns of interaction led to different rates of upselling also resonated with *some* existing theory and empirical evidence. In other words, the explanation was plausible given past research on (1) interaction's effects on other types of outcomes, like the formation of identities or the accomplishment of group goals, and (2) variations across different types of buyers in their price outcomes.

Ultimately, any causal claim is, as Iddo Tavory and Stefan Timmermans put it, "assessed by its use. . . . Ethnographers thus do not have the final word: their work advances a research-based explanation generalizing patterns of meaning making to be taken up or ignored by the community of inquiry" (2013:709). This is why I continue to develop the interactional approach used in *Upsold* elsewhere.[7] *Upsold* is not the final word on whether and why interaction matters for economic outcomes; future research must continue to test theories and explore alternative possibilities.

GATHERING QUALITATIVE DATA

Respondents were initially gathered through my own social network: I posted on social media and asked friends to put me in touch with any real estate agents they knew. I also filed a Freedom of Information Law (FOIL) request with the New York Department of State to obtain the names and business addresses of every licensed real estate salesperson in the state. I randomized this list and contacted agents for interviews. At the end of every interview, I would ask the respondent if he or she knew of other agents who would be willing to be interviewed for the project.

After interviewing five salespeople—including two who had not represented a buyer in the previous year—I decided that respondents should be interviewed only if they had represented at least one buyer searching for a house in the last year. I made this decision to better pursue the answer to a puzzle that began to emerge in these early interviews: Agents reported that prospective buyers usually stated that they wanted to take their time in looking for a house, but typically made offers within weeks of starting their searches. What was happening to buyers that convinced them to quickly commit to a house? To answer this question, I continued interviewing, but I also immersed myself in the world of sales, becoming an observer of the real estate market to better understand agents' effects.

My ethnographic research involved shadowing agents from various parts of the New York City metropolitan area. For twenty-seven months I sat with various agents in their offices while they posted ads, searched for listings, and read the *New York Times* Real Estate section. I traveled with them on the subway and in cabs, Ubers, Lyfts, and their own cars to meet buyers at open houses, at coffee shops, and for strolls around neighborhoods. I listened and watched as they conversed with interested buyers about neighborhoods, architectural styles, buyers' preferences, and the historically spectacular rise in prices that was taking place within the city. I observed how they avoided the appearance of bias in housing sales and how aspects of buyers' identities like gender, sexuality, and occupation influenced agents' decisions about what units to show. I analyzed how agents and buyers talked about different units, paying particularly close attention to their discussions of prices. I followed agents and buyers back to agents' offices, where they compared the units they had visited and discussed making offers, closing times, and negotiation strategies. Some of these interactions were recorded, and I took notes on my phone as they occurred. Quotes presented during interactions are therefore sometimes verbatim if they were recorded. In other cases, quotations are close reconstructions from field notes, often taken as the exchange occurred. Indeed, it was not unusual for phones to be in hand and in use for the parties to a housing search. Agents generally made efforts to appear attentive when talking with buyers, but when buyers were preoccupied with looking, agents would often take out their phone to text and email. Buyers often used their phones to take pictures of the units they were viewing. In some quotes I have removed extra words or fillers like "um" for readability, and I have sometimes combined quotes from different points in an interview, noted with an ellipsis—most of these note a removal of my own, usually affirmative response to statement from an respondent, like "OK," "I see," or "mm-hmm." For each interaction I observed between agents and buyers I would type a memo. These memos usually began as the notes I had taken on my phone as the interactions occurred that I would email myself and then expand.

Overall, twelve agents and fifty-seven of their clients allowed me to accompany them during the sales process. I met the twelve agents initially through gathering interviews in New York City. As described in the introduction, agents worked with clients who were broadly demographically similar. Agents too shared some demographic similarities with their clients—particularly race and ethnicity. Chandra, who worked mostly in the middle-class, predominantly black neighborhood of Jamaica, Queens, identified as black. All the other agents identified as white except Miguel, who identified as Latino, and Lucy, who identified as part white and part Asian American. Aside from Chandra, all agents, including Miguel and Lucy, reported that their clients were mostly white. Agents sometimes differed from their clients in socioeconomic status, especially if the agent worked at the higher end of the market.[8] In other words, there seemed to be a larger class gap between agents and buyers when buyers were searching for more expensive homes. Four agents who had represented buyers searching for homes listed at over $1 million reported in informal conversations that they could not afford to buy a home listed at that price themselves.

Agents would ask their clients in advance if I could shadow them during their housing search. All agents and clients were assured anonymity.[9] In addition to the twelve agents who did allow me to observe their interactions, I asked sixteen other agents who did not. None refused outright; instead they said they would ask clients and then either didn't respond to my follow-up requests or reported that their clients refused. With agents who did invite me to showings with buyers, I figured it was best to let the agents determine how to introduce me to their clients. Most reported telling their clients about my interest in the housing market, while some reported telling their clients that I was interested in becoming a real estate agent or a real estate agent in training. While I did take the classes necessary to become a licensed real estate salesperson, this was not true. However, I did not feel it was appropriate for me to correct agents' descriptions of me to their clients, since agents generated income from these relationships. In other words, I felt I should not do anything that might affect the agents' relationships with their clients and instead tried to do everything possible to minimize my obtrusiveness and presence in general during the search.[10]

Actual interactions between agents and buyers were often temporally limited in the sense that agents and buyers would meet at predetermined times and locations of open houses or, more rarely, arranged private showings of available units. The longest time spent at an open house was close to one hour; the shortest was about five minutes. Agents and buyers would view units, often multiple units in one day, and then discuss their merits. These interactions occurred at the available units as well as at restaurants and coffee shops where agents would offer to take clients after viewing and, sometimes, at agents' offices. One clear limitation of my data is that they do not include all the private correspondence agents and buyers may have had outside their face-to-face meetings. Agents and buyers did occasionally describe the content of emails or text message conversations—all reported that phone conversation were rare except when negotiating after an offer had been made—but undoubtedly there are communications I did not witness. The amount of observations between agents and clients varied. At one end of the spectrum, I observed an agent interact with two different buyers; at the other, I observed one interact with ten. For all other agents, the number fell somewhere between (see table A.1).

These agents worked in a variety of neighborhoods and at vastly different price points. For example, Chandra had two years of experience as an agent. She specialized in Jamaica, a middle-class neighborhood in Queens. When we first met, the most one of Chandra's clients had ever spent on a house, according to her, was $335,000 for what she described as "a three-

TABLE A.1. OBSERVED REAL ESTATE AGENTS

Agent	Neighborhoods worked in	Number of clients observed*
Chandra	Jamaica / Forest Hills, Queens	2 (1 single, 1 couple)
Don	Prospect Heights / Crown Heights, Brooklyn	3 (1 single, 2 couples)
Thomas	East Village / Lower East Side / FiDi, Manhattan	7 (6 singles, 1 couple)
Miguel	Prospect Heights / Crown Heights / Bed-Stuy, Brooklyn	4 (2 singles, 2 couples)
Luis	Prospect Heights / Crown Heights / Clinton Hill, Brooklyn; Lower East Side, Manhattan	4 (1 single, 3 couples)
Liz	Williamsburg / Greenpoint / Bushwick, Brooklyn; Lower East Side / FiDi, Manhattan	10 (8 singles, 2 couples)
Sarah	Flatiron / Midtown, Manhattan; Long Island City, Queens	3 (1 single, 2 couples)
Lucy	Downtown / Brooklyn Heights / Carroll Gardens / Cobble Hill / Boerum Hill / Fort Greene / Clinton Hill, Brooklyn	5 (2 singles, 3 couples)
Brandon	TriBeCa / West Village / Battery Park City / The Bowery, Manhattan	9 (3 singles, 6 couples)
Nancy	Flatiron / Murray Hill / Midtown / Upper East Side, Manhattan	3 (2 singles, 1 couple)
Johnny	Prospect Heights / Park Slope, Brooklyn	4 (1 single, 3 couples)
Kim	West Village, Manhattan; Park Slope, Brooklyn	3 (3 couples)

* While, as Liz's interaction with her single female client in chapter 3 shows, agents might treat single buyers who were in relationships as couples, here buyers are counted as single if they approached agents alone and told agents they were planning on being the only permanent resident in the housing unit immediately after purchase.

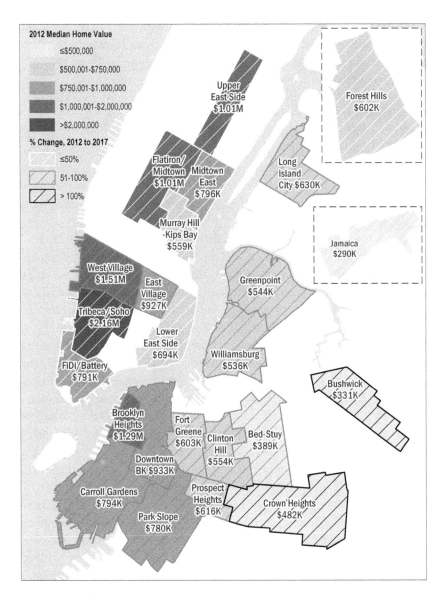

2012 Median Home Value

- ≤$500,000
- $500,001–$750,000
- $750,001–$1,000,000
- $1,000,001–$2,000,000
- >$2,000,000

% Change, 2012 to 2017

- ≤50%
- 51–100%
- > 100%

Upper East Side $1.01M

Forest Hills $602K

Flatiron/ Midtown $1.01M

Midtown East $796K

Long Island City $630K

Murray Hill -Kips Bay $559K

Jamaica $290K

West Village $1.51M

East Village $927K

Greenpoint $544K

Tribeca/Soho $2.16M

Lower East Side $694K

Williamsburg $536K

FiDi/Battery $791K

Bushwick $331K

Brooklyn Heights $1.29M

Fort Greene $603K

Clinton Hill $554K

Bed-Stuy $389K

Downtown BK $933K

Carroll Gardens $794K

Prospect Heights $616K

Crown Heights $482K

Park Slope $780K

FIGURE A.1. Prices in the New York City neighborhoods where I observed agents and buyers searching for houses for purchase. These neighborhoods, mostly in Manhattan and Brooklyn and mostly very high priced, saw high rates of increasing prices during and after my fieldwork. The neighborhood boundaries drawn on the map are neighborhood tabulation areas (NTAs) from combined census tracts, rather than informants' categories. NTAs are quite useful for measuring aggregate data, but they may not necessarily fit with residents' or agents' common conceptions of neighborhoods.

bedroom stand-alone house with a small backyard." In contrast, Brandon had worked as an agent for twenty-five years, mostly in downtown Manhattan. Brandon reported that the largest deal in which he had been involved over the course of his career was a six-bedroom apartment that was purchased for over $20 million. I witnessed transactions covering a wide range of geographies, housing types, and prices.

Of the fifty-seven buyers I followed, forty-nine eventually made offers on houses, ranging from $415,000 to $13.5 million. These offers were between $7,000 and $3.4 million more than what these buyers had initially said they wanted to spend. Buyers indicated in interviews that the price ceilings they stated in their early interactions with agents were indeed what they expected and desired to spend.[11]

During the fieldwork, I continued to interview agents I was not observing ethnographically. In addition to the 12 agents I observed ethnographically, I interviewed 45 real estate agents from across the state. Of these, 25 were from the randomized list of licensed agents in New York State—21 of these were contacted directly from the randomized list, and 4 were referred by an agent contacted from the list. In total, I contacted over 275 agents from the randomized list. I generated an additional 20 interviews from my social network and snowball sampling in New York City. I asked friends, in person and via social media, to refer any real estate agents they knew. As the project continued, I was connected to additional interviewees through more social connections, including a professor at another institution whom I spoke to about the project at an academic conference. Of the 20 New York City interviewees, 7 were real estate brokers. All interviewees, whether salespeople or brokers, were asked about the same general set of themes regarding interactions with buyers. Brokers were asked additional questions about supervising salespeople. The goal of these interviews was to delve into how agents think about pricing, race/ethnicity, and neighborhoods, as well as to identify processes of their work. Not only is New York City more diverse than the other parts of the state in terms of race/ethnicity; it is also a place where neighborhood meaning is particularly salient and segregation is high.[12] Indeed the particular circumstances of New York City allow for a deeper understanding of the mechanisms that lead to the broader quantitative findings related to neighborhood inequality discussed in chapter 4.[13] Overall, interview respondents worked in an array of rural, suburban, and urban markets, ranged in age from twenty-four to sixty-eight, and in experience from just over one to forty years. These agents' prior-year income ranged from $24,000 to $300,000. The sample consisted of 29 women and 16 men, with 30 identifying as white, 6 as black, 6 as Asian American, and 3 as Latino.

The broad topics covered in interviews were (1) work location and local organization of sales, including if and how much of their work occurred near their offices, if and why local organization was beneficial, and how and why agents matched clients with neighborhoods; (2) evaluation of units and buyers' price points, including how and why clients spend higher or lower amounts than their initially stated price limits and how agents thought buyers should value houses; and (3) fair housing practices. In order to gain insight into the fair housing practices of real estate, interviewees were asked to respond to hypothetical situations where buyers or sellers asked for information about the racial or ethnic makeup of particular neighborhoods. These hypothetical situations often elicited agents' real-life experiences of dealing with the issue of race or ethnicity in their work. If the respondent offered no examples, they were asked explicitly if they had ever been a situation where a client had made a request that violated fair housing laws.

Of the fifty-seven buyers I observed in their search for houses, I interviewed twenty-five. Twenty-one of these buyers had made offers on a unit and were interviewed within six weeks of making their offers. The remaining four buyers I interviewed did not make offers on houses using the agents with whom I had seen them interact. In addition to these twenty-five buyers, I interviewed four buyers who searched for and purchased houses without the assistance of a real estate agent. These four buyers were contacted through my own personal social network as well as through buyers I observed during my fieldwork. My questions focused on the specifics of the buyers' relationships with their particular agent and their views of how the search process went.

In retrospect, I wish I had tried harder to interview all the buyers I observed and had collected more specific financial data from each of them. More in-depth financial data could have yielded deeper background information on how buyers formed their initially stated price ceilings.[14] In other words, I wonder how exactly buyers, especially ones with vast amounts of capital, formed their price ceilings before the search process began. However, asking individuals about their assets and the sources of their income is socially difficult, and I did not want to make any of the buyers feel uncomfortable.[15]

While the interview data in general helped triangulate the observational data and more broadly provided insights into how agents and buyers thought about their actions,[16] I also observed other aspects of the housing market and real estate agent training to further contextualize agent–buyer interactions. I visited eighty-seven open houses in 2012–13 throughout the New York City metro area. This included open houses in all five boroughs,

TABLE A.2. INITIALLY STATED PRICE CEILINGS VS. PRICE OFFERINGS*

Ceiling	Offered	Difference
$399,000	$415,000	$16,000
$400,000	$420,500	$20,500
$470,000	$510,000	$40,000
$500,000	$609,999	$109,999
$550,000	$576,000	$26,000
$550,000	$565,000	$15,000
$550,000	$565,895	$15,895
$590,000	$612,000	$22,000
$600,000	$634,000	$34,000
$600,000	$650,000	$50,000
$625,000	$632,200	$7,200
$630,000	$661,500	$31,500
$650,000	$655,000	$5,000
$650,000	$698,000	$48,000
$660,000	$689,000	$29,000
$675,000	$685,000	$10,000
$680,000	$699,000	$19,000
$690,000	$710,000	$20,000
$699,000	$723,000	$24,000
$700,000	$702,500	$2,500
$700,000	$710,000	$10,000
$700,000	$725,000	$25,000
$750,000	$761,000	$11,000
$750,000	$760,000	$10,000
$780,000	$799,999	$19,999
$790,000	$810,000	$20,000
$800,000	$812,000	$12,000

Ceiling	Offered	Difference
$800,000	$845,000	$45,000
$900,000	$1,200,000	$300,000
$1,000,000	$1,380,000	$380,000
$1,000,000	$1,459,000	$459,000
$1,000,000	$1,650,000	$650,000
$1,050,000	$2,199,999	$1,149,999
$1,250,000	$1,750,000	$500,000
$1,250,000	$2,130,000	$880,000
$1,990,000	$2,750,000	$760,000
$2,100,000	$2,895,000	$795,000
$2,500,000	$2,960,000	$460,000
$2,700,000	$3,100,000	$400,000
$2,750,000	$3,059,000	$309,000
$2,900,000	$3,906,000	$1,006,000
$3,000,000	$3,493,000	$493,000
$3,900,000	$5,210,000	$1,310,000
$4,750,000	$5,299,000	$549,000
$6,750,000	$8,250,000	$1,500,000
$8,000,000	$8,750,000	$750,000
$8,500,000	$9,399,000	$899,000
$10,500,000	$13,900,000	$3,400,000
$12,000,000	$13,509,900	$1,509,900

*The stated price ceilings for the eight buyers who did not make offers during my fieldwork were $500,000, $680,000, $750,000, $900,000, $1 million, $3.5 million, $4.5 million, and $16.5 million.

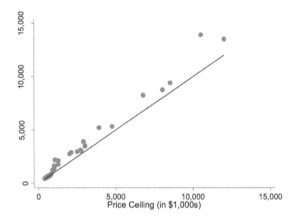

FIGURE A.2. Price ceiling and price paid in all forty-nine transactions I observed that culminated in an offer. (There is extreme clustering and therefore visual overlap at the lower left.) The *x*-axis is buyers' stated price ceiling, and the *y*-axis is the prices buyers offered (in $1,000s). While all buyers offered more than their initially stated price ceilings (above the diagonal line), the difference between price ceiling and actual price offered increases with buyers' initially stated price ceiling.

three cities in New Jersey (Hoboken, Jersey City, and Union City), and four New York cities off the Metro-North Railroad (Scarborough, Cold Spring, Hudson, and Catskill). At these open houses I looked around the units and conversed with listing agents about the properties. I asked about comparable units in the area and recent price trends. Lastly, I attended classes at three different real estate licensing schools. Under New York State law, all real estate licensing schools must teach the same seventy-five hours of required subjects for licensing real estate salespeople. I did this fieldwork at licensing schools to get a better sense of the occupational requirements as well as the content of required knowledge. I was particularly interested in what agents in training were told about valuation and fair housing. At these classes I acted as a student during instruction time and occasionally chatted informally with other students and instructors.

SAMPLE INTERVIEW QUESTIONS FOR AGENTS

Interviews were semi-structured, and questions were dynamic and dependent on the answers provided by the respondent. In other words, not all interviewees were asked the exact same questions. The questions below, however, provide a broad overview of the types of topics covered in the interviews.

Questions

How long have you been a real estate agent?

Why did you become a real estate agent / how did you get into the business?

Did you know many real estate agents before you started working as one?

> Did these acquaintances make being a real estate agent seem like a good job?

Did you have any jobs before becoming a real estate agent that you think prepared you for the work?

Where did you take your licensing classes?

How did you choose your brokerage?

Did your brokerage offer further instruction when you joined?

> (If yes) What kind of instruction/training?

Have you worked at the same brokerage for your entire career?

> (If not) Why did you change brokerages?

How often do you talk to your broker about work?

> Do you think your broker gives good/helpful advice?

What is the commission arrangement between you and broker?

> About how much money did you make from your broker last year?

What are the other agents at your brokerage firm like?

Do you enjoy the work?

> What aspects of your job do find particularly rewarding / what do you like most about being a real estate agent?
>
> If any, what aspects of your job do you not like / find boring?
>
> What would you change about your job?

Could you tell me about what you do during a typical workday?

Do you own your home?

> (If yes) What have been the biggest benefits of owning your home?
>
> (If not) Would you like to own a home soon?

Do you think homeownership is a good thing? (Why?)

Do you work mostly in sales or rentals?

How many units have you been the listing agent for in the last year? last five years?

> How many of these units sold?
>
> How quickly?
>
> Where were these units located?

Do you generally work in one neighborhood or part of the city?

> Why or why not?
>
> Is it close to where your office is?
>
> Do you think it helps to specialize in one neighborhood or part of the city?
>
> Do most agents you know tend to specialize in one neighborhood or area?

How many buyers have you represented in the last year? last five years?

> How did you get these buyers as clients?
>
> Do buyers usually come into the search knowing what they want? (price, location, search duration, etc.)
>
> Is there anything buyers usually don't know about how to look for a house that you think they should before they start?
>
> Of the buyers you've worked with recently, how many ended up purchasing houses? Where?
>
> How long was the time between your first meetings with these buyers to when they made offers on houses?
>
> Did buyers think the search was fast? slow?
>
> Did you agree?

Of the buyers you've worked with recently, what were the prices of the houses they purchased?

> Were these amounts what they expected to pay when they started their searches?
>
> Do buyers usually come in with very hard price ceilings?
>
> Did any of these buyers change their minds about where they wanted to buy or how much they wanted to spend while you were searching for houses?

Different neighborhoods have different kinds of amenities. Are buyers generally aware of these differences when they search for houses?

> Is it part of a real estate agent's job to let buyers know about these differences?

When you search for a house with a buyer, what do you tell them to think about when comparing units?

How do you help buyers cope with the potential stress of buying a house?

There have been a lot of dramatic changes in the housing market in the last five years. Have these changes affected your work?

> Do you think these changes have affected what buyers are looking for in houses?

Do you stay in contact with buyers after they purchase a house?

> Would you say you like most of the buyers you've represented?
>
> Do you think it's important for buyers to like you personally?

(If they have not mentioned referrals yet) Some agents I've interviewed talk a lot about referrals. How do you generate referrals?

    Do you ever give your clients gifts?

    Do you or your brokerage provide other kinds of services for buyers while they're looking for a house?

How has the popularity of real estate websites like Zillow.com affected your work?

    Do you think buyers know more about the market because of real estate websites?

    Does this make your work easier or harder?

    Do you think the information on real estate websites is generally correct?

    Do you think real estate websites will ever replace real estate agents?

Recent data from the census shows that places like Long Island, Westchester, Buffalo, Syracuse, New York City are very segregated by race/ethnicity. Why do you think that is?

    If a buyer asked you a question about the racial makeup of a particular neighborhood, what would you tell them?

    If a seller told you she'd prefer to sell her house to someone like her, what would you tell her?

    Have you ever heard these kinds of comments and questions from clients?

    Have other agents you know experienced these kinds of comments and questions?

    Have buyers ever asked you questions that you knew you legally could not answer?

    Do you feel like the classes you took on fair housing prepared you for the kinds of questions you get from clients?

    Do you think co-op boards discriminate against certain types of buyers?

Demographic questions

How old are you?

What is your race/ethnicity?

What's your highest educational degree?

QUANTITATIVE MODELS

DATA SOURCES AND CONTROLS

After gathering the addresses of licensed real estate salespeople in New York State through a FOIL request (n=55,770), we geocoded them and matched each to its census tract. We then gathered tract median home values for owner-occupied units and other characteristics from the five-year estimates of the 2017 American Community Survey. Additional demographic data including educational attainment (i.e., percentage of high school and college graduates), poverty rate, median age of householders, share of households that had a single parent, population, unemployment, and racial and ethnic makeup (majority non-Hispanic white, non-Hispanic black, non-Hispanic Asian, and Latino/Hispanic) were collected from the ACS, as well as housing characteristics likely to affect home values including ownership rate, percentage of single-unit structures, vacancy rate, and percentage of structures with fifty or more units. Because real estate agents are likely drawn to "hot" markets, the analyses also included a measure of the percent change in median home price since 2000. Because agents were concentrated in commercial centers, we added the number of commercial establishments to the statistical models as well as dummy variables for whether a tract is in the primary city of a metropolitan area and a measure of each tract's area (square miles). These variables capture some of the difference between central city markets and other markets in which agents may be less geographically concentrated.

COUNTY FIXED EFFECTS AND SPATIAL CROSS-REGRESSION

In interviews, agents reported that geographic specialization was an important aspect of their expertise, hence their work in highly local markets. Respondents reported that the location of their offices was generally near where the majority of their business was conducted. This was broadly true of the agents I observed as well. This finding motivated a series of statistical models estimating the geographic relationship between agents and home values, beginning with the bivariate relationship between the natural log of owner-occupied home values and the number of agents within a tract. Data exploration suggested that agent distribution and home values had a quadratic relationship, so analyses included the squared number of agents as well.[1] Next, county fixed effects were added to the model to account for regional variation within New York. Additionally, controlling for unobservable characteristics of each county helps estimate how agent concentration and home prices covary within similar markets.

Because the local nature of agent business sometimes spilled across census tract boundaries, spatial cross-regressive models, which include spatially lagged measures of independent variables, were used for the analysis.[2] We created a spatial weights matrix that described the geographic proximity between each census tract and every other census tract. Following the model presented in Crowder and South (2008), we capped the inverse-distance weights at 100 miles.[3] That is, the relationship between two census tracts was defined as one divided by the distance between the centroids of the two tracts. Tracts farther than 100 miles apart were given weights of zero. Weights were row standardized, so the sum of all weights for a specific census tract equals 1. These weights were used to create spatially lagged measures of real estate agent concentration—both the linear and squared terms—by multiplying the $k{\times}k$ spatial weights matrix by the $k{\times}2$ vector of real estate concentration, where k is equal to the number of census tracts in New York. This matrix algebra generated, for each census tract, a weighted average of the number of real estate agents and that number squared for all nearby census tracts. Because inverse distance was used, closer census tracts are assigned higher statistical importance. We then incorporated these values into regression models. Finally, we added in the covariates described above.

While across all models in table B.1 the relationship between agent concentration and house prices is in the expected direction, the covariates

TABLE B.1. FULL-SAMPLE OLS AND FIXED-EFFECTS MODELS OF THE RELATIONSHIP BETWEEN HOME PRICES AND NUMBER OF REAL ESTATE AGENTS WITHIN CENSUS TRACTS IN NEW YORK STATE

	Model 1	Model 2	Model 3	Model 4	Model 5	Model 6
Num. realtors	0.007393***	0.003426***	0.000716	0.002337***	0.000919**	0.001349**
	(0.000586)	(0.000309)	(0.000471)	(0.000314)	(0.000392)	(0.000258)
Num. realtors squared	−0.000011***	−0.000005***	−0.000002*	−0.000004***	−0.000001**	−0.000002**
	(0.000002)	(0.000001)	(0.000001)	(0.000001)	(0.000001)	(0.000000)
Num. realtors—extra-local			0.266938***	0.130111***	0.225757***	0.019650*
			(0.008300)	(0.011941)	(0.012993)	(0.010367)
Num. realtors squared—extra-local			−0.000413***	−0.000220***	−0.000404***	−0.000016
			(0.000025)	(0.000033)	(0.000042)	(0.000027)
Population					−0.000000	−0.000013**
					(0.000007)	(0.000005)
Majority black					0.378374***	−0.082997**
					(0.029609)	(0.020093)
Majority Asian					−0.087007*	0.035150
					(0.048863)	(0.035951)
Majority Latino					0.396704***	0.029470
					(0.033993)	(0.023145)
% single parent					−1.932133***	−0.655671**
					(0.107160)	(0.075863)
Median age					−0.000867	0.001038
					(0.001621)	(0.001062)
% college grads					−0.170273	0.837744**
					(0.114640)	(0.070929)
% high school grads					−1.301273***	−0.431011**
					(0.136622)	(0.084652)
Poverty rate					−0.527959***	0.218735*
					(0.122172)	(0.079907)
Unemployment rate					−0.750545***	−0.382706**
					(0.210407)	(0.127154)
Commercial establishments					−0.000035**	0.000009
					(0.000016)	(0.000011)
% owner-occupied					−0.287127***	−0.690222*
					(0.078996)	(0.053331)

BLE B.1. (CONTINUED)

	Model 1	Model 2	Model 3	Model 4	Model 5	Model 6
of structures with 1 unit					−0.332780***	0.412239***
					(0.053332)	(0.040215)
of structures with 50+ ts					−0.767565***	−0.843489***
					(0.067241)	(0.051697)
ancy rate					−0.295585***	−0.140098**
					(0.101825)	(0.064404)
change in median home ue					0.006460***	−0.000307
					(0.002505)	(0.001492)
central city					0.240959***	−0.152836***
					(0.025896)	(0.023353)
area					−0.079596***	0.065547***
					(0.006540)	(0.005172)
nstant	12.519533***	12.553363***	10.332722***	11.502322***	13.306058***	11.810806***
	(0.012814)	(0.006137)	(0.060025)	(0.081247)	(0.206916)	(0.127193)
unty fixed effects	No	Yes	No	Yes	No	Yes
servations	4443	4443	4443	4443	4443	4443
	0.038	0.786	0.384	0.807	0.703	0.891

< 0.10, ** $p < 0.05$, *** $p < 0.01$ (two-tailed tests). Robust standard errors in parentheses.

(added in Model 5 and Model 6) account for some of the correlation. The outcome in these models is the natural log of the median price of owner-occupied houses in the census tract, so the coefficients represent the expected change in log of median home prices for each additional real estate agent in the census tract, holding all other variables at any fixed value. If we undo the logarithmic transformation, the coefficients have an interpretation in percent changes. The fixed-effects model not only controls for geographic variation across the state but slightly changes how to interpret the coefficients for the covariates.

The first model, which estimates a linear and squared relationship between the phenomena without any controls, suggests that tracts with larger concentrations of real estate agents also have higher home prices, but this relationship flattens out at high values. When county fixed effects are added (Model 2)—to account for any systematic variation across counties in the state—the relationship between agents and home prices is substantively the same, though somewhat attenuated. Each additional ten real estate agents is associated with a 3 percent higher median home price (or approximately $10,700 on a home worth $356,400). The coefficient for the squared term is negative, also suggesting the relationship flattens out or reverses in high-priced neighborhoods, perhaps due to a saturation of high-end local markets with many real estate agents.

The next two models (Model 3 and Model 4) contain extra-local, or spatially weighted, measures of real estate concentration, to see if agent concentration is correlated with housing prices in nearby census tracts as well. In Model 3, the within-tract relationship between agents and home values shrinks to insignificance. However, the coefficients for spatially weighted measures of agents are significant and follow the same functional form as in Model 1. Areas with a higher number of real estate agents in nearby tracts have significantly higher home values. When these relationships are measured within counties (Model 4), the numbers of both local and extra-local agents vary significantly with home values. It is also worth noting that the sizes of the coefficients for extra-local real estate agents / square mile are much larger than those describing the local relationship, which demonstrates that the generalized relationship between agents and prices is geographically expansive beyond census tract boundaries.

While Model 5 (OLS) compares census tracts across the entire state, Model 6 (fixed effects) compares within counties. These two models contain tract-level social, economic, housing, and geographic covariates. In all of these models, the relationship between agents and home prices is broadly similar to that of the simpler models—though the additional variables in the last two models account for some of the correlation. For example, higher rates of college completion are significantly associated with higher home prices only within counties. Conversely, the local poverty rate is significantly negatively associated with home prices only in Model 5. It is possible that these distinctions result from issues of statistical power or differences in dynamics across statewide and within-county dynamics.

The relationship between house prices and racial and ethnic makeup shows interesting variation across model specifications. Statewide, prices are higher in majority black and Latino tracts, but these relationships become insignificant once county fixed effects are added. Perhaps the within-county correlations are driven by the concentration of people of color in high-cost urban areas such as New York City. Home prices in areas with greater shares of single-parent families and higher unemployment are generally lower.

Housing characteristics also have strong relationships with home prices. Prices are lower in census tracts with higher proportions of larger buildings (i.e., those with fifty or more units). Within counties, home values are negatively associated with the homeownership rate and positively associated with the presence of single-unit structures.[4] The coefficient for whether a census tract is within a central city is negative in the county fixed-effects model, indicating that areas within counties outside of central cities have relatively higher home values. Statewide, geographically larger census tracts have lower home prices, while the opposite is true within counties. Interpreted together, the relationships between home prices, housing characteristics, and geography suggest that suburban areas have the highest home prices, as described above. The percent change in median home value between 2000 and the 2013–17 ACS values is only significant before county fixed effects are added.

<h2 style="text-align:center">SUBSAMPLES</h2>

Estimating the county fixed-effects model within particular subsamples of census tracts tests whether the relationship between real estate agents and home prices varied across neighborhood type. The first and second columns of table B.2 contain output from models using samples restricted to census tracts within New York City and outside, respectively.[5] These subsamples were chosen because New York City is a unique housing market that could possibly skew the estimates. The results suggest only a slight difference between neighborhoods within and outside New York City. The results hold when outliers (i.e., the top 1 percent of the distribution of agents) and/or census tracts without any agents are removed. The same relationship exists when the sample is stratified based on whether a census tract is within any city statewide. The third column, which includes only tracts in Long Island,[6] shows similar results, as does the fourth column, which excludes tracts in New York City and Long Island. Racial and ethnic heterogeneity were analyzed by subsampling by majority non-Hispanic white, majority black, and majority Latino census tracts. There was an insufficient number of majority Asian tracts to run these analyses. Dynamics in predominantly non-Hispanic white and black tracts mirrored those in the full sample: agent concentration was positively associated with house prices. Latino tracts displayed the opposite relationship, whereby agents are negatively associated with house prices except at higher values.

TABLE B.2. SUBSAMPLE MODELS OF THE RELATIONSHIP BETWEEN HOME PRICES AND NUMBER OF REAL ESTATE AGENTS WITHIN CENSUS TRACTS IN NEW YORK STATE

	NYC	Outside NYC	Long Island	Upstate	Maj. White	Maj. Black	Maj. Lat
Num. realtors	0.001466***	0.001113***	0.000848***	0.001204***	0.000776***	0.002479	−0.008783
	(0.000508)	(0.000262)	(0.000240)	(0.000440)	(0.000216)	(0.002546)	(0.004041
Num. realtors squared	−0.000003**	−0.000002***	−0.000001***	−0.000002*	−0.000001***	−0.000028	0.000158
	(0.000001)	(0.000000)	(0.000000)	(0.000001)	(0.000000)	(0.000034)	(0.000073
Num. realtors— extra-local	0.024523**	0.091813***	0.067308***	0.112216***	0.010364	0.201814**	0.125924
	(0.011306)	(0.014011)	(0.013261)	(0.020897)	(0.010882)	(0.081236)	(0.035905
Num. realtors squared— extra-local	−0.000007	−0.000182***	−0.000121***	−0.000371***	−0.000009	0.000088	−0.000302
	(0.000028)	(0.000030)	(0.000024)	(0.000078)	(0.000028)	(0.000399)	(0.000104
Population	−0.000026***	0.000000	−0.000009	0.000006	−0.000007**	−0.000045**	−0.000000
	(0.000009)	(0.000003)	(0.000005)	(0.000004)	(0.000003)	(0.000019)	(0.00001
Majority black	−0.132901***	−0.099668***	−0.082963**	−0.119655***			
	(0.025906)	(0.029418)	(0.034888)	(0.036764)			
Majority Asian	0.045520						
	(0.034877)						
Majority Latino	−0.074726***	0.091485**	0.006107	0.104186*			
	(0.028330)	(0.036515)	(0.035710)	(0.057820)			
% single parent	−0.465431***	−0.764236***	−0.335919**	−0.761320***	−0.975965***	−0.413828**	−0.283447
	(0.106940)	(0.106913)	(0.161189)	(0.115987)	(0.104344)	(0.192339)	(0.19103
Median age	−0.002341	0.001291	0.005939***	0.000583	0.000293	−0.006821	−0.00356
	(0.001927)	(0.001125)	(0.002189)	(0.001264)	(0.001130)	(0.004360)	(0.00552
% college grads	0.377131***	1.261943***	0.914377***	1.282157***	0.827175***	0.782280***	−0.05281
	(0.094174)	(0.103673)	(0.158911)	(0.123577)	(0.121434)	(0.234922)	(0.23097
% high school grads	−0.441579***	−0.102441	−0.614462***	0.017430	−0.525919***	0.055202	−0.115359
	(0.116214)	(0.121477)	(0.184239)	(0.141025)	(0.142303)	(0.270748)	(0.20161
Poverty rate	0.213863**	0.152194	−0.168555	0.206014	0.162547	0.105584	0.45364
	(0.103891)	(0.124718)	(0.227666)	(0.132552)	(0.112303)	(0.178104)	(0.21854
Unemployment rate	−0.034010	−0.481592***	−0.127439	−0.472909***	−0.658960***	−0.392766	0.44052
	(0.176352)	(0.164635)	(0.281652)	(0.183349)	(0.180868)	(0.248514)	(0.30452
Commercial establishments	−0.000012	0.000026**	0.000031**	0.000043***	0.000025**	−0.000058	−0.00000
	(0.000016)	(0.000011)	(0.000013)	(0.000015)	(0.000011)	(0.000050)	(0.00003

TABLE B.2. *(CONTINUED)*

	NYC	Outside NYC	Long Island	Upstate	Maj. White	Maj. Black	Maj. Latino
owner-occupied	−0.631886***	−0.644363***	−0.379735***	−0.720691***	−0.497624***	−1.040145***	−0.422290**
	(0.068442)	(0.072324)	(0.109403)	(0.084053)	(0.066365)	(0.197373)	(0.167861)
of structures with 1 unit	0.451853***	0.380698***	0.246518***	0.493235***	0.286189***	0.286886***	0.315613
	(0.061786)	(0.056874)	(0.081765)	(0.068932)	(0.051025)	(0.105360)	(0.223595)
of structures with 50+ units	−0.798250***	−0.216963	−0.242529	−0.204170	−0.870758***	−0.995885***	−0.816494***
	(0.057684)	(0.136904)	(0.181305)	(0.153841)	(0.067386)	(0.212400)	(0.131992)
vacancy rate	0.049172	−0.029015	0.356132***	−0.111738*	0.034989	−0.730608***	0.023453
	(0.151711)	(0.060204)	(0.127060)	(0.062236)	(0.061346)	(0.218414)	(0.315094)
change in median home value	−0.004624	0.002616	−0.002423	0.055024***	−0.000898	−0.015028*	−0.015813
	(0.004046)	(0.002539)	(0.002492)	(0.011203)	(0.001613)	(0.007786)	(0.012044)
central city		−0.072165***		−0.049814**	−0.076729***	−0.046646	0.276699***
		(0.021232)		(0.021159)	(0.024207)	(0.160010)	(0.089910)
log area	0.045621***	0.057816***	0.038117***	0.061203***	0.052409***	−0.039218	0.002635
	(0.013597)	(0.004521)	(0.013365)	(0.005164)	(0.004581)	(0.033810)	(0.035132)
constant	12.938475***	10.442378***	11.497051***	10.192861***	11.819148***	11.974253***	12.221256***
	(0.205852)	(0.159799)	(0.257378)	(0.187246)	(0.159941)	(0.555436)	(0.463120)
county fixed effects	Yes	Yes	N/A	Yes	Yes	Yes	Yes
observations	1774	2669	577	2092	2901	542	347
	0.681	0.922	0.780	0.904	0.925	0.903	0.592

< 0.10, ** p < 0.05, *** p < 0.01 (two-tailed tests). Robust standard errors in parentheses

AGENT CONCENTRATION AND PRICE CHANGE

Given that upselling appeared endemic to agents' work, further analyses explored the relationship between agent concentration and change in house prices over time. Unlike in the previous models, where the dependent variable was simply house price, these models calculated change in house price using ACS data from nonoverlapping survey periods, 2009–12 and 2013–17. Since the agent concentration data is from 2012, this offered the opportunity to measure whether agent concentration in 2012 is in fact associated with house price changes over the next five years. In analyses using the

TABLE B.3. FULL-SAMPLE OLS AND FIXED-EFFECTS MODELS OF THE RELATIONSHIP
BETWEEN CHANGES IN HOME PRICES (2012-2017) AND NUMBER OF REAL ESTATE AGENTS
WITHIN CENSUS TRACTS (2012) IN NEW YORK STATE

	Model 1	*Model 2*	*Model 3*	*Model 4*
Num. realtors	0.000287*	0.000458***	0.000274*	0.000307*
	(0.000159)	(0.000165)	(0.000165)	(0.000164)
Num. realtors squared	−0.000000	−0.000001**	−0.000001	−0.000001
	(0.000000)	(0.000000)	(0.000000)	(0.000000)
Population			−0.000006*	−0.000007**
			(0.000003)	(0.000003)
Majority black			−0.023712*	−0.054748***
			(0.013643)	(0.015256)
Majority Asian			0.007793	0.010643
			(0.026705)	(0.027010)
Majority Latino			0.001883	0.008933
			(0.021783)	(0.023008)
% single parent			−0.207080***	−0.088997
			(0.049670)	(0.055759)
Median age			0.000761	0.000664
			(0.000711)	(0.000719)
% college grads			0.108238**	0.082729
			(0.051663)	(0.051209)
% high school grads			−0.056828	−0.060751
			(0.060052)	(0.060902)
Poverty rate			0.218318***	0.205893***
			(0.063244)	(0.065264)
Unemployment rate			0.171713	0.245221**
			(0.115150)	(0.115337)
Commercial establishments			0.000017***	−0.000011*
			(0.000006)	(0.000006)
% owner-occupied			−0.031337	−0.045888
			(0.031605)	(0.032134)
% of structures with 1 unit			−0.049329**	0.013316
			(0.019939)	(0.022884)

TABLE B.3. (*CONTINUED*)

	Model 1	*Model 2*	*Model 3*	*Model 4*
% of structures with 50+ units			−0.054571	−0.056420
			(0.036896)	(0.035723)
Vacancy rate			−0.021515	0.005434
			(0.037492)	(0.041325)
% change in median home value			−0.001694	−0.002146
			(0.001554)	(0.001559)
In central city			0.064963***	0.009369
			(0.008363)	(0.013066)
ln (area)			0.008823***	0.011186***
			(0.002431)	(0.003183)
Constant	−0.025020***	−0.026457***	−0.050657	−0.220204***
	(0.003322)	(0.003271)	(0.072023)	(0.081831)
County fixed effects	No	Yes	No	Yes
Observations	4443	4443	4443	4443
R2	0.001	0.123	0.086	0.152

* $p < 0.10$, ** $p < 0.05$, *** $p < 0.01$ (two-tailed tests). Robust standard errors in parentheses.

same modeling strategies and controls as before, it is apparent that agent concentration in 2012 is associated with higher changes in house prices between 2012 and 2017. Across all subsamples, the relationship between agent concentration in 2012 and price in the next five years is positive, and is strongest and largest in New York City tracts.

The outcome in these models is the change between the natural log of owner-occupied house prices in 2012 and the natural log of owner-occupied house prices in 2017. The coefficients represent the expected change in log of median home prices from 2012 to 2017 for each additional real estate agent in the census tract in 2012, with all other variables held at any fixed value. If we undo the logarithmic transformation, the coefficients have an interpretation in percent changes. The first model, which estimates a linear and squared relationship between the phenomena without any controls, suggests that tracts with larger concentrations of real estate agents in 2012 also experienced higher home price increases between 2012 and 2017. An additional ten real estate agents in a given neighborhood is associated with a .3 percent increase in median house price.

When county fixed effects are added (Model 2)—to account for any systematic variation across counties in the state—the relationship between agents and changes in home prices is larger. Each additional ten real estate agents in 2012 is associated with a .5 percent higher median home price change from 2012 to 2017. The coefficient for the squared term is negative. Again, this suggests that the relationship flattens out or reverses in high-priced neighborhoods, likely because high-end local markets are saturated with many real estate agents. The next two models (Model 3 and Model 4) contain tract-level social, economic, housing and geographic covariates. In all of these models, the relationship between agent concentration in 2012 and changes in home prices from 2012 to 2017 is broadly similar to the simpler models. These findings are robust to controlling for the number of real estate agents in the neighboring tracts (i.e., adding spatially weighted linear and quadratic terms accounting for the number of agents in extra-local tracts).

NOTES

INTRODUCTION

1. See Pattillo 2013.
2. Akerlof and Shiller 2015; Pattillo 2013.
3. McCabe 2016; Shlay 2015; Sullivan 2018. For how housing stratifies American society economically see Spilerman 2000; Oliver and Shapiro 2006. For explorations of the meaning of housing in philosophy and literature, see Bachelard [1958] 1994; Garber 2000.
4. The Marxist geographer David Harvey (2014:22) describes the contemporary housing market in this way:

> Housing provision under capitalism has moved, we can conclude, from a situation in which the pursuit of use values dominated to one where exchange values moved to the fore. . . . The provision of adequate housing use values (in the conventional consumption sense) for the mass of the population has increasingly been held hostage to these ever-deepening exchange value considerations. The consequences for the provision of adequate and affordable housing for an increasing segment of the population have been disastrous.

Overall, the retrenchment of the state from providing traditional forms of welfare has increased reliance on homeownership for financial stability (Conley 1999; Conley and Gifford 2006; Oliver and Shapiro 2006; Orzechowski and Sepielli 2003), meaning that the use and exchange value of housing—at least for consumers in a nation where the majority of the population owns their homes—have become increasingly inextricable.

The sociologist Viviana Zelizer (1994; 2005; 2011; 2012) provides a way to theorize interests in economic markets more generally that might be useful for scholars of housing. Instead of thinking about use and exchange as hostile or competing sets of value—as some of the literature on housing does—Zelizer argues that people are always combining and working through the contradictions between the two in economic transactions. Economic actors cannot separate their culturally influenced values from their monetary interests. In fact, pure monetary interest may not exist at all; what we value is highly contingent on the historical moment in which we live as well as how various economic activities take on different meanings depending on who is transacting. Put differently, the distinct separation of use and exchange is likely not how individuals *experience* the marketplace. The sociologist Debbie Becher (2014), in her analyses of outcomes in the use of eminent domain, shows how complicated housing is as a commodity. She demonstrates that local governments seizing residential private property are more likely to quell opposition and achieve legitimate compensation packages when they recognize that property owners are losing both the market value of their houses and the emotional and social value of their homes. She advocates for a "value pluralism" framework for understanding housing as a commodity (Becher 2014:250).

5. McCabe 2016.

6. Howard 1997; Jackson 1987; A. Schwartz 2010.

7. Hutchinson 1997; Lands 2008; Lauster 2010; Luken and Vaughn 2005 and 2006.

8. Halle 1984; Kefalas 2003; Newman 1989; Pattillo 2007; Townsend 2002.

9. Brownstein 2011.

10. Owning a home can also affect an individual's psychological health, though the mechanisms behind the connection are not well defined. See Clapham 2005; Rohe and Stegman 1994; Zavisca and Gerber 2016.

11. Importantly, these repeated encounters overlay economic deals with what the pioneering scholar of networks Mark Granovetter (1985:490) described as "social content that carries strong expectations of trust and abstention from opportunism."

12. Dore 1992.

13. Podolny 1993 and 2005.

14. In reference to economic markets, the sociologist Jens Beckert (2011:771) calls culture "the normative preconditions necessary for goods or services to become legitimate objects for market exchange and thereby to have prices attached to them."

15. DiMaggio 1994; Weber [1930] 1992; Zelizer 1979; 1985.

16. So can political interests, political mobilization, and public policy. See Fligstein 1996 and 2002.

17. Beckert and Aspers 2011; Biggart and Beamish 2003; Bourdieu 1993; Fourcade 2011; Karpik 2010; Lamont 2012; Zuckerman 1999 and 2012.

18. See Bessy and Chauvin 2013. Some readers—particularly ones who study brokerage—might ask why I do not refer to these agents as brokers. Sociologists and anthropologists have long used the term *broker* to refer to an actor or organization who brings two previously unconnected actors or organizations together. Within organizations, brokers fill structural holes—that is, the broker occupies a particular position at the intersection of two separate networks and can benefit from controlling the flow of information and resources between the networks (Burt 1992 and 2005; see also Stovel and Shaw 2012; Cohen and Comaroff 1976; Geertz 1960; James 2011; Simmel 1950; Wolf 1956).

However, the term has some limitations. First, it is *too* broad. Brokerage encapsulates so much action—connecting people to other people or organizations or resources—that a more specific term for what happens in economic markets is perhaps necessary. The category of "market intermediaries"—those who are tasked with explaining a market and facilitating deals in that market—is more defined, circumscribed, and attendant to the practical ways that valuation occurs as economic transactions unfold (see Dewey 1939). Second, brokerage is too often conceptualized as an act as opposed to an ongoing process (Obstfeld, Borgatti, and Davis 2014; Small 2009b). The term *market intermediary* better captures the dynamic ways particular actors interact with buyers and sellers and take them through the process of exchange.

19. Besbris 2016b; Chan 2009. See also Bandelj 2009 and 2012; Fligstein 2001; C. W. Smith 1989.

20. See, for example, Calhoun 1994; Desmond 2007; Ermakoff 2008; Fine 1996 and 2012; Glaeser 2010; Khan 2011; Mische 2008; Ridgeway and Smith-Lovin 1999; Sewell 1996; Tavory 2016; West and Zimmerman 1987.

21. National Association of Realtors 2016; see also Rutherford and Yavas 2012.

22. House's research is more concerned with the nature of service work than with economic processes like valuation, but his point about the potential influence real estate agents have on home buyers' decisions is borne out in decades' worth of research. In a survey of homebuyers in the late 1960s, the economist Douglas Hempel (1969) found that homebuyers rated real estate agents as either the most influential or the second most influential source of information on the "fair" value of a home, price range to be considered, and preferred neighborhood or location. More recent work by Maria Krysan (2008) also shows that aside from buyers' own research, real estate professionals are the most used source of information in the search for housing. But real estate agents' central position is not guaranteed. According to the most recent American Housing Survey—a biennial survey of America's housing stock conducted by the US Census and the Department of Housing and Urban Development—people living in urban areas in the United States now cite the internet as the most important source of information for their housing search.

23. Hornstein 2005.

24. Bourdieu shows how this expertise leads to the stratification of consumption and taste in the housing market; homeseekers are systematically steered toward certain types of houses that match their status so that their home—the physical space in which they live—is consistent with their overall tastes and class position.

25. The question of agents' influence over the sales process has also motivated scholarship in housing market economics. While some economists argue that agents hoard information to increase prices (Crocket 1982; Yinger 1981; Zumpano and Hooks 1988), others claim they produce fair and competitive markets (Mantrala and Zabel 1995). In one sense, the mere existence and persistence of real estate agents can be taken to mean they must be worth their while. In other words, if real estate agents were not efficient and useful, market forces would have eliminated them. However, most economists do not hold this view, and a great deal of research is concerned with both the inefficiencies they create for individual homebuyers and sellers and how

their labor market is itself inefficient (Hseih and Moretti 2003). Generally, economists strike a middle ground, pointing out that "agents provide a bundle of services besides just valuation information, and these services are worth the commission cost despite the distortions" (Levitt and Syverson 2008:610). Economists have also documented how agents shape the transaction, making search times shorter and price concessions by sellers more likely (Elder, Zumpano, and Baryla 2000; Witte, Grunhagen, and Gentry 2008).

Empirical research on the effects of individual agents on prices is, however, mixed. Individual agent characteristics have insignificant effects on prices, though agent specialization in tasks, e.g., working more with sellers or working more with buyers, tends to yield better prices for clients (Turnbull and Dombrow 2007). For a succinct summary of the kinds of questions about real estate agents that tend to preoccupy economists, see Benjamin, Jud, and Sirmans 2000. See also Clark 1982.

While this work reveals that agents affect outcomes in the housing market, it does not assess the interactive work that agents do with buyers, and it cannot account for variation across individual decisions. Furthermore, it assumes that homes are investments like any other and that individual homebuyers react to agents in the same fashion across transactions. As a result, prior research is unable to address two concerns laid out by Bourdieu (2005:159), who in *The Social Structures of the Economy* notes that the real estate agent "does, in fact, contribute crucially to the production of the product: what the buyer is offered is not just a house, but a house accompanied by the discourse surrounding it."

26. Faulkner and Becker 2009; Goffman 1959 and 1967.

27. Wynn 2016; see also Desmond 2014.

28. See Bruch and Feinberg 2017 for summary.

29. Bettman, Luce, and Payne 1998; Lichtenstein and Slovic 2006; Sen 1973 and 1993; Slovic 1995.

30. This demonstrates how value is a social construct and contains a certain amount of arbitrariness (Ariely, Loewenstein, and Prelec 2006; see also Simmel 1978).

31. For more on theoretical differences between economic sociology and behavioral economics see Bandelj, Wherry, and Zelizer 2017.

32. Additionally, the book fits within a growing sociological literature examining decision-making as flexible, prospective, and situationally dependent, e.g., Abend 2018a and 2018b; Daipha 2015; see also Beckert 2016; Dewey 1922 and 1939; Martin 2011.

33. Blumer 1969; Goffman 1983. See also Eliasoph and Lichterman 2003.

34. Jerolmack and Khan 2014.

35. Becker and Geer 1957; Katz 2015.

36. The list was obtained through a Freedom of Information Law request from the New York Department of State.

37. While I did not intentionally filter out any types of buyers—their inclusion was through their real estate agents—the fact that so few had school-aged children meant that perceptions of local school quality were not driving buyers' decision-making.

Recent evidence on how important local schools are to residential decision-making is mixed. Some work shows that parents with school-aged children are likely making residential decisions based on school performance and school district boundaries and increasing racial/ethnic and income segregation when doing so (Owens 2016 and 2017; Rich and Jennings 2015; see also Goldstein and Hastings 2019). Other research shows that these decisions may not be overtly about schools but instead result from households' reliance on information gleaned from their social networks when choosing where to live (Lareau 2014; Lareau and Goyette 2014).

38. Kwate et al. 2013.

39. McPherson, Smith-Lovin, and Cook 2001.

40. Similar methods have been used to analyze how individuals evaluate their own decision-making processes, especially regarding consequential selection processes like why employers make offers to certain job candidates (Rivera 2015a and 2015b) and why elite colleges admit certain applicants over others (Stevens 2007).

41. Affordability here is measured as the median house price divided by the gross before tax median household income—what is called the "Median Multiple."

42. See Cox and Pavletich 2013. This price metric does not account for what *kind* of house one might be purchasing in different cities or the square footage that one obtains for a given price. The housing market may be slightly less affordable overall in Los Angeles than it is in New York City, but houses in Los Angeles tend to be larger. And while this measure might place the affordability of a place like Sacramento near that of larger coastal cities, it does not mean that the actual prices in Sacramento are comparable. In the second quarter of 2018, for example, the median price of a house listed for sale on Zillow.com in Sacramento was $350,000, compared to $660,000 for New York City, $674,000 for Los Angeles, and $1,334,800 for San Francisco.

43. Rao 2014.

44. See Cox and Pavletich 2017. While affordability and even median price in the housing market in New York City were comparable to those of some other cities, the sources of capital investment and rates of occupancy in the local market may be different. The New York housing market has a high rate of purchases by limited liability corporations—or shell companies—instead of individuals. About half of all houses that cost over $5 million in the United States are purchased by shell companies, with the rate even higher in places like Manhattan and Los Angeles (Story 2016). During my fieldwork there was some media attention paid to the inflow of foreign investment into New York's housing market (see Story and Saul 2015). While these types of transactions are not examined here, their actual effect on prices is an interesting and open question. The growth in prices for property since the Great Recession also likely reflects the availability of credit and quantitative easing by the Federal Reserve (Harvey 2017). Surplus capital must find new "fixes" to the problem of overaccumulation and the spectacular rise in investment in property markets—as well as other speculative markets like the stock market or the market for art—is a way in which investors can put their money to work. This book, in part, seeks to elucidate this process as well as describe, particularly in chapter 4, some of the forms of inequality produced as a result.

45. For example, see DeLuca, Garboden, and Rosenblatt 2013; Desmond 2016; Rosen 2014 and 2017; Sullivan 2017; 2018; though see Krysan and Crowder 2017; Kimelberg 2014; Lareau 2014.

46. Allard 2017; Chetty and Hendren 2018; Chetty et al. 2014; Frickel and El-liott 2018; Gibbons and Yang 2014; Kohler-Hausmann 2018; Levine 2016; Logan and Molotch 1987; Marwell 2007; Massey and Fischer 2006; Nuru-Jeter and LaVeist 2011; Peterson and Krivo 2010; Quillian 2014; Rich and Jennings 2015; R. J. Sampson 2012; Sharkey 2013; Sharkey and Faber 2014; Sharkey, Besbris, and Friedson 2016; Williams and Collins 2001.

47. Bischoff and Reardon 2014; Dwyer 2007; Jargowsky 1996 and 2018; Owens 2015 and 2016; Reardon and Bischoff 2011; Reardon et al. 2018; Reardon, Fox, and Townsend 2015.

48. UC Berkeley's Urban Displacement Project and the California Housing Part-nership 2018a, 2018b, and 2018c.

49. For more on why studying high-end or elite environments is necessary for understanding stratification processes, see Cousin, Khan, and Mears 2018; Harrington 2016; Khan 2011 and 2012; Rivera 2012 and 2015b; Sherman 2017.

50. For the history of the real estate profession, see Hornstein 2005. I draw heavily from Hornstein's work, particularly in chapter 1.

51. *Upsold* is not an ethnography of a particular job in the traditional sense. By this I mean ethnographies that describe the historical development of a particular occu-pation, explain the daily flows of action and tasks necessary for completing the work, analyze the institutional and individual attributes that contribute to successfully doing the work, and often elaborate the pleasures and failures of the job as well as how the job reproduces some social phenomena. For excellent examples see Bearman 2005; Davis 1959; Gambetta and Hamill 2005; Harrington 2016; Leidner 1993; Nadeem 2011; Ocejo 2017; Sallaz 2009; Sherman 2007; Viscelli 2016; C. L. Williams 2006.

While many aspects of the occupation are considered—including education and myriad work practices—I do not make arguments about dispositions particular to indi-viduals who are real estate agents. Aside from their interactions with clients, I have not included many descriptions of what agents are doing in their day-to-day work. A lot of what agents do is fairly predictable and not particularly interesting. Descriptions of them checking emails, looking at real estate websites that provide them with analytics, or simply reading the news and checking social media—much of what I witnessed when I was with real estate agents in their offices or waiting to meet clients—could maybe tell us something about the nature of contemporary service work, but I doubt the insights would be that novel. So while the book is about the work of market inter-mediaries, work here is generally in reference to the outward-facing parts of the labor process where intermediaries and clients are interacting.

And because the focus of the book is on interactions between agents and clients, there is also not a great deal of character development. Readers will learn a bit about agents' and buyers' personal lives as they pertain to particular interactions being de-scribed, but the book does not contain in-depth personal histories. This is partially because I want to obscure the actual identities of the agents and buyers who agreed to participate in this research as much as possible. But it is also because the book privileges interaction over individuals. Individuals are analytically important insofar as they are party to the interaction, so readers should not expect to "get to know" the individuals participating in much of the interaction. As the sociologist Andrew Abbott (1995:863) puts it: "Previously-constituted actors enter interaction but have no ability to traverse the interaction inviolable. They ford it with difficulty and in it many disappear. What comes out are new actors, new entities, new relations."

52. The process was a way for agents to manipulate housing prices to increase their profit and an explicit policy of racial control—many real estate associations required agents to show homes to black buyers only in black or transitioning blocks. This avoided the "haphazard" entry of blacks into white neighborhoods (Helper 1969:4; 224–38). For how federal laws created, encouraged, and sanctioned residential racial and ethnic segregation, see Jackson 1987; Massey and Denton 1993; Rothstein 2017.

53. See Besbris and Faber 2017; Galster and Godfrey 2005; Massey and Denton 1993; Yinger 1995. While the intensity of some of these practices has ebbed somewhat in recent decades, an audit study conducted by the Department of Housing and Urban Development from as recently as 2012 shows they still exist throughout the country, raising the costs of searching for nonwhite homeseekers (Turner et al. 2013:xi). These steering practices contribute to the concentration of racial/ethnic minorities in high-poverty and highly polluted neighborhoods (Christensen and Timmins 2018). The sociologist Elizabeth Korver-Glenn (2018a; 2018b) has provided deep insights into how racial and ethnic stereotypes among housing market actors, including real estate agents, contribute to sustained inequalities between whites and nonwhites and between white and nonwhite neighborhoods. She shows how the US racial and ethnic hierarchy is ingrained in the structure of the US housing market. For more on how real estate advertising is involved in racially and ethnically defined placemaking, see Perkins, Thorns, and Newton 2008; Williams, Qualls, and Grier 1995.

CHAPTER ONE

1. Gallup 2015.

2. Other surveys on the trustworthiness of agents find similar results (Beale 2013), even in other countries (Cross 2014).

3. Americans' dim view of real estate agents likely stems from their role as intermediaries. When information is not widely available, intermediaries and brokers more generally fill what social scientists call a structural hole. In other words, they provide a conduit through which information can flow from one party to another (Burt 1992). Yet because the parties who need this information cannot access it on their own, they may be suspicious that the intermediary is not entirely forthcoming (Bailey 1963; Friedman and Podolny 1992; Stovel, Golub, and Milgrom 2011; see also Simmel 1950). Brokers and intermediaries have "a clear opportunity to gain at the expense of either or both of the groups for whom [they are] brokering" (Stovel and Shaw 2012:154). For much of the history of the occupation, real estate agents have had unique access to

information about the housing market, and their entire occupation is predicated on profiting from this access (see Bishop 2004).

4. Action 4 News Staff 2013; Barnett 2015; Bennett 2008; Chung 2006; Harding 2013; Kalfus 2018; Kurhi 2013; P. Sampson 2013; Streitfeld 2008.

5. See Abbott 1988; Eyal 2013.

6. While the National Association of Realtors has a Code of Ethics & Standards and Practices for members, membership in the association is voluntary and not required by any state to be a licensed real estate salesperson.

7. Hornstein 2005. The sociologist C. Wright Mills predicted that work in general would shift away from valuing skills to valuing personalities. In his dazzling study of postwar middle-class society in the United States, *White Collar* (1951:182), Mills wrote:

> In a society of employees dominated by the marketing mentality, it is inevitable that a personality market should arise. For in the great shift from manual skills to the art of "handling," selling, and servicing people, personal or even intimate traits of employees are drawn into the sphere of exchange and become commodities in the labor market. . . . Kindness and friendliness become aspects of personalized service or of public relations of big firms, rationalized to further the sale of something. With anonymous insincerity, the Successful Person thus makes an instrument of his own appearance and personality.

As more and more jobs become less like traditional models of company work and freelancing, part-time, and commission-based work become more common (Besbris and Petre 2019; Collins 2013; Kalleberg 2011; Leicht and Fennell 2001; Smith 2001), real estate agents provide an example not only of a typical economic intermediary but also of entrepreneurial labor. Indeed, in their day-to-day work, real estate agents have become a paradigmatic case of what the sociologist J. D. House (1977) called "contemporary entrepreneurs." That is, real estate agents expend time and effort in face-to-face encounters with clients to build a strong reputation which yields referrals. Because real estate agents profit from commissions and referrals, it is essential that they keep their good reputations within local housing markets.

8. The powerful Chicago Real Estate Board set the model that would become the norm for payment in real estate transactions in early 1900s. Sellers sign an exclusive listing agreement with a brokerage, which earns a fee that is a percentage of the sale price (Hornstein 2005). The listing brokerage will split the fee, usually in half, between the listing agent and the buyer's agent. This model quickly became the norm for real estate boards across the country and generally holds today. For sellers, the broker's fee is specified in the listing agreement and is legally always subject to negotiation—although individual agents will often tell prospective clients that their brokerage firm has rules that mandate all sales require a 6 percent fee. The 6 percent charge is standard practice. (For real estate agent commissions in other countries see Delcoure and Miller 2002.) It is also not uncommon to lower this fee to 5 percent if the listing agent and the buyer's agent are the same person or are both employed by the same brokerage—i.e., there is only one real estate brokerage firm participating in the sale. The norm of a 6 percent

fee is, however, very strong. Brokerages that regularly charge less than the standard 6 percent grow more slowly than those that do, and the houses they list sell less quickly, indicating that while price collusion is illegal, brokerages charging fees different from the norm are less desirable transaction partners (Barwick, Pathak, and Wong 2015).

9. In his doctoral dissertation on the Chicago Real Estate Board, the sociologist Everett C. Hughes ([1931] 1979) described a conscious effort by the board's founders to help their members become professional advocates for property owners. His early research demonstrates the usefulness of examining real estate agents' work to understand broader themes of sociological interest including occupations, institutions, and the role of market intermediaries in maintaining stratification (Abbott 1999; Chapoulie 1996).

10. The board helped the newly established Department of Commerce produce and distribute guides like "How to Own Your Own Home," which reached over 300,000 consumers (McCabe 2016). This kind of political work not only used government resources to help promote homeownership, but also continued the professionalization of real estate agents and increased their political clout.

11. Spillman 2012. According to the Center for Responsive Politics, the National Association of Realtors spent over $50 million on lobbying in 2018.

12. For how professional organizations were instrumental in the professionalization process in the late 1800s and early 1900s, see Abbott 1988; Freidson 2001; Larson 1977; Starr 1982.

13. All together, the rules, laws, and institutions advocated for by professional real estate associations have helped create and maintain extremely high rates of ethnoracial and income segregation in American cities (Gotham 2002; Jackson 1987; Krysan and Crowder 2017; Massey and Denton 1993: Rothstein 2017). See chapter 4.

14. *Mortgage Fraud Blog* 2013; Buckshot 2015.

15. Boeing and Waddell 2017; Schachter and Besbris 2017.

16. Zillow's data—on neighborhood boundaries as well as prices—are already being used by scholars looking at various urban processes (Boeing 2018; see also Besbris et al. 2015 and 2018).

17. Zillow does indeed publish yearly median percentage errors in its estimates for over twenty major metropolitan areas and for the nation as a whole. In 2015 the typical difference between Zillow's estimate and a unit's actual price in NYC was over $34,000; for the nation as a whole it was close to $18,000. In 2016 the company reduced the error to about $28,000 and $14,000 respectively.

18. Akerlof and Shiller 2015.

19. DiMaggio and Louch 1998.

20. It should be noted that in this case John and Steven's meeting with Lucy did not obligate them to use her representation during their housing purchase. In New York State, buyers and agents can sign various types of agreements after their initial contact. Open buyer-agency agreements allow buyers to deal with other agents, and the agent receives a commission only if she finds the unit the buyer eventually purchases. Exclusive buyer-agency agreements require that the agent earn a commission regardless of whether the buyer or the agent find the unit that is eventually purchased.

Exclusive-agency buyer-agency agreements require a commission to be paid to a bro-ker if any agent under contract with that broker finds the buyer a house and secures the sale. Despite these various types of possible agreements, and recommendations from the New York Department of State that agents disclose their role in writing to buyers at their first substantive contact, agents rarely asked buyers to sign anything at their initial meetings. In fact, most agents and buyers went through the search process assuming they were working exclusively together even though they were under no legal obligation to do so.

21. In an expansive study of how people chose where to live and how these choices maintain ethnoracial segregation, sociologists Maria Krysan and Kyle Crowder (2017) show that individuals are generally familiar with a very limited set of neighborhoods in their city (see also Krysan and Bader 2009). Other research has shown that in general middle- and upper-class homeseekers generally have very little specific knowledge about the neighborhoods they move to beyond broad reputations as being good places to live where current residents are by and large like them (Lareau 2014). The pre-search knowledge that buyers do have is structured by homeseekers' existing social networks. Since most aspects of social life are segregated by race/ethnicity and class, homeseekers' basic knowledge about potential places to live are constrained and lim-ited by race/ethnicity and class even before the search begins in earnest. An additional factor that narrows the scope of individual home searches is that real estate agents tend to concentrate in a relatively narrow geography. Agents do so because it increases their specific knowledge about a particular neighborhood, which can lead to more sales completed more quickly (see Besbris and Faber 2017).

22. See, for example, Anteby 2010; Quinn 2008; Zelizer 2005.

23. One of the main insights of the morals and markets literature is that institu-tional actors work to make certain products into legitimate market objects (Chan 2012; Fourcade and Healy 2007). In other words, whether they truly believe in their beneficence or not, actors with financial interests have sought to rhetorically frame new and morally dubious products in ways that highlight various types of returns for market participants. For rhetorical and practical legitimation in the market for sex, see Bernstein 2007; Besbris 2016a; Hoang 2015; Rosen and Venkatesh 2008; in the market for sporting violence, see Wacquant 1998 and 2001.

24. McCabe 2016; Zavisca and Gerber 2016. The commodification of land is, in fact, "necessary to the perpetuation of capitalism" (Harvey 1982:371; see also Polanyi 1944). Many scholars and activists have, however, long questioned the morality of commodified housing (Engels 1935 and [1845] 1993; Harvey and Wachsmuth 2012; Madden and Marcuse 2016).

25. See Fridman and Luscombe 2018; Healy 2006; Lainer-Vos 2013; Rossman 2014.

26. A "closing" is the meeting where the seller transfers the deed to the buyer. Closings are often drawn-out affairs that include final walk-throughs as well as paying the fees for real estate attorneys, taxes, and sometimes move-in costs charged by a particular apartment building.

27. Biggs 2017.

28. See Lainer-Vos 2011 and 2014; Mauss 1967. Even in less consequential and more fleeting interactions between consumers and market intermediaries, intermediaries act in certain ways to create a sense of mutual obligation and increase the likelihood of completing a transaction. For example, in their study of interactions between customers and salespeople in a chain computer and electronics store, the sociologists Asaf Darr and Trevor Pinch (2013) reveal how salespeople are often willing to listen to superfluous information from potential buyers—details about buyers' personal lives—because it further obliges the buyer to make a purchase.

29. When it came to listing houses, agents reported being as attentive and eager to give gifts to sellers as they are in their dealings with buyers. However, there is some evidence that agents provide better service when the seller is not moving out of the city. If a seller is leaving the city, the agent may believe he or she will be less able to provide referrals in the future, compared to sellers who are just moving to a different house in the same city. As a result, agents might put less effort into selling the house; indeed houses of sellers moving out of the city tend to sell for less than those of sellers who aren't (Shi and Tapia 2015).

30. Kaufman 2019.

31. In cases where deeper and more involved relationships developed, agents and their clients shared similar social characteristics like age, race, family status, and socioeconomic status. The sociologist Brooke Harrington (2016) studied how wealth managers established trust with their clients and found that relationships between financial service providers and their clients were often facilitated through a shared habitus, similar social dispositions and consumption practices, or even shared racial/ethnic or religious identities. Some agents reported shared experiences or identities as helpful although not necessary for them to do their work. Unlike wealth managers, whose relationships with their clients last decades and span generations, agents' interactions with their clients are generally more contained and circumscribed, with a clear goal of completing a single transaction. Moreover, most agents do not often have the luxury of being able to turn clients down, regardless of whether they share similar dispositions. It should be reiterated again, however, that the sorting processes that lead clients to agents—through particular neighborhoods and social networks—are broadly segregated, meaning that agents and their clients likely share some social identity characteristics, particularly race/ethnicity (Krysan 2008; Krysan and Crowder 2017; Kwate et al. 2013).

32. See Macaulay 1963. This "implied agency"—where the buyer–agent relationship is established through words and acts instead of written documents—was the norm and is technically legally binding if terms were discussed (see New York State General Obligations Law § 5-701[a][1]). In other words, to be legally enforced, implied agency must have established that the agent was asked to perform a search with the expectation of payment upon completion—in legal terms, there must be a "meeting of the minds" between the agent and the buyer about compensation (see Procidano v. Mautner, 70 Misc. 2d 891, 335 N.Y.S.2d 17, 20, 1972 N.Y. Misc. LEXIS 2352 [N.Y.C. Civ. Ct. N.Y. County 1972]). Despite the ubiquity of implied agency on behalf of buyers, one

of the textbooks provided by a real estate licensing school warns that "New York courts do not easily enforce implied agency agreements." However, because buyer's agents are usually paid through the listing broker, and because most buyers came through referrals, agents rarely established terms in early meetings with buyers. The exceptions were agents who worked for brokerage firms that were exclusively buyer brokerages; these buyers'-only agents always required buyers to sign exclusive buyer-agency agreements. In contrast, almost all agents reported signing agency documents when they represented a seller.

33. Agents who also worked with renters liked social media posts by their clients as well. Agents generally kept lease dates in the calendars, and a few reported more social media engagement with renters three months before the end of the lease, the time at which landlords in New York City are obligated to notify tenants if they plan on raising the rent.

34. To reiterate, individual agents are not paid directly from the sale; instead, payment goes to the broker who holds their license. Individual listing agents therefore rarely keep the entire 3 percent (splitting 6 percent with a buyer's agent). The entire commission is paid to the listing broker, who then pays a portion to the agent who listed the property—an independent contractor with the brokerage—and a portion to the buyer's agent's brokerage, which then pays a portion to the buyer's agent. Many brokerage firms use incentive programs where they increase the percentage to the agent as the agent's volume or dollar amount of deals increases.

35. There is a cottage industry within real estate economics examining the various conflicts of interest that afflict the real estate industry. The first concerns dual-agency arrangements. "Dual-agency" arrangements in which only one brokerage—either the same agent or agents from the same brokerage firm—facilitates both ends of the sale are legal in forty-two states. Most of these, including New York, require the broker to disclose their dual agency and what that entails to both seller and buyer in writing. Even in the eight states that have outlawed dual-agency arrangements, other agent–client relationships allow single agents or brokers to represent both buyers and sellers in a single transaction (Carter and Brambila 2012). Laws governing real estate agent and broker behavior are complex; nonrepresentative surveys by the National Association of Realtors and the private real estate news company *Inman* both showed that many agents "don't seem to understand dual agency, can't explain it to their clients, and don't make the required disclosures" (Carter 2011). Recent increases in the number of buyers'- and sellers'-only brokers may indicate some movement away from the dual-agency model (Carter 2011; Stellin 2011).

Within economics, a number of scholars have examined the so-called principal-agent problem that is inherent in real estate brokerage. That is, how can agents, who are usually legally obligated to represent the interests of the client, do so when there are likely times when the best thing for a buyer or seller is to say no to an offer or take a lower price—lowering or forgoing an agent's commission? There is some evidence that the problem is, in fact, real at least for agents and sellers. Studies that compare the outcomes of when real estate agents sell others' houses to when they sell their own find that agents get higher prices when they sell their own houses (Levitt and

Syverson 2008; Rutherford, Springer, and Yavas 2005; see also Hendel, Nevo, and Ortalo-Magné 2009).

36. For more on how agents enjoy scheduling flexibility, see C. S. Wharton 2002.

37. Akerlof and Schiller 2015.

38. Mendes 2013. There is no shortage of examples of individual elected officials disparaging the body in which they serve.

CHAPTER TWO

1. Broadly, identity and emotions are deeply intertwined with economic decision-making (Bandelj 2009; Bourdieu 2005; Peters 2006; Slovic et al. 2006).

2. For psychological studies of emotions and consumer behavior, see Lerner and Tiedens 2006; O'Shaughnessy and O'Shaughnessy 2003; P. Williams 2014. Echoing sociological explanations of consumption behavior (Bourdieu 1984; 2005; Zukin and Maguire 2004), recent psychological research shows consumers make purchases that resonate with their perceptions of self to reaffirm certain identity characteristics, which in turn provides emotional satisfaction (Coleman and Williams 2013).

3. Bourdieu 1984; Wherry 2008. An additional perspective useful in understanding how consumers distinguish between products comes from the "qualification" approach to pricing, most clearly associated with the work of the sociologist Michel Callon (Callon 1998; Callon, Meadel, and Rabeharisoa 2002; Callon and Muniesa 2005; Muniesa, Millo, and Callon 2007; see also Caliskan 2007). This approach focuses on the acts of "singularization" that make pricing possible. Callon and Muniesa elaborate:

> Singularizing a product . . . means linking it to other products in the same space or on the same list. This is a process of classification, clustering and sorting that makes products both comparable and different. The consumer can make choices only if the goods have been endowed with properties that produce distinctions. . . . The good has been placed in a frame with other goods. Relations have been established between them, leading to new classifications that allow forms of comparison: the good can finally be calculated. All these operations constitute the material base for the extraction of a result (a price, a classification, a choice). (2005:1235)

4. Many types of economic action, particularly acts of consumption, are fundamentally interpersonal processes mediated by market intermediaries who actively try to shape the choices of consumers (Prus 1989), so understanding how intermediaries affect buyers' emotional responses to products is essential for developing more valid accounts of purchasing. This is not to say that scholars have ignored emotions' role in the economy. For decades researchers have examined emotional labor, or the processes by which individuals must manage and perform emotions at work (Hochschild 1979 and 1983; A. Wharton 2009). Until recently, however, sociologists left emotions out of analyses of other parts of economic life (Bandelj 2012; Berezin 2005; Stets 2012). Similarly, economics has largely ignored the role of emotions for much of its history (Elster

1998; Frank 1998) even though emotions act as a guide that narrows individuals' conceptions of what an optimal outcome is and what are the least risky means of achieving it (Damasio 1994; Kahneman, Slovic, and Tversky 1982; Slovic et al. 2004). Research in behavioral economics, psychology, and consumer research that does invoke emotion often ignores social context because it isolates particular decision-making processes in lab experiments (Bruch and Feinberg 2017:208). In contrast, sociological analyses argue that emotions are more than just another mechanism of rational action. For sociologists studying economic decision-making and market action, emotions are a core way that economic actors cope with issues of trust and uncertainty (Pixley 2004 and 2009; Barbalet 2009; DiMaggio 2002; Tuckett 2011). Emotions are therefore not just a resource for achieving market goals but also a way that actors create meaning and value in economic transactions (Chong and Tuckett 2015; Pixley, McCarthy, and Wilson 2014).

Where, however, do emotions come from? Sociologist Nina Bandelj (2009 and 2012) theorizes that interaction is a key place to look. She argues that because economic transactions are not cut off from other parts of life, individuals' complex relationships with and feelings about other transactors play a fundamental part in organizing economic action. Put another way, because emotions are the outcomes of interpersonal exchanges, they should vary along with interactional flows (Besbris 2016b; Katz 1999; Rivera 2015a).

5. Data through 2017 show that median prices in the city's most expensive neighborhoods had plateaued, although prices in general continued to rise (Marino 2017). While the S&P/CoreLogic/Case-Shiller home price index showed continued growth in New York, by 2019 it had certainly attenuated. In the country overall, real home prices were up 35% from 2012–18, while real rents were only up 13% (Shiller 2019:223), indicating some potential divergence between supply and demand constraints and beliefs about housing prices and future desirability (see Zuckerman 2012).

6. Toy 2012.

7. Keil and Golding 2014.

8. Higgins 2015 and 2016.

9. Rice 2014.

10. Kaysen 2015. Constant media coverage of rising prices reinforced a consistent narrative that New York real estate was a good investment. This kind of speculation in home prices is what the economist Robert Shiller (2019) calls a "perennial economic narrative." Such narratives, because they are expressed so exuberantly and catch on through media so easily, can affect policy and drive prices. As Shiller (2019:223) notes, the boom in home prices leading up the Great Recession "far exceeded anything that could be attributed to increased or unmet demand for housing services." He goes on to to explain that after the Great Recession these durable narratives about the value of urban real estate quickly reemerged and prices started "taking off again in a new boom that continues to 2019."

11. Irwin 2018. According to the Joint Center for Housing Studies at Harvard, typical sale price of an existing single-family home in 2017 was 4.2 times greater than the median household income, up from 3.3 in 2011 though slightly lower than the 4.7 price-

to-income ratio in 2005, right before the Great Recession. In the New York metro area, the price-to-income ratio was over 5. However, incomes have risen faster for the very highest earners, so income growth at the high end has more closely tracked changing home prices, especially in places like New York with low inventory and high competition (see Hermann 2018).

12. Market actors selectively pick up information that supports their desired outcomes and ignore disconfirming data so that they may continue to participate in certain transactions that may be unsound (see Zuckerman 2012). In more recent work, Shiller (2019) stresses that narratives and ideas about the economy—whether they are valid or fallacious—have a real power to shape economic outcomes when a critical mass of actors believes in them. Bubbles, in other words, are fueled by sustained *attention* on a booming asset. Other research on markets has shown how seemingly objective market conditions are responsive to the on-the-ground behavior and rhetoric of market actors (see Abolafia 1996; Chan 2012; Zaloom 2006).

13. Desmond (2016:150–51) found similar talk among landlords in Milwaukee after the recession.

14. Howard 1997; McCabe 2016; A. Schwartz 2010.

15. Been et al. 2011.

16. For how sequencing affects consumer choice, see Ariely and Zauberman 2000; Diehl and Zauberman 2005. Sequencing is ubiquitous in markets, particularly in retail, in the sense that most stores organize their products so that consumers will experience them in a particular order (D. Miller 1998).

17. Dellaert and Häubl 2012; B. Schwartz 2004.

18. For how neighborhoods are associated with certain demographic groups, behaviors, and institutions, see Besbris, Faber, and Sharkey 2019; Besbris et al. 2015 and 2018; Kimelberg 2014; Krysan and Bader 2007; Quillian and Pager 2001; Rich and Jennings 2015; R. J. Sampson 2012; Sampson and Raudenbush 2004; Small 2004; Small and McDermott 2006. For how neighborhoods are associated with particular identities and, in turn, shape these identities, see Brown-Saracino 2018; Ghaziani 2014. For how neighborhoods are associated with particular consumption practices or lifestyles associated with particular identities, see Deener 2012; Ghaziani 2015; Lloyd 2005; Ocejo 2014; Zukin 1982.

19. Zukin 1982.

20. In 2017 Nobu moved to the Financial District and Bouley closed. However, Tribeca has no shortage of new incredibly expensive and trendy restaurants.

21. The sociologist Richard Ocejo (2017) describes a similar process he calls "service teaching." Service workers—especially high-end cultural ones—attempt to educate consumers about the products and the labor required to produce them.

22. This conversation took place several years before the New York Metropolitan Transit Authority announced that starting in the spring of 2019, the L train would close for over a year to repair damage sustained after Hurricane Sandy. In early 2019, New York governor Andrew Cuomo canceled plans for the closure.

23. For more on how the Lower East Side became an elite consumption space, see Mele 2000; Ocejo 2014.

24. Bushwick, a neighborhood in North Brooklyn, has a reputation as a gentrifying (or gentrified) neighborhood. Between 2000 and 2015, the black population declined by 5 percent, the Latino population declined by 12 percent, and the annual median household income increased by $10,000 (Austensen et al. 2016).

25. For more on symbolic boundaries, neighborhoods, and place see Anderson 2012 and 2015; Bauder 2002; Besbris et al. 2018; Garrido 2013; Hunter 1974; Hwang 2016; Jones and Jackson 2012; Logan and Molotch 1987; R. J. Sampson 2012; Small 2004; Suttles 1972; Wacquant 2008; Wirth [1928] 1998; Zorbaugh [1929] 1976; see also Lamont and Molnar 2002.

26. Hawthorne 2016.

27. I looked up all of the one-bedroom listings on the market for Williamsburg, the neighborhood in Brooklyn where the search occurred, from Trulia.com and Zillow .com for the three months when the search was taking place to compare the square footage of the units Liz selected and classify them as above or below the average.

28. The sociologist Lauren Rivera, in her study of how emotions affect hiring decisions, makes a distinction between liking and excitement. "Excitement is a high-arousal, forward-looking state in which one anticipates receiving future social or material rewards. . . . Liking is a lower-arousal, more generalized positive evaluative sentiment toward another" (2015a:1365).

29. The fact that they came to Lucy with some neighborhoods already in mind is in keeping with theories of staged decision-making that suggest that homeseekers have some preknowledge that makes them aware of some neighborhoods—ones that match them demographically—but not others (see Bruch and Swait 2019; Krysan and Bader 2009; Krysan and Crowder 2017).

30. As a heuristic cue indicating value, scarcity changes how individuals allocate attention (Lynn 1992a; Shah, Mullainathan, and Shafir 2012). Highlighting scarcity is an integral part of some markets where the quantity of the product is inherently limited or uncertain (Karpik 2010; Mears 2011; Velthuis 2005). Indeed consumers are sensitive to time limits on purchases or limits to the quantity of a particular good that accentuate value in transactions (Inman, Peter, and Raghubir 1997). Marketing research has revealed that scarcity induces consumers to act in more competitive ways and broadens their sense of acceptable outcomes (Roux, Goldsmith, and Bonezzi 2015), but less is known about how consumers become aware of scarcity.

31. There is some research on scarcity's effects on housing market searches, particularly for people who hold housing market vouchers (Rosen 2014). The sociologists Eva Rosen and Stefanie DeLuca and colleagues have shown how homeseekers' evaluations of housing units and their mobility decisions are highly contingent on their material circumstances. Those with fewer resources do not have the time or luxury to filter out neighborhoods in the same way as do higher-income homeseekers, their choice sets are limited to poorer-quality places. As a result, they focus more on their own abilities to deal with challenges that might arise from their selections (Darrah and DeLuca 2014; Rhodes and DeLuca 2014; Rosen 2017; Rosenblatt and DeLuca 2012; see also Krysan and Crowder 2017:144–45).

32. According to the National Association of Realtors (2005), purchase offers gen-

erally aren't confidential. Sellers can direct their listing agent to disclose the terms of an existing offer to anyone. In some cases, sellers may make other buyers aware that an offer is in hand, or even disclose details about one buyer's offer to another in hope of convincing the second buyer to outbid the first. It is illegal, however, to misrepresent existing offers in New York State. See also New York State Association of Realtors Code of Ethics (2015), articles 1–9.

33. Lynn 1992b.

34. The emotion-generating processes outlined are also likely found in other types of transactions. Advertising, for instance, is meant to produce excitement in consumers and match parts of their identities to particular products but it is not innocuous since cultural tastes are a powerful exclusionary force (Bourdieu 1984; Zukin 2004). For how cultural matching creates inequality in various settings see Childress 2017; Childress and Nault 2018; Rawlings and Childress 2019; Rivera 2012; Schor et al. 2016.

CHAPTER THREE

1. My definition of upselling focuses on buyers' decisions. I consider buyers to be upsold when they begin the sales process with a particular price in mind as the maximum they want to spend, but eventually make an offer above that stated price ceiling. This is different from having the price of a particular unit increase above the listed price. In other words, my definition is about individuals and the prices they pay, not houses and the amounts paid for them.

2. Despite its centrality in markets, sociologists have tended to avoid studying price directly (Beckert 2011).

3. Logan and Molotch 1987. For how the relationship between housing supply and prices is weak see Freemark 2019; Rodríguez-Pose and Storper 2019. For a more general discussion of how objective conditions and subjective interpretations of them affect valuation, see Zuckerman 2012.

4. Granovetter 1985; Zbaracki and Bergen 2010.

5. Uzzi 1999. The standard division of social ties into gradations, e.g., embedded/arm's-length or close/distant, has led to multiple insights regarding the ways network structure drives market outcomes like price. Network ties matter in a vast array of markets since consumers and suppliers have relationships that vary in their intimacy and can influence their decisions about how to set or pay prices. In other words, consumers do not automatically switch their loyalties when prices change since they have previously established relationships with suppliers whom they trust (Dore 1992; Zbaracki et al. 2004).

6. Uzzi and Lancaster 2004.

7. In particular, the accrual of relationships with high-status producers or consumers in a given market translates into a continued accrual of more ties, also known as the "Matthew Effect," and, as a result, the ability to charge higher prices (Podolny 1993).

8. These findings on price highlight what has historically been the dominant approach to studying markets and economic action more broadly within sociology. It

conceives of markets as networks and is concerned largely with the position of a supplier in relation to other suppliers within the network (White 1981).

9. Krippner 2001; see also Krippner and Alvarez 2007.

10. Zelizer 2012.

11. DiMaggio 1994; Zelizer 1994; 2005; 2011. In other words, network analysis lacks a coherent understanding of both the content of relational ties and the context that surrounds them (see Biggart and Beamish 2003; Chan 2009; Emirbayer and Goodwin 1994).

12. Beckert and Aspers 2011; Degenshein 2017; Chan 2012; Karpik 2010; Lamont 2012; Velthuis 2005; Zelizer 1979 and 1985.

13. Formal institutions are also key ways that culture gets filtered into pricing (Fourcade 2011).

14. Studies of distinction and discrimination in markets further highlight how cultural norms affect the setting, distribution, and meaning of prices (see Bourdieu 1984; Hanser 2010; Ody-Brasier and Vermeulen 2014; Wherry 2008). Factors as varied as race, gender, and place of residence trigger discrimination and affect prices and opportunity in economic exchanges (Ayres and Siegelman 1995; Besbris 2015; Besbris et al. 2015; Besbris, Faber, and Sharkey 2019; Pager and Shepherd 2008). Put differently, aspects of an individual's identity beyond her capacity and willingness to pay produce varying prices within the same market.

15. See Spillman (2012) and Spillman and Strand (2013). For example, the pricing of male and female genetic material varies because of cultural norms regarding gender and parenting, as well as the more specific organizational structure of sperm and egg donation centers (Almeling 2007). Even within a single market, different organizations can develop different pricing mechanisms for the same goods based on their historic orientation to different cultural values (Anteby 2010; Reich 2014). Status also matters in the cultural approach to understanding economic action. Within the cultural approach, status is generally conceptualized as the ability to arbitrate taste. That is, within a given market, certain individuals or organizations have more or less power to compare goods and establish hierarchies (Karpik 2010). The more experts exalt a particular product over others, the more consumers will be willing to pay for that product.

16. Some scholars have indeed encouraged combining them—since there is clearly overlap—to better understand economic exchange. See MacKenzie and Millo 2003.

17. Simmel 1978. This is not to say that structure and culture are irrelevant. On the contrary, they explain a great deal of why buyers seek out certain goods. However, looking at only the network positions of actors, the classifications they make across goods, and the devices they use when doing so, yields too rigid understanding of demand. Examining interaction, including the context of transactions, allows for a clearer picture of how the prices actors offer—or the meanings ascribed around economic activity that the cultural account of economic action seeks to uncover—are the result of the "demand characteristics" of the given situation (Faulkner and Becker 2009:31; see also Fine and Fields 2008; Jerolmack and Khan 2014).

18. Biggart and Beamish 2003. These sequences not only reify identities but do so in relation to other actors, bolstering a sense of order (Collins 2004; Fine 1996). How-

ever, because it entails responding to others under particular constraints (e.g., power relations, cultural value systems), interaction is necessarily dynamic—a practically limited garden of forking paths where each situation has the potential to be unique as actors are continuously and skillfully working together to agree on what will come next (Goffman 1969; Tavory and Eliasoph 2013).

19. See table A.2 in appendix A for the difference between all buyers' initially stated price preference and the actual amount they ended up offering for a house.

20. Buyers who expressed a preference for spending amounts between $800,000 and $1 million were sometimes treated with deference by agents and sometimes were not, but the further buyers' price points diverged from this range in either direction, the more clearly distinct the differences in interaction became.

21. See Ho 2009; Khan 2011; Rivera 2015b; though see Jack 2019. While this is generally the case for institutions serving elite people, intermediaries are not always so deferential. The sociologist Rachel Sherman (2011) found that personal concierges serving wealthy clients sometimes overtly attempted to shape their consumption choices. They arbitrated good and bad taste and steered their clients away from products they deemed ugly, tacky, obvious, and cheesy.

22. For more on deference and what it reveals about power relations in interactions, see Goffman 1967.

23. See Harrington 2016:98 for similar examples of financial service providers avoiding direct price talk with wealthy elites.

24. Sherman 2007.

25. See Sherman 2017.

26. J. Miller 2014 and 2015.

27. See Carruthers 2013; Guseva and Rona-Tas 2001.

28. Williamsburg is a neighborhood with much higher prices than those of Bushwick. The implication is that buyers searching in less wealthy neighborhoods cannot go far beyond their stated ceilings, whereas buyers looking in wealthier neighborhoods presumably have more flexibility and capital to spend.

29. The observed relationship is nonlinear. A bivariate regression of the difference between offered price and initial price ceiling over the natural log of the initial price ceiling shows that an increase by one in the log of the initial price ceiling is correlated with a $530,500 increase in the difference between initial price ceiling and price offered ($p<.001$). There was also a strong, positive, and significant correlation between the logged difference in price ceiling and price offered and the logged price ceiling .80 ($p<.001$). A corresponding bivariate regression of the logged difference and the logged price ceiling revealed that a 1 percent increase in price ceiling would yield an expected 1.69 percent increase in the difference between price ceiling and price paid, and this is statistically significant. This means that both in terms of dollar amount and in terms of percentage differences, buyers with higher initially stated price ceilings are more likely to have higher differences between their price ceilings and the amounts they offer.

30. There were no discernible differences in the duration of the search or the number of units seen across less wealthy and wealthier buyers.

31. Under New York State law, even though Brandon had not asked the buyer to

sign any agreement, if the buyer had made an offer on one of the houses shown by Brandon, this would be implied agency.

32. Levitt and Syverson 2008.

33. See Hanser 2008. Future research should look for upselling and similar mechanisms in other markets that determine the prices buyers are willing to pay.

34. Like the higher rates of upselling for wealthier buyers described above, other recent studies have found similar patterns and asked why, against intuition, wealthier buyers pay more than expected. Networks can play a role—buyers who are connected to individuals who experience higher house price increases are more likely to buy larger, more expensive houses—as can aggregate differences in buyers' dispositions at varying levels of wealth—"wealthy individuals demand higher-valued homes but prefer not to expend the time and energy needed to bargain aggressively, and so do worse" (Harding, Rosenthal, and Sirmans 2003:185). See also Bailey et al. 2018.

35. We might expect upselling to play out differently in markets that are not commission driven or when upselling is more or less tied to intermediaries' occupational identity. In contrast, salespeople working in markets or with products that demand high levels of education or skill (see Darr 2006) may reject upselling, while in other cases upselling might be facilitated by actors who are not explicit intermediaries but nonetheless feel obliged to upsell clients on behalf of others with whom they are socially connected (see Mears 2015:1112–13). Other potential comparisons include occupations where there is high variance in the price of the product (for example, sommeliers) or where the relationship between the customer and the intermediary has the potential to last decades (for example, family financial planners).

36. See, for example, Conti 2014; Mears 2015; P. Sampson 2013.

CHAPTER FOUR

1. Ultan 2009.

2. Kaysen 2015; see also Berger 2005; Budin 2015; Morris 2015; Sisson 2017.

3. For how and why certain types of interactions and patterns of behavior aggregate up and how they reproduce inequality, see Collins 1988 and 2000.

4. Faber 2018; 2019; Krysan and Crowder 2017; Lichter, Parisi, and Taquino 2015; Logan and Stults 2011; Massey and Denton 1993; Quillian 2014; Reardon and Bischoff 2011; Small and McDermott 2006.

5. Herbert, McCue, and Sanchez-Moyano 2014; Massey and Denton 1993; Oliver and Shapiro 2006; Pattillo 2013; R. J. Sampson 2012; Shapiro 2017; Sharkey and Faber 2014; Squires and Kubrin 2006. The consequences of residential sorting are widely studied. For most Americans, particularly members of racial and ethnic minorities, home equity makes up the largest share of total assets, and stratification scholars point to differences in asset holdings, especially houses, as a crucial aspect of racial inequality, responsible for numerous other disparities in such outcomes as education and employment (Conley 1999; Shapiro 2004; Spilerman 2000). Recent analyses have shown that interracial gaps have grown substantially due to the tumult of the housing

market beginning in 2008 (Faber and Ellen 2016; Rugh 2015; Taylor et al. 2011). On racial disparities in home equity, see Cutler, Glaeser, and Vigdor 1999; Flippen 2004; Kim 2003; Anacker 2010; Howell and Korver-Glenn 2018. On how the housing market remains a site of intense stratification see Flippen 2010; Massey 2015.

6. Charles 2003; Gotham 2002; Jackson 1987; Rothstein 2017; Squires 1994; Taylor 2019.

7. Bobo and Charles 1996; Charles 2003; Emerson, Chai, and Yancey 2001; Krysan and Farley 2002; Lewis, Emerson, and Klineberg 2011. See also Krysan and Crowder 2017; Lareau and Goyette 2014; Molotch 1972; Roscigno, Karafin, and Tester 2009.

8. I do not want to overstate the role of individual-level bias. Current segregation results from government policy (Rothstein 2017) as well as from existing segregation that narrows individuals' social experiences and knowledge of places by race and ethnicity (Krysan and Crowder 2017). Therefore changing individuals' housing preferences will not end segregation.

9. Galster 1990; Yinger 1995.

10. Galster and Godfrey 2005; Turner et al. 2013; see also Massey 2005; Yinger 1997.

11. Squires, Friedman, and Saidat 2002.

12. Galster and Godfrey 2005.

13. Other audit studies have shown that real estate agents not only share less information on units with nonwhites but also decline to show white buyers properties in diverse neighborhoods and provide less information on financing to black homeseekers. See Galster 1990; Ondrich, Ross, and Yinger 2003; Ross and Turner 2005; Turner et al. 2013; Yinger 1995.

14. Anglin and Arnot 1991; Arnold 1992.

15. Kiel and Zabel 1999.

16. Baryla and Zumpano 1995; Elder, Zumpano, and Baryla 2000; Jud 2003; Levitt and Syverson 2008.

17. Brastow, Springer, and Waller 2011.

18. Bischoff and Reardon 2014; Jargowsky 1996 and 2018. Sean Reardon and Kendra Bischoff (2011) document how increasing income inequality—the unequal distribution of income across the US population—accounts for a substantial part of the increase in income segregation but cannot account for all of it. By their estimates, rising income inequality accounts for 40–80 percent of the increase in income segregation from 1970 to 2000. Their work suggests that there are endogenous mechanisms within local housing markets that might also drive rising income segregation—mechanisms like upselling.

19. See Moretti 2013. The increase in housing prices in already expensive neighborhoods is not unique to high-cost cities. For example, the neighborhood with highest increase in the cost of housing from 2010 to 2016 in Houston, TX—a city with relatively low housing costs overall—was River Oaks, the neighborhood that already had the highest housing costs in 2010. There is some debate among scholars as to the severity of this trend: according to the sociologist John Logan and his colleagues (2018), the findings of increased income segregation since 2000 may be due to measurement

error from small sample sizes used in the American Community Survey. Reardon et al. (2018) maintain that the increase is real.

20. Dwyer 2007; Owens 2015 and 2016; Reardon, Fox, and Townsend 2015.

21. Reardon, Townsend, and Fox 2017.

22. Block 2012; Akerlof and Shiller 2015.

23. New York State provides an excellent case study for multiple reasons. First, the state's geography is quite varied, containing the country's largest city, several midsized cities (e.g., Syracuse, Buffalo), stretches of suburbs (Long Island, the Hudson Valley), and swaths of rural land. Second, the state's demographic diversity, particularly in New York City, allows for analyses of agent concentration in neighborhoods that are majority white, black, Latino, and Asian. (See appendix B for in-depth descriptions of data and analyses.)

24. Brastow, Springer, and Waller 2011; Hornstein 2005.

25. Flippen 2012.

26. T-tests of these racial and ethnic differences are statistically significant ($p<0.1$) with the exception of the difference between majority Black and Latino tracts. See Besbris and Faber 2017.

27. When neighborhoods are broken down into quintiles by average home value, the average number of real estate agents is as follows: Q1: 3.6; Q2: 7.6; Q3: 8.1; Q4: 12.5; Q5: 18.6.

28. See Besbris and Faber 2017. In this earlier work we used a mix of OLS, county fixed effects, and spatial cross-regressive models.

29. We measured county-level segregation of blacks and Latinos using dissimilarity and isolation indices (Massey and Denton 1993) using the same data as in the tract-level analyses. Dissimilarity reflects how uneven racial and ethnic distribution is across census tracts within a county and can be thought of as the percentage of a group that would have to move to create an even distribution. Isolation measures the homogeneity of a typical area for the typical person of a particular race or ethnicity within a county. We found a positive and significant relationship between the number of real estate agents within a county and both measures of segregation, net of other demographic, housing, economic, and geographic characteristics.

30. Since the earlier analyses were based on home price data that were aggregated from surveys administered between 2010 and 2014 and the data on real estate agent concentration is from 2012, the datasets overlapped. This means that while these earlier analyses could measure some association between agent concentration and home price, they could not tell if agent concentration was associated with longer-term effects in the housing market. More recent ACS data, however, can supplement these earlier findings.

31. We also obtained data on agent geographic distribution in 2017. Agents were located by and large in the same places five years later. We ran models comparing the change in agent distribution to the change in home prices, but did not find a significant effect, likely because there was not much change in agent distribution over the period. However, this is a promising research question that may simply require administrative data on real estate agent distribution over a longer period of time.

32. In New York City, a seventy-five-hour salesperson licensing classes costs $300–$500.

33. See Helper 1969.

34. Korver-Glenn 2018a.

35. Kwate et al. 2013.

36. This, of course, does not mean that individual agents did not hold racist attitudes. If they did, however, it is not surprising that they were unwilling to express them to a sociologist asking them directly about race, though see Korver-Glenn 2018b.

37. See Korver-Glenn 2018b.

38. From 2000 to 2015, the percentage of black residents in Crown Heights dropped from 78.1 percent to 55.5 percent, while the white population nearly tripled, from 7.4 percent to 21.6 percent (Austensen et al. 2016).

39. Ironically, many of Lee's films highlight interracial friction and animosity. For more on differences in how residents draw neighborhood boundaries, see Brown-Saracino 2009; Hwang 2016.

40. In a study of real estate agents in gentrifying neighborhoods in Syndey, Australia, Gary Bridge (2001) also finds that agents draw taste boundaries not only in terms of space but also in terms of style—i.e., agents and buyers articulate distinctions about what architectural elements of buildings mark them as more or less appropriate for gentrifiers and for resale.

41. Donnelly 2017; Freeman 2006.

42. Other studies have shown that nonwhite agents are willing to facilitate minority buyers' preferences for neighborhoods with demographics that mirror their own because it affords access to particular cultural amenities like same-ethnic restaurants (Korver-Glenn 2018b).

43. Logan and Stults 2011.

44. Though see Korver-Glenn (2018b) for racial-spatial talk and boundary making among same-raced agents and clients.

45. For more on how race/ethnicity is the prism through which homeseekers see the city, see Krysan and Bader 2007 and 2009; Krysan and Crowder 2017.

46. For example, see Gibson 2015.

47. Chung 2006; Scott 2006. Fair housing laws prevent agents from discussing school quality, but agents were encouraged in licensing classes to direct buyers to myriad sources of information about local schools available online.

48. In her study of suburban middle-class blacks, the sociologist Karyn Lacy (2007:100–110) found that many black homeseekers of means did not think discrimination was a problem. However, those middle-class blacks who assumed they would experience discrimination in the housing market or reported interactions with agents that were discriminatory said that the race of agent was not determinant; both white and black agents might steer black homeseekers by only showing them houses in predominantly black neighborhoods.

49. See Krysan and Crowder 2017. These strategies contrast with some evidence on how black job seekers look for employment. While black job seekers may respond to expected discrimination in hiring by casting a wider search and applying to more

positions (Pager and Pedulla 2015), reports from black homeseekers indicate that they deal with expected discrimination by relying heavily on within-network references and avoiding situations and interactions in the housing market in which they might experience discrimination.

50. For why certain types of neighborhoods are more or less likely to gentrify, see Hwang and Sampson 2014.

51. Logan and Molotch 1987; R. J. Sampson 2012; Wacquant 2008; 2010; Wacquant, Slater, and Pereira 2014; see also Lamont and Molnar 2002.

52. Shiller 2015.

53. It is possible that the micro-level dynamics described here and in previous chapters (e.g., steering, upselling) vary based on the identity of the agent, the buyer, the seller, and combinations of the three. If so, it is likely that the neighborhood-level relationships between real estate agents and house prices depend on the ethnoracial mix of agents within and in surrounding neighborhoods interacting with buyer and seller identities. While the quantitative data set used here lacks information on the race and ethnicity of agents, interviews suggest that the same incentives operate among real estate agents of all ethnoracial groups (see also Korver-Glenn 2018a). Additionally, the findings are limited by the lack of available data on house value disaggregated by race and ethnicity and the reliance on data aggregated at the census tract. Subsequent work could leverage hedonic regression models using actual transaction data at the property level and including a measure of proximity to real estate agents to see if there is indeed a negative relationship between agent concentration and the ratio of black- and Latino-to-non-Hispanic-white median home value as well as reveal any heterogeneity of agent effects within neighborhoods. Future work should also observe the mechanisms outlined above over time; multiple years of house price, segregation, and agent geographic distribution data could be used to better measure the causal direction of the relationships between real estate agent geographic concentration and house prices.

54. Better regulation of real estate agents alone will not end segregation, since segregation is the product of law, policy, and decades of existing segregation that has fundamentally separated individuals' everyday experiences by race. The historian Richard Rothstein (2017) argues that Americans must be taught that segregation is the outcome of racist policy. The sociologists Maria Krysan and Kyle Crowder (2017) advocate for inclusionary zoning, more affordable housing, and expanding access to information. However, addressing the impacts of real estate agents, who are a key source of information for homeseekers, must be part of any comprehensive plan in the fight against segregation and neighborhood inequality.

55. There are, of course, many visions of how to ameliorate inequality in the housing market. Regressive policies that tend to benefit wealthier homeowners like the home mortgage interest deduction should be removed from the tax code, and pro-tenant laws that protect renters and allow them to remain in place should be strengthened (Desmond 2016; McCabe 2016). Collective forms of land ownership that remove the profit motive from the housing market can reduce economic precarity, leading to better lives (Engels 1935 and 1993; Harvey and Wachsmuth 2012; Madden and Marcuse 2016; Sullivan 2018).

CONCLUSION

1. Bruch and Feinberg 2017. As Zelizer (2011:315) notes, economic transactions are marked by "dynamic, meaningful, incessantly negotiated interactions" where individuals are continually reassessing their own and others' interests in the context of unequal access to information and resources.

2. In her theoretically rich book on how meteorologists make weather predictions and deal with uncertainty, the sociologist Phaedra Daipha (2015:201) notes, "When the typical decision-making heuristics and techniques do not seem to apply, it is the empirical context of action that will determine, first and foremost, how the challenge can be resolved." Here Daipha is referring in particular to rarely made decisions for which we have little experience or knowledge. See also Bandelj 2012.

3. Beckert 2016; Tavory and Eliasoph 2013.

4. For other examples of the routinized way market intermediaries and other service workers do their work, including categorizing clients, see Bearman 2005; Davis 1959; Gambetta and Hamill 2005; Leidner 1993; Prus 1989; Sherman 2007 and 2011.

5. Block 2012; Zelizer 2012. See also Collins 1988 and 2000.

6. Looking beyond economic markets, an interactional approach also reorients scholarship on brokerage and decision-making. By and large the literature on brokerage is focused on the benefits individuals, groups, or organizations accrue by virtue of their position in a social network. Being connected to two actors who aren't connected to each other means that a broker will have access to a wider set of information than either of the actors the broker is connected to. This conceptualization is not concerned with social action; brokers broker because of who they are connected to—their position in a network. Some have suggested that future scholarship on brokerage might move away from conceptualizing it as a role to understanding it as a process (Obstfeld, Borgatti, and Davis 2014; Small 2009b). An interactional approach aids in such a move since it directs attention to what actors are doing in order for brokerage to move forward. In other words, future work should look not just at the structural position and capacity of a broker but at what patterns of interaction allow the broker to fulfill this capacity.

An interactional approach also allows for empirical comparisons across a wide array of brokered processes (see Childress 2017). For example, the sociologist John Meyer (2017:793) points out that many things that get described as 'decisions' are not choices in the conventional sense (see also Abend 2018a and 2018b). Meyer argues: "Any good student in a prestigious American university ought to be able, almost instantaneously, to write some paragraphs about 'why I decided to go to college.' But on inspection, it turns out that almost none of these students actually decided to go to college, as they had never contemplated any alternative. Going to college was taken for granted."

If high school students from advantaged backgrounds take going to college for granted—i.e., do not *decide* to go to college—how do they end up in particular higher education institutions? The answer may lie in how high school college counselors do their work. How do they decide what schools are appropriate matches for students, how do they curate students' experiences, and how do they communicate the meaning of different schools to students?

7. Chetty and Hendren 2018; Chetty et al. 2014; de Souza Briggs 2005; Peterson and Krivo 2010; R. J. Sampson 2012; Squires and Kubrin 2006.

8. Logan and Molotch 1987.

9. Krysan and Crowder 2017.

10. Howell and Korver-Glenn 2018; Korver-Glenn 2018b.

11. Besbris et al. 2015 and 2018; Besbris, Faber, and Sharkey 2019; Sharkey and Faber 2014.

12. See Lamont, Beljean, and Clair 2014.

13. Shiller 2015.

14. See Zuckerman 2012. As Robert Shiller (2019:217) notes, housing price increase "appears to be driven less by future expectations than by the proliferation of stories and talk that draw attention to the asset that is booming, thereby fueling the bubble."

15. Casselman 2018.

16. Irwin 2018.

APPENDIX A

1. Small 2013.

2. Tavory and Timmermans 2013; see also Gross 2009; Reiss 2009.

3. Variation across similar situations or interactions, or "data set variation," is one of three types of variation outlined by sociologists Iddo Tavory and Stefan Timmermans (2013). The other two are "variation over time," where ethnographers examine how the same individuals make meaning over a prolonged temporal landscape, and "inter-situational variation," where ethnographers follow something—often individuals—across situations to understand variation in the ways they make meaning under varying circumstances. I use all of three of these in *Upsold* to some extent. I have followed up with home buyers years after their purchases to see if the meanings they made during their search processes still resonated (variation over time), and I examined meaning making vis-à-vis housing not just during housing transactions but also in real estate agent training, among buyers who did not use real estate agents, and in media accounts of the housing market (intersituational variation). However, the most sustained and focused type of variation throughout the book has been dataset variation, and it is this type of variation that has yielded the book's most important analytic insights.

4. Katz 2001.

5. Besbris and Khan 2017; Ermakoff 2017; Katz 2015.

6. See Katz 2002 and 2015.

7. See Besbris and Wohl 2019.

8. According to the Bureau of Labor Statistics, the average annual income of real estate agents in the New York–White Plains–Wayne NY–NJ Metropolitan Division was $87,810 in 2012. The median was $70,920. For real estate brokers in the same region at that time, the average was $119,120 and the median was $102,120.

9. This anonymity includes assigning pseudonyms and, since sales prices are public record, not reporting the final price paid by buyers but instead their initial offer prices as an indication of what they were willing to spend. It also means that I sometimes refer to agents or buyers in the text without any identifier (e.g., "one agent said"). While I have not provided vivid descriptions of agents or buyers, I have also not altered any demographic characteristics that would affect the argument (see Sherman 2017:256; cf. Jerolmack and Murphy 2017).

10. See Chan 2012:201–2.

11. It is certainly possible that buyers had reservation prices that were higher than their stated price preferences and that they did not reveal these reservation prices even after offers had been made. What seems more plausible is that the price points home buyers have change over time—that there is a sequence and history to the formation of individual preferences and that preferences cannot be accounted for without reference to the contexts in which they arise (Sen 1973 and 1993).

12. Logan and Stults 2011.

13. See Small 2009a.

14. More comparative work across cities with varying levels of affordability and price is needed to further unpack not only the interactional dynamics of upselling and price increase described in chapters 3 and 4 but also if and how changes in the sources of investment affect prices. A recent investigation by the *New York Times* found that about half of all houses that cost more than $5 million in the United States are purchased not by named individuals but by shell companies in the form of limited liability corporations (Story 2016; Story and Saul 2015). The rate is even higher in places with the highest house prices, like Los Angeles and Manhattan. This indicates that the wealthy elite—from all over the world, not just the United States—see urban real estate markets as attractive places to park capital. What drives the changing composition of investment capital into cities—particularly in the wake of the Great Recession? What effect, if any, does the different composition of investment have on prices?

15. Sherman 2017.

16. Miles and Huberman 1994:266–67. See also Jerlomack and Khan 2014; Swidler 2001.

APPENDIX B

1. The long right tail of the agents' distribution led to explorations of several transformation options, including agents per capita, the natural log of agents, and the number of agents squared. Comparing fit statistics across models using different transformations reinforced the decision to use linear and quadratic terms. The relationship between house prices and agent concentration is substantively identical across transformations, with the exception that we do not see diminishing returns to their concentration without the squared term.

2. Anselin 2001 and 2003; Crowder and South 2008.

3. While the 100-mile threshold may seem large, this follows the example of pre-

vious work exploring neighborhood-level dynamics (e.g., Crowder and South 2008). Furthermore, the inverse-distance weighting ensures that closer agents have a much stronger statistical effect than those farther away.

4. The negative relationship between homeownership and home values is due in part to multicollinearity. The two variables are positively and strongly correlated in a county fixed-effects model regressing home value on only the homeownership rate (b=0.466 and s.e.=0.029). Including the measure of homeownership rate in the final model improves overall model fit (the AIC is 621.5 with it and 927.9 without it).

5. The variable for whether a tract is in a central city is omitted from the New York City model, since all tracts are within a central city. Since there were no majority-Asian tracts outside New York City, that variable was omitted from the "Outside NYC" subsample.

6. Because there are only two counties on Long Island, we were unable to estimate county fixed effects in this model.

REFERENCES

Abbott, Andrew. 1988. *The System of Professions*. Chicago: University of Chicago Press.

Abbott, Andrew. 1995. "Things of Boundaries." *Social Research* 62:857–82.

Abbott, Andrew. 1999. *Department and Discipline: Chicago Sociology at One Hundred*. Chicago: University of Chicago Press.

Abend, Gabriel. 2018a. "The Limits of Decision and Choice." *Theory and Society* 47:805–41.

Abend, Gabriel. 2018b. "Outline of a Sociology of Decisionism." *British Journal of Sociology* 69:237–64.

Abolafia, Mitchell. 1996. *Making Markets: Opportunism and Restraint on Wall Street*. Cambridge, MA: Harvard University Press.

Action 4 News Staff. 2013. "Police: Real Estate Agent Launders Money for Drug Trafficker." http://valleycentral.com/news/local/police-real-estate-agent-launders-money-for-drug-trafficker.

Akerlof, George A., and Robert J. Shiller. 2015. *Phishing for Phools: The Economics of Manipulation and Deception*. Princeton, NJ: Princeton University Press.

Allard, Scott W. 2017. *Places in Need: The Changing Geography of Poverty*. New York: Russell Sage.

Almeling, Rene. 2007. "Selling Genes, Selling Gender: Egg Agencies, Sperm Banks, and the Medical Market in Genetic Material." *American Sociological Review* 72:319–40.

Anacker, Katrin. 2010. "Still Paying the Race Tax?" *Journal of Urban Affairs* 32:55–77.

Anderson, Elijah. 2012. "The Iconic Ghetto." *Annals of the American Academy of Political and Social Sciences* 642:8–24.

Anderson, Elijah. 2015. "The White Space." *Sociology of Race and Ethnicity* 1:10–21.

Anglin, Paul M. and Richard Arnott. 1991. "Residential Real Estate Brokerage as a Principal-Agent Problem." *Journal of Real Estate Finance and Economics* 4:99–125.

Anselin, Luc. 2001. "Spatial Econometrics." In *A Companion to Theoretical Econometrics*, edited by B. H. Baltagi, 310–30. Malden, MA: Blackwell.

Anselin, Luc. 2003. "Spatial Externalities, Spatial Multipliers, and Spatial Economet-rics." *International Regional Science Review* 26:153–66.

Anteby, Michel. 2010. "Markets, Morals, and Practices of Trade: Jurisdictional Disputes in the U.S. Commerce in Cadavers." *Administrative Science Quarterly* 55:606–38.

Ariely, Dan, George Loewenstein, and Drazen Prelec. 2006. "Tom Sawyer and the Construction of Value." In *The Construction of Preference*, edited by Sarah Lichten-stein and Paul Slovic, 271–81. Cambridge: Cambridge University Press.

Ariely, Dan, and Gal Zauberman. 2000. "On the Making of an Experience: The Effects of Breaking and Combining Experiences on Their Overall Evaluation." *Journal of Behavioral Decision Making* 13:219–32.

Arnold, Michael A. 1992. "The Principal-Agent Relationship in Real Estate Brokerage Services." *Real Estate Economics* 20:89–106.

Aspers, Patrik, and Asaf Darr. 2011. "Trade Shows and the Creation of Market and Industry." *Sociological Review* 59:758–78.

Austensen, Max, Vicki Been, Luis Inaraja Vera, Gita Khun Jush, Katherine M. O'Regan, Stephanie Rosoff, Traci Sanders, Eric Stern, Michael Suher, Mark A. Willis, and Jessica Yager. 2016. *State of New York City's Housing and Neighborhoods 2016*. New York: NYU Furman Center. http://furmancenter.org/files/sotc/SOC_2016 _Full.pdf.

Ayres, Ian, and Peter Siegelman. 1995. "Race and Gender Discrimination in Bargaining for a New Car." *American Economic Review* 85:304–21.

Bachelard, Gaston. [1958] 1994. *The Poetics of Space*. Boston: Beacon.

Bailey, F. G. 1963. *Politics and Social Change in Orissa in 1959*. Berkeley: University of California Press.

Bailey, Michael, Ruiqing Cao, Theresa Kuchler, and Johannes Stroebel. 2018. "The Eco-nomic Effects of Social Networks: Evidence from the Housing Market." *Journal of Political Economy* 126:2224–276.

Bandelj, Nina. 2009. "Emotions in Economic Action and Interaction." *Theory and Society* 38:347–66.

Bandelj, Nina. 2012. "Relational Work and Economic Sociology." *Politics & Society* 40:175–201.

Bandelj, Nina, Frederick F. Wherry, and Viviana A. Zelizer. 2017. "Introduction: Advancing Money Talks." In *Money Talks: Explaining How Money Really Works*, edited by Nina Bandelj, Frederick F. Wherry, Viviana A. Zelizer, 1–24. Princeton, NJ: Princeton University Press.

Barbalet, Jack. 2009. "A Characterization of Trust, and Its Consequences." *Theory and Society* 38:367–82.

Barnett, Kyle. 2015. "Real Estate Agent Accused of Heightening Commission on $700k Sale without Knowledge of Client." *Louisiana Record*, April 8, http://louisianarecord.com/stories/510585869-real-estate-agent-accused-of-heightening -commission-on-700k-sale-without-knowledge-of-client.

Barwick, Panle Jia, Parag A. Pathak, and Maisy Wong. 2015. "Conflicts of Interests and the Realtor Commission Puzzle." NBER Working Paper 21489, http://www.nber .org/papers/w21489.

Baryla, Edward, and Leonard Zumpano. 1995. "Buyer Search Duration in the Residential Real Estate Market: The Role of the Real Estate Agent." *Journal of Real Estate Research* 10:1–13.

Bauder, Harald. 2002. "Neighborhood Effects and Cultural Exclusion." *Urban Studies* 39:89–93.

Beale, Laruen. 2013. "Most Americans Don't Trust Real Estate Agents, Poll Finds." *Los Angeles Times*, November 13, http://www.latimes.com/business/la-fi-mo-most -distrust-real-estate-agents-20131113-story.html#axzz2kdX5zqfE.

Bearman, Peter. 2005. *Doormen*. Chicago: University of Chicago Press.

Becher, Debbie. 2014. *Private Property and Public Power: Eminent Domain in Philadelphia*. New York: Oxford University Press.

Becker, Howard S. and Blanche Geer. 1957. "Participant Observation and Interviewing: A Comparison." *Human Organization* 16:28–32.

Beckert, Jens. 2011. "Where Do Prices Come From? Sociological Approaches to Price Formation." *Socio-economic Review* 9:757–86.

Beckert, Jens. 2016. *Imagined Futures*. Cambridge, MA: Harvard University Press.

Beckert, Jens, and Patrik Aspers. 2011. "Value in Markets." In *The Worth of Goods: Valuation and Pricing in the Economy*, edited by J. Beckert and P. Aspers, 3–40. New York: Oxford University Press.

Been, Vicki, et al. 2011. *State of New York's Housing and Neighborhoods 2011*. New York: Furman Center for Real Estate and Urban Policy, http://furmancenter.org/files /sotc/SOC_2011.pdf.

Benjamin, John D., G. Donald Jud, and D. Stacy Sirmans. 2000. "What Do We Know about Real Estate Brokerage?" *Journal of Real Estate Research* 20:5–30.

Bennett, Kelly. 2008. "Jury Says Realtor Not to Blame for Purchase Price." *Voice of San Diego*, April 11, http://www.voiceofsandiego.org/all-narratives/housing/jury-says -realtor-not-to-blame-for-purchase-price/.

Berezin, Mabel. 2005. "Emotions and the Economy." In *The Handbook of Economic Sociology*, 2nd ed., edited by N. Smelser and R. Swedberg, 109–31. New York: Russell Sage Foundation / Princeton, NJ? Princeton University Press.

Berger, Joseph. 2005. "Goodbye South BronxBlight, Hello SoBro." *New York Times*, June 24, https://www.nytimes.com/2005/06/24/nyregion/goodbye-south -bronxblight-hello-sobro.html.

Bernstein, Elizabeth. 2007. *Temporarily Yours: Intimacy, Authenticity, and the Commerce of Sex*. Chicago: University of Chicago Press.

Besbris, Max. 2015. "Stigma." In *The Sage Encyclopedia of Economics and Society*, edited by Frederick F. Wherry and Juliet Schor, 1532–34. Thousand Oaks, CA: Sage.

Besbris, Max. 2016a. "Revanchist Masculinity: Gender Attitudes in Sex Work Management." *Sociological Quarterly* 57:711–32.

Besbris, Max. 2016b. "Romancing the Home: Emotions and the Interactional Creation of Demand in the Housing Market." *Socio-economic Review* 14:461–82.

Besbris, Max, and Jacob William Faber. 2017. "Investigating the Relationship between Real Estate Agents, Segregation, and House Prices: Steering and Upselling in New York State." *Sociological Forum* 32:850–73.

Besbris, Max, Jacob William Faber, Peter Rich, and Patrick Sharkey. 2015. "Effect of Neighborhood Stigma on Economic Transactions." *Proceedings of the National Academy of Sciences* 112:4994–98.

Besbris, Max, Jacob William Faber, Peter Rich, and Patrick Sharkey. 2018. "The Geography of Stigma: Experimental Methods to Identify the Penalty of Place." In *Audit Studies: Behind the Scenes with Theory, Method and Nuance*, edited by S. Michael Gadiss, 159–77. New York: Springer.

Besbris, Max, Jacob William Faber, and Patrick Sharkey. 2019. "Disentangling the Effects of Race and Place in Economic Transactions." *City & Community* 18:529–55.

Besbris, Max, and Shamus Khan. 2017. "Less Theory. More Description." *Sociological Theory* 35:147–53.

Besbris, Max, and Caitlin Petre. 2019. "Professionalizing Contingency: How Journalism Schools Adapt to Deprofessionalization." *Social Forces*, June 21, doi:10.1093/sf/soz094.

Besbris, Max, and Hannah Wohl. 2019. "Moments of Valuation: An Interactional Approach to Economic Action." Unpublished manuscript.

Bessy, Christian, and Pierre-Marie Chauvin. 2013. "The Power of Market Intermediaries: From Information to Valuation Processes." *Valuation Studies* 1:83–117.

Bettman, James R., Mary Frances Luce, and John W. Payne. 1998. "Constructive Consumer Choice Processes." *Journal of Consumer Research* 25:187–217.

Biggart, Nicole W. 1989. *Charismatic Capitalism: Direct Selling Organizations in America*. Chicago, IL: University of Chicago Press.

Biggart, Nicole, and Thomas Beamish. 2003. "The Economic Sociology of Conventions: Habit, Custom, Practice, and Routine in Market Order." *Annual Review of Sociology* 29:443–464.

Biggs, Caroline. 2017. "Brokers Who Go Big with Their Closing Gifts." *New York Times*, May 22, https://www.nytimes.com/2017/12/22/realestate/brokers-closing-gifts.html.

Bischoff, Kendra, and Sean F. Reardon. 2014. "Residential Segregation by Income, 1970–2009." In *Diversity and Disparities: America Enters a New Century*, edited by John. R. Logan, 208–33. New York: Russell Sage Foundation.

Bishop, Paul. 2004. "Despised, Slippery and Untrustworthy? An Analysis of Reputation in Estate Agency." *Housing Studies* 19:21–36.

Block, Fred. 2012. "Relational Work in Market Economies: Introduction." *Politics & Society* 40:135–44.

Blumer, Herbert. 1969. *Symbolic Interactionism*. Berkeley: University of California Press.

Bobo, Lawrence, and Camille L. Zubrinsky Charles. 1996. "Attitudes on Residential Integration: Perceived Status Differences, Mere In-Group Preference, or Racial Prejudice?" *Social Forces* 74:883–909.

Boeing, Geoff. 2018. "A Multi-scale Analysis of 27,000 Urban Street Networks: Every U.S. City, Town, Urbanized Area, and Zillow Neighborhood." *Environment and Planning B: Urban Analytics and City Science*, August 8, doi:10.1177/2399808318784595.

Boeing, Geoff, and Paul Waddell. 2017. "New Insights into Rental Housing Markets across the United States: Web Scraping and Analyzing Craigslist Rental Listings." *Journal of Planning Education and Research* 37:457–76.

Bourdieu, Pierre. 1984. *Distinction: A Social Critique of the Judgment of Taste.* Cambridge, MA: Harvard University Press.

Bourdieu, Pierre. 1993. *The Field of Cultural Production.* New York: Columbia University Press.

Bourdieu, Pierre. 2005. *The Social Structures of the Economy.* Malden, MA: Polity.

Brastow, Raymond T., Thomas M. Springer, and Bennie D. Waller. 2011. "Efficiency and Incentives in Residential Brokerage." *Journal of Real Estate Finance and Economics* 45:1041–61.

Bridge, Gary. 2001. "Estate Agents as Interpreters of Economic and Cultural Capital: The Gentrification Premium in the Sydney Housing Market." *International Journal of Urban and Regional Research* 25:87–101.

Brown-Saracino, Japonica. 2009. *The Neighborhood That Never Changes.* Chicago: University of Chicago Press.

Brown-Saracino, Japonica. 2018. *How Place Makes Us: Novel LBQ Identities in Four Small Cities.* Chicago: University of Chicago Press.

Brownstein, Ronald. 2011. "A Solid Foundation: Why Americans Still Long for Their Own Homes." *National Journal,* March 19.

Bruch, Elizabeth, and Fred Feinberg. 2017. "Decision-Making Processes in Social Contexts." *Annual Review of Sociology* 43:207–27.

Bruch, Elizabeth, and Joffre Swait. 2019. "Choice Set Formation in Residential Mobility and Its Implications for Segregation Dynamics." *Demography* 56:1665–92.

Buckshot, Sarah Moses. 2015. "Fabius Real Estate Agent Sentenced in $1 Million Fraud Case." Syracuse.com, May 21, http://www.syracuse.com/crime/index.ssf/2015/05/fabius_real_estate_agent_to_be_sentenced_in_1_million_fraud_case.html.

Budin, Jeremiah. 2015. "Mott Haven's Transition into New Dumbo/Williamsburg Is Nigh." *Curbed New York,* March 9, http://ny.curbed.com/2015/3/9/9983170/mott-havens-transition-into-new-dumbo-williamsburg-is-nigh.

Burt, Ronald. 1992. *Structural Holes: The Social Structure of Competition.* Cambridge, MA: Harvard University Press.

Burt, Ronald. 2005. *Brokerage and Closure: An Introduction to Social Capital.* New York: Oxford University Press.

Calhoun, Craig. 1994. *Neither Gods Nor Emperors: Students and the Struggle for Democracy in China.* Berkeley: University of California Press.

Caliskan, Koray. 2007. "Price as a Market Device: Cotton Trading in Izmir Mercantile Exchange." In *Market Devices,* edited by Michel Callon, Yuval Millo, and Fabian Muniesa, 241–60. Oxford: Blackwell.

Callon, Michel. 1998. "Introduction: The Embeddedness of Economic Markets in Economics." In *The Laws of the Market,* edited by Michel Callon, 1–57. Oxford: Blackwell.

Callon, Michel, Cécile Méadel, and Vololona Rabehariso. 2002. "The Economy of Qualities." *Economy and Society* 31:194–217.

Callon, Michel, and Fabian Muniesa. 2005. "Peripheral Vision: Economic Markets as Calculative Collective Devices." *Organization Studies* 26:1229–50.

Calltharp, Bret. 2014. "Can You Explain to Buyers and Sellers Why Technology Hasn't Made Real Estate Brokers Obsolete?" Inman.com, April 11, http://www.inman.com/2014/04/11/can-you-explain-to-buyers-and-sellers-why-technology-has-not-made-real-estate-brokers-obsolete/#.U4TOcpRdVbv.

Carruthers, Bruce. 2013. "From Uncertainty toward Risk: The Case of Credit Ratings." *Socio-economic Review* 11:525–51.

Carter, Matt. 2011. "Dual Agency and 'Double-Dipping' Still Risky Business." Inman.com, November 1, https://www.inman.com/2011/11/01/dual-agency-and-double-dipping-still-risky-business/.

Carter, Matt, and Andrea V. Brambila. 2012. "Buyer and Seller Beware: Your Agent May Not Represent Your Best Interests." Inman.com, February 24, http://www.inman.com/2012/02/24/buyer-and-seller-beware-your-agent-may-not-represent-your-best-interests/.

Casselman, Ben. 2018. "Housing Market Slows, as Rising Prices Outpace Wages." *New York Times*, September 29, https://www.nytimes.com/2018/09/29/business/economy/home-prices-housing-market-slowdown.html.

Chan, Cheris Shun-ching. 2009. "Invigorating the Content in Social Embeddedness: An Ethnography of Life Insurance Transactions in China." *American Journal of Sociology* 115:712–54.

Chan, Cheris Shun-ching. 2012. *Marketing Death: Culture and the Making of a Life Insurance Market in China.* Oxford: Oxford University Press.

Chapoulie, Jean-Michel. 1996. "Everett Hughes and the Chicago Tradition." *Sociological Theory* 14:3–29.

Charles, Camille. 2003. "The Dynamics of Racial Residential Segregation." *Annual Review of Sociology* 29:167–207.

Chetty, Raj, and Nathaniel Hendren. 2018. "The Impacts of Neighborhoods on Intergenerational Mobility I: Childhood Exposure Effects." *Quarterly Journal of Economics* 133:1107–62.

Chetty, Raj, Nathaniel Hendren, Patrick Kline, and Emmanuel Saez. 2014. "Where Is the Land of Opportunity? The Geography of Intergenerational Mobility in the United States." *Quarterly Journal of Economics* 129:1553–623.

Childress, Clayton. 2017. *Under the Cover: The Creation, Production, and Conception of a Novel.* Princeton, NJ: Princeton University Press.

Childress, Clayton, and Jean-Francois Nault. 2018. "Encultured Biases: The Role of Products in Pathways to Inequality." *American Sociological Review* 84:115–41.

Chong, Kimberly, and David Tuckett. 2015. "Constructing Conviction through Action and Narrative: How Money Managers Manage Uncertainty and the Consequence for Financial Market Functioning." *Socio-economic Review* 13:309–30.

Christensen, Peter, and Christopher Timmins. 2018. "Sorting or Steering: Experimental Evidence on the Economic Effects of Housing Discrimination." NBER Working Paper 24826.

Chung, Jen. 2006. "Fair Housing Group Says Corcoran Doesn't Care about Black

People." *Gothamist*, October 11, http://gothamist.com/2006/10/11/fair_housing _gr.php.

Clapham, David. 2005. *The Meaning of Housing: A Pathways Approach*. Bristol, UK: Policy.

Clark, W. A. V. 1982. *Modeling Housing Market Search*. London: Croom Helm.

Cohen, A. P., and J. L. Comaroff. 1976. "The Management of Meaning: On the Phenomenology of Political Transactions." In *Transaction and Meaning: Directions in the Anthropology of Exchange and Symbolic Behavior*, edited by Bruce Kapferer, 87–107. Philadelphia: Institute for the Study of Human Issues.

Coleman, Nicole, and Patti Williams. 2013. "Feeling like My Self: Emotion Profiles and Social Identity." *Journal of Consumer Research* 40:203–22.

Collins, Randall. 1988. "The Micro Contribution to Macro Sociology." *Sociological Theory* 6:242–53.

Collins, Randall. 2000. "Situational Stratification: A Micro-Macro Theory of Inequality." *Sociological Theory* 18:17–43.

Collins, Randall. 2004. *Interaction Ritual Chains*. Princeton, NJ: Princeton University Press.

Collins, Randall. 2013. "The End of Middle Class Work: No More Escapes." In *Does Capitalism Have a Future?*, by I. Wallerstein, R. Collins, M. Mann, G. Derluguian, and C. Calhoun, 37–70. Oxford: Oxford University Press.

Condron, Dennis J., Daniel Tope, Christina R. Steidl, and Kendralin J. Freeman. 2013. "Racial Segregation and the Black/White Achievement Gap, 1992 to 2009." *Sociological Quarterly* 54:130–157.

Conley, Dalton. 1999. *Being Black, Living in the Red: Race, Wealth, and Social Policy in America*. Berkeley: University of California Press.

Conley, Dalton, and Brian Gifford. 2006. "Homeownership, Social Insurance, and the Welfare State." *Sociological Forum* 16:263–80.

Conti, Alie. 2014. "Prostitutes Steal Millions and Walk Free." *Miami New Times*, January 23, http://www.miaminewtimes.com/2014-01-23/news/south-florida -prostitutes-steal-millions-and-walk-free/2/.

Cousin, Bruno, Shamus Khan, and Ashley Mears. 2018. "Theoretical and Methodological Pathways for Research on Elites." *Socio-economic Review* 16:225–49.

Cox, Wendell, and Hugh Pavletich. 2013. "9th Annual Demographia International Housing Affordability Survey: 2013." http://www.demographia.com/dhi2013.pdf.

Cox, Wendell, and Hugh Pavletich. 2017. "13th Annual Demographia International Housing Affordability Survey: 2017." http://www.demographia.com/dhi2017.pdf.

Crocket, John. H. 1982. "Competition and Efficiency in Transacting: The Case of Residential Real Estate Brokers." *Real Estate Economics* 10:209–27.

Crowder, Kyle, and Scott J. South. 2008. "Spatial Dynamics of White Flight: The Effects of Local and Extralocal Racial Conditions on Neighborhood Out-Migration." *American Sociological Review* 73:792–812.

Cross, Steven. 2014. "Less than 1 in 10 believe agents are trustworthy." *Real Estate Business* [REB], April 14, http://www.realestatebusiness.com.au/breaking-news /7525-less-than-1-in-10-believe-agents-are-trustworthy.

Cutler, David, Edward Glaeser, and Jacob Vigdor. 1999. "The Rise and Decline of the American Ghetto." *Journal of Political Economy* 107:455–506.

Daipha, Phaedra. 2015. *Masters of Uncertainty: Weather Forecasters and the Quest for Truth*. Chicago: University of Chicago Press.

Damasio, Antonio. 1994. *Descartes' Error: Emotion, Reason, and the Human Brain*. New York: Harper Collins.

Darr, Asaf. 2006. *Selling Technology: The Changing Shape of Sales in an Information Economy*. Ithaca, NY: Cornell University Press.

Darr, Asaf, and Trevor Pinch. 2013. "Performing Sales: Material Scripts and the Social Organization of Obligation." *Organization Studies* 34:1601–21.

Darrah, Jennifer, and Stefanie DeLuca. 2014. "'Living Here Has Changed My Whole Perspective': How Escaping Inner-City Poverty Shapes Neighborhood and Housing Choice." *Journal of Policy Analysis and Management* 33:350–84.

Davis, Fred. 1959. "The Cabdriver and His Fare: Facets of a Fleeting Relationship." *American Journal of Sociology* 65:158–65.

Deener, Andrew. 2012. *Venice: A Contested Bohemia in Los Angeles*. Chicago: University of Chicago Press.

Degenshein, Anya. 2017. "Strategies of Valuation: Repertoires of Worth at the Financial Margins." *Theory and Society* 46:387–409.

Delcoure, Natalya, and Norm G. Miller. 2002. "International Residential Real Estate Brokerage Fees and Implications for the US Brokerage Industry." *International Real Estate Review* 5:12–39.

Dellaert, Benedict G. C., and Gerald Häubl. 2012. "Searching in Choice Mode: Consumer Decision Processes in Product Search with Recommendations." *Journal of Marketing Research* 49:277–88.

DeLuca, Stefanie, Philip M. E. Garboden, and Peter Rosenblatt. 2013. "Segregating Shelter: How Housing Policies Shape the Residential Location of Low-Income Minority Families." *Annals of the American Academy of Political and Social Science* 647:268–99.

DePillis, Lydia. 2013. "Why Do Real Estate Agents Still Exist?" *Washington Post*, August 22, https://www.washingtonpost.com/news/wonk/wp/2013/08/22/why-do-real-estate-agents-still-exist/?utm_term=.c410939075f5.

Desmond, Matthew. 2007. *On the Fireline: Living and Dying with Wildland Firefighters*. Chicago: University of Chicago Press.

Desmond, Matthew. 2014. "Relational Ethnography." *Theory and Society* 43:547–79.

Desmond, Matthew. 2016. *Evicted: Poverty and Profit in the American City*. New York: Crown.

de Souza Briggs, Xavier. 2005. *The Geography of Opportunity: Race and Housing Choice in Metropolitan America*. Washington, DC: Brookings Institution Press.

Dewey, John. 1922. *Human Nature and Conduct: An Introduction to Social Psychology*. New York: Holt.

Dewey, John. 1939. *Theory of Valuation*. Chicago: University of Chicago Press.

Diehl, Kristin, and Gal Zauberman. 2005. "Searching Ordered Sets: Evaluations from Sequences under Search." *Journal of Consumer Research* 31:824–32.

DiMaggio, Paul. 1994. "Culture and Economy." In *The Handbook of Economic Sociology* edited by Neil Smelser and Richard Swedberg, 27–57. New York: Russell Sage Foundation / Princeton, NJ: Princeton University Press.

DiMaggio, Paul. 2002. "Endogenizing 'Animal Spirits': Toward A Sociology of Collective Response to Uncertainty and Risk." In *The New Economic Sociology*, edited by M. Guillen, R. Collins, P. England, and M. Meyer, 79–101. New York: Russell Sage Foundation.

DiMaggio, Paul, and Hugh Louch. 1998. "Socially Embedded Consumer Transactions: For What Kinds of Purchases Do People Most Often Use Networks?" *American Sociological Review* 63:619–37.

Donnelly, Kathleen. 2017. "The Gentrifier's Dilemma: Narrative Strategies and Self-Justifications of Incoming Residents in Bedford-Stuyvesant, Brooklyn." *City & Community* 17:374–93.

Dore, Ronald. 1992. "Goodwill and the Spirit of Market Capitalism." In *The Sociology of Economic Life*, edited by Mark Granovetter and Richard Swedberg, 159–81. Boulder: Westview.

Drake, St. Clair, and Horace R. Cayton. 1945. *Black Metropolis: A Study of Negro Life in a Northern City*. Chicago: University of Chicago Press.

Dwyer, Rachel E. 2007. "Expanding Homes and Increasing Inequalities: U.S. Housing Development and the Residential Segregation of the Affluent." *Social Problems* 54:23–46.

Elder, Harold, Leonard Zumpano, and Edward Baryla. 2000. "Buyer Brokers: Do They Make a Difference? Their Influence on Selling Price and Search Duration." *Real Estate Economics* 28:337–62.

Eliasoph, Nina, and Paul Lichterman. 2003. "Culture in Interaction." *American Journal of Sociology* 108:735–94.

Elster, Jon. 1998. "Emotions and Economic Theory." *Journal of Economic Literature* 36:47–74.

Emerson, Michael O., Karen J. Chai, and George Yancey. 2001. "Does Race Matter in Residential Segregation? Exploring the Preferences of White Americans." *American Sociological Review* 66:922–35.

Emirbayer, Mustafa. 1997. "Manifesto for a Relational Sociology." *American Journal of Sociology* 103:281–317.

Emirbayer, Mustafa, and Jeff Goodwin. 1994. "Network Analysis, Culture, and the Problem of Agency." *American Journal of Sociology* 99:1411–54.

Engels, Friedrich. 1935. *The Housing Question*. New York: International Publishers.

Engels, Friedrich. [1845] 1993. *The Condition of the Working Class in England*. Oxford: Oxford University Press.

Ermakoff, Ivan. 2008. *Ruling Oneself Out: A Theory of Collective Abdications*. Durham, NC: Duke University Press.

Ermakoff, Ivan. 2017. "Shadow Plays: Theory's Perennial Challenges." *Sociological Theory* 35:128–37.

Eyal, Gil. 2013. "For a Sociology of Expertise: The Social Origins of the Autism Epidemic." *American Journal of Sociology* 118:863–907.

Faber, Jacob William. 2018. "Segregation and the Geography of Creditworthiness: Racial Inequality in a Recovered Mortgage Market." *Housing Policy Debate* 28:215–47.

Faber, Jacob William. 2019. "Segregation and the Cost of Money: Race, Poverty, and the Prevalence of Alternative Financial Institutions." *Social Forces*, February 4, doi:10.1093/sf/soy129.

Faber, Jacob William, and Ingrid Gould Ellen. 2016. "Race and the Housing Cycle: Differences in Home Equity Trends among Long-Term Homeowners." *Housing Policy Debate* 26:456–73.

Faulkner, Robert R., and Howard S. Becker. 2009. *"Do You Know . . . ?" The Jazz Repertoire in Action.* Chicago: University of Chicago Press.

Fine, Gary Alan. 1996. *Kitchens: The Culture of Restaurant Work.* Berkeley: University of California Press.

Fine, Gary Alan. 2012. "Group Culture and the Interaction Order: Local Sociology on the Meso-Level." *Annual Review of Sociology* 38:159–79.

Fine, Gary Alan, and Corey D. Fields. 2008. "Culture and Microsociology: The Anthill and the Veldt." *Annals of the American Academy of Political and Social Science* 619:130–48.

Fligstein, Neil. 1996. "Markets as Politics: A Political-Cultural Approach to Market Institutions." *American Sociological Review* 61:656–73.

Fligstein, Neil. 2001. "Social Skill and the Theory of Fields." *Sociological Theory* 19:105–25.

Fligstein, Neil. 2002. *The Architecture of Markets: An Economic Sociology of Twenty-First Century Capitalist Societies.* Princeton, NJ: Princeton University Press.

Flippen, Chenoa. 2004. "Unequal Returns to Housing Investments? A Study of Real Housing Appreciation among Black, White, and Hispanic Households." *Social Forces* 82:1523–51.

Flippen, Chenoa. 2010. "The Spatial Dynamics of Stratification: Metropolitan Context, Population Redistribution, and Black and Hispanic Homeownership." *Demography* 47:845–68.

Flippen, Chenoa. 2012. "Housing and Immigration: United States." In *International Encyclopedia of Housing and Home*, edited by Susan J. Smith, Marja Elsinga, Lorna Fox O'Mahony, Ong Seow Eng, Susan Wachter, and Peter M. Ward, 4:16–21. Oxford: Elsevier.

Fourcade, Marion. 2011. "Cents and Sensibility: Economic Valuation and the Nature of 'Nature.'" *American Journal of Sociology* 116:1721–77.

Fourcade, Marion, and Kieran Healy. 2007. "Moral Views of Market Society." *Annual Review of Sociology* 33:285–311.

Frank, Robert. 1998. *Passions within Reason.* New York: W. W. Norton.

Freeman, Lance. 2006. *There Goes the 'Hood: Views of Gentrification from the Ground Up.* Philadelphia: Temple University Press.

Freemark, Yonah. 2019. "Upzoning Chicago: Impacts of Zoning Reform on Property Values and Housing Construction." *Urban Affairs Review*, January 29, doi:10.1177/1078087418824672.

Freidson, Eliot. 2001. *Professionalism: The Third Logic*. Chicago: University of Chicago Press.

Frickel, Scott, and James R. Elliott. 2018. *Sites Unseen: Uncovering Hidden Hazards in American Cities*. New York: Russell Sage.

Fridman, Daniel, and Alex Luscombe. 2018. "Gift-Giving, Disreputable Exchange, and the Management of Donations in a Police Department." *Social Forces* 96:507–28.

Friedman, Raymond A., and Joel Podolny. 1992. "Differentiation of Boundary Spanning Roles: Labor Negotiations and Implications for Role Conflict." *Administrative Science Quarterly* 37:28–47.

Gallup. 2015. "Honesty/Ethics in Professions" survey tabulation, http://www.gallup.com/poll/1654/honesty-ethics-professions.aspx, accessed February 29, 2016.

Galster, George. 1990. "Racial Steering by Real Estate Agents: Mechanisms and Motives." *Review of Black Political Economy* 19:39–63.

Galster, George, and Erin Godfrey. 2005. "By Words and Deeds: Racial Steering by Real Estate Agents in the U.S. in 2000." *Journal of the American Planning Association* 71:251–68.

Gambetta, Diego, and Heather Hamill. 2005. *Streetwise: How Taxi Drivers Establish Their Customers' Trustworthiness*. New York: Russell Sage.

Garber, Marjorie. 2000. *Sex and Real Estate: Why We Love Houses*. New York: Anchor Books.

Garrido, Marco. 2013. "The Sense of Place behind Segregating Practices: An Ethnographic Approach to the Symbolic Partitioning of Metro Manila." *Social Forces* 91:1343–62.

Geertz, Clifford. 1960. "The Javanese Kijaji: The Changing Role of a Cultural Broker." *Comparative Studies in Society and History* 2:228–49.

Ghaziani, Amin. 2014. *There Goes the Gayborhood?* Princeton, NJ: Princeton University Press.

Ghaziani, Amin. 2015. "'Gay Enclaves Face Prospect of Being Passé': How Assimilation Affects the Spatial Expressions of Sexuality in the United States." *International Journal of Urban and Regional Research* 39:756–71.

Gibbons, Joseph, and Tse-Chuan Yang. 2014. "Self-Rated Health and Residential Segregation: How Does Race/Ethnicity Matter?" *Journal of Urban Health* 91:648–60.

Gibson, D. W. 2015. "'I Put in White Tenants': The Grim, Racist (and Likely Illegal) Methods of One Brooklyn Landlord." *New York Magazine*, May, http://nymag.com/daily/intelligencer/2015/05/grim-racist-methods-of-one-brooklyn-landlord.html.

Glaeser, Andreas. 2010. *Political Epistemics: The Secret Police, the Opposition, and the End of East German Socialism*. Chicago: University of Chicago Press.

Goffman, Erving. 1959. *The Presentation of Self in Everyday Life*. New York: Anchor Books.

Goffman, Erving. 1967. *Interaction Ritual*. New York: Pantheon Books.

Goffman, Erving. 1969. *Strategic Interaction*. New York: Ballantine Books.

Goffman, Erving. 1974. *Frame Analysis*. Boston: Northeastern University Press.

Goffman, Erving. 1983. "The Interaction Order: American Sociological Association, 1982 Presidential Address." *American Sociological Review* 48:1–17.

Goldstein, Adam, and Orestes Hastings. 2019. "Buying In: Positional Competition, Schools, Income Inequality, and Housing Consumption." *Sociological Science* 6:416–45.

Gotham, Kevin Fox. 2002. *Race, Real Estate, and Uneven Development: The Kansas City Experience, 1900–2000.* Albany: State University of New York Press.

Granovetter, Mark. 1985. "Economic Action and Social Structure: The Problem of Embeddedness." *American Journal of Sociology* 91:481–510.

Gross, Neil. 2009. "A Pragmatist Theory of Social Mechanisms." *American Sociological Review* 74:358–79.

Guseva, Alya, and Akos Rona-Tas. 2001. "Uncertainty, Risk, and Trust: Russian and American Credit Card Markets Compared." *American Sociological Review* 66: 623–46.

Halle, David. 1984. *America's Working Man.* Chicago: University of Chicago Press.

Hanser, Amy. 2008. *Service Encounters: Class, Gender, and the Market for Social Distinction in Urban China.* Stanford, CA: Stanford University Press.

Hanser, Amy. 2010. "Uncertainty and the Problem of Value: Consumers, Culture and Inequality in Urban China." *Journal of Consumer Culture* 10:307–32.

Harding, David. 2013. "Real Estate Agent Turned Home He Was Supposed to Be Selling into Sex Pad: Lawsuit." *New York Daily News*, December 23, http://www.nydailynews.com/news/national/real-estate-agent-customers-home-sex-pad-suit-article-1.1556428.

Harding, John P., Stuart S. Rosenthal, and C. F. Sirmans. 2003. "Estimating Bargaining Power in the Market for Existing Homes." *Review of Economics and Statistics* 85:178–88.

Harrington, Brooke. 2016. *Capital without Borders: Wealth Managers and the One Percent.* Cambridge, MA: Harvard University Press.

Harvey, David. 1982. *The Limits to Capital.* Chicago: University of Chicago Press.

Harvey, David. 2014. *Seventeen Contradictions and the End of Capitalism.* Oxford: Oxford University Press.

Harvey, David, 2017. *Marx, Capital, and the Madness of Economic Reason.* Oxford: Oxford University Press.

Harvey, David, and David Wachsmuth. 2012. "What Is to Be Done? And Who the Hell Is Going to Do It?" In *Cities for People, Not for Profit: Critical Urban Theory and the Right to the City*, edited by N. Brenner, P. Marcuse, and M. Mayer, 264–74. New York: Routledge.

Hawthorne, Fran. 2016. "Prospect Heights, Where Historic Meets Brand New." *New York Times*, February 21, https://www.nytimes.com/2016/02/21/realestate/prospect-heights-brooklyn-where-historic-meets-brand-new.html.

Healy, Kieran. 2006. *Last Best Gifts: Altruism and the Market for Human Blood and Organs.* Chicago: University of Chicago Press.

Helper, Rose. 1969. *Racial Policies and Practices of Real Estate Brokers.* Minneapolis: University of Minnesota Press.

Hempel, Donald J. 1969. *The Role of the Real Estate Broker in the Home Buying Process.* Storrs, CT: Center for Real Estate and Urban Economic Studies.

Hendel, Igal, Aviv Nevo, and François Ortalo-Magné. 2009. "The Relative Performance of Real Estate Marketing Platforms: MLS versus FSBOMadison.com." *American Economic Review* 99:1878–98.

Hermann, Alexander. 2018. "Price-to-Income Ratios Are Reaching Historic Highs." *Housing Perspectives* (Joint Center for Housing Studies blog), September 13, https://www.jchs.harvard.edu/blog/price-to-income-ratios-are-nearing-historic-highs/.

Herbert, Christopher E., Daniel T. McCue, and Rocio Sanchez-Moyano. 2014. "Is Homeownership Still an Effective Means of Building Wealth for Low-Income and Minority Households?" In *Homeownership Built to Last: Balancing Access, Affordability, and Risk After the Housing Crisis,* edited by E. S. Belsky, C. E. Herbert, and J. H. Molinsky, 50–98. New York: Brookings Institute.

Higgins, Michelle. 2015. "Manhattan Apartment Prices Near Million Dollar Mark, Report Says." *New York Times,* October 1, https://www.nytimes.com/2015/10/01/realestate/manhattan-apartment-prices-near-million-dollar-mark-reports-say.html.

Higgins, Michelle. 2016. "Manhattan Apartment Prices Reached $1.15 Million Mark in 2015, Report Says." *New York Times,* October 5, https://www.nytimes.com/2016/01/05/nyregion/manhattan-apartment-prices-reached-1-15-million-mark-in-2015-reports-say.html.

Ho, Karen. 2009. *Liquidated: An Ethnography of Wall Street.* Durham NC,: Duke University Press.

Hoang, Kimberly Kay. 2015. *Dealing in Desire: Asian Ascendancy, Western Decline, and the Hidden Currencies of Global Sex Work.* Berkeley: University of California Press.

Hochschild, Arlie R. 1979. "Emotion Work, Feeling Rules, and Social Structure." *American Journal of Sociology* 85:551–75.

Hochschild, Arlie R. 1983. *The Managed Heart: Commercialization of Human Feeling.* Berkeley: University of California Press.

Hornstein, Jeffrey M. 2005. *A Nation of Realtors: A Cultural History of the Twentieth-Century American Middle Class.* Durham, NC: Duke University Press.

House, J. D. 1977. *Contemporary Entrepreneurs: The Sociology of Residential Real Estate Agents.* Westport, CT: Greenwood.

Howard, Christopher. 1997. *The Hidden Welfare State.* Princeton, NJ: Princeton University Press.

Howell, Junia, and Elizabeth Korver-Glenn. 2018. "Neighborhoods, Race, and the Twenty-First-Century Housing Appraisal Industry." *Sociology of Race and Ethnicity* 4:473–90.

Hseih, Chang-Tai, and Enrico Moretti. 2003. "Can Free Entry Be Inefficient? Fixed Commissions and Social Waste in the Real Estate Industry." *Journal of Political Economy* 111:1076–122.

Hughes, Everett C. [1931] 1979. *The Growth of an Institution: The Chicago Real Estate Board.* New York: Arno.

Hunter, Albert. 1974. *Symbolic Communities: The Persistence of Change in Chicago's Local Communities*. Chicago: University of Chicago Press.

Hutchinson, Janet. 1997. "Building for Babbit: The State and the Suburban Home Ideal." *Journal of Policy History* 9:184–210.

Hwang, Jackelyn. 2016. "The Social Construction of a Gentrifying Neighborhood." *Urban Affairs Review* 53:98–128.

Hwang, Jackelyn, and Robert J. Sampson. 2014. "Divergent Pathways of Gentrification." *American Sociological Review* 79:726–51.

Inman, J. Jeffrey, Anil C. Peter, and Priya Raghubir. 1997. "Framing the Deal: The Role of Restrictions in Accentuating Deal Value." *Journal of Consumer Research* 24:68–79.

Irwin, Neil. 2018. "Why the Housing Market Is Slumping Despite a Booming Economy." *New York Times*, November 15, https://www.nytimes.com/2018/11/15/upshot/housing-market-slumping-despite-booming-economy.html.

Jack, Anthony Abraham. 2019. *The Privileged Poor: How Elite Colleges and Failing Disadvantaged Students*. Cambridge, MA: Harvard University Press.

Jackson, Kenneth T. 1987. *Crabgrass Frontier: The Suburbanization of the United States*. New York: Oxford University Press.

James, Deborah. 2011. "The Return of the Broker: Consensus, Hierarchy, and Choice in South African Land Reform." *Journal of the Royal Anthropological Institute* 17:318–38.

Jargowsky, Paul A. 1996. "Take the Money and Run: Economic Segregation in U.S. Metropolitan Areas." *American Sociological Review* 61:984–98.

Jargowsky, Paul A. 2018. "The Persistence of Segregation in the 21st Century." *Law & Inequality: A Journal of Theory and Practice* 36:307–30.

Jerolmack, Colin, and Shamus Khan. 2014. "Talk Is Cheap: Ethnography and the Attitudinal Fallacy." *Sociological Methods & Research* 43:178–209.

Jerolmack, Colin, and Alexandra Murphy. 2017. "The Ethical Dilemmas and Social Scientific Trade-Offs of Masking in Ethnography." *Sociological Methods & Research*, March 30, doi:10.1177/0049124117701483.

Jones, Nikki, and Christina Jackson. 2012. "'You Just Don't Go Down There': Learning to Avoid the Ghetto in San Francisco." In *The Ghetto: Contemporary Global Issues and Controversies*, edited by Ray Hutchinson and Bruce D. Haynes, 83–110. Boulder: Westview.

Jud, G. Donald 2003. "Real Estate Brokers and the Market for Residential Housing." *Real Estate Economics* 11:69–82.

Kahneman, Daniel, Paul Slovic, and Amos Tversky. 1982. *Judgment under Uncertainty: Heuristics and Biases*. New York: Cambridge University Press.

Kalfus, Marilyn. 2018. "Jury: Coldwell Banker Real Estate Agent Did Not Mislead Buyer in Mansion Dispute." *Orange County Register*, April 5, https://www.ocregister.com/2018/04/05/jury-coldwell-banker-real-estate-agent-did-not-mislead-buyer-in-mansion-dispute/.

Kalleberg, Arne. 2011. *Good Jobs, Bad Jobs: The Rise of Polarized and Precarious Em-*

ployment Systems in the United States, 1970s–2000s. New York: Russell Sage Foundation.

Karpik, Lucien. 2010. *Valuing the Unique: The Economics of Singularization.* Princeton, NJ: Princeton University Press.

Katz, Jack. 1999. *How Emotions Work.* Chicago: University of Chicago Press.

Katz, Jack. 2001. "From How to Why: On Luminous Description and Causal Inference in Ethnography (Part 1)." *Ethnography* 2:443–73.

Katz, Jack. 2002. "From How to Why: On Luminous Description and Causal Inference in Ethnography (Part 2)." *Ethnography* 3:63–90.

Katz, Jack. 2015. "Situational Evidence: Strategies for Causal Reasoning from Observational Field Notes." *Sociological Methods & Research* 44:108–44.

Kaufman, Joanne. 2019. "The Romance of Real Estate." *New York Times*, January 25, https://www.nytimes.com/2019/01/25/realestate/the-romance-of-real-estate.html.

Kaysen, Ronda. 2015. "The South Bronx Beckons." *New York Times*, September 20, https://www.nytimes.com/2015/09/20/realestate/the-south-bronx-beckons.html.

Kefalas, Maria. 2003. *Working-Class Heroes.* Berkeley: University of California Press.

Keil, Jennifer Gould, and Bruce Golding. 2014. "Manhattan Real Estate Prices Rise above 2008 Pre-recession Record." *New York Post*, April 1, https://nypost.com/2014/04/01/manhattan-real-estate-prices-rise-above-2008-pre-recession-record/.

Khan, Shamus. 2011. *Privilege: The Making of an Adolescent Elite at St. Paul's School.* Princeton, NJ: Princeton University Press.

Khan, Shamus. 2012. "The Sociology of Elites." *Annual Review of Sociology* 38:361–77.

Kiel, Katherine A., and Jeffery E. Zabel. 1999. "The Accuracy of Owner-Provided House Values: The 1978–1991 American Housing Survey." *Real Estate Economics* 27:263–98.

Kim, Sunwoong. 2003. "Long-Term Appreciation of Owner-Occupied Single-Family House Prices in Milwaukee Neighborhoods." *Urban Geography* 24:212–31.

Kimelberg, Shelley McDonough. 2014. "Middle-Class Parents, Risk, and Urban Public Schools." In *Choosing Homes, Choosing Schools*, edited by Annette Lareau and Kimberly Goyette, 207–36. New York: Russell Sage.

Kohler-Haussman, Issa. 2018. *Misdemeanorland: Criminal Courts and Social Control in an Age of Broken Windows Policing.* Princeton, NJ: Princeton University Press.

Korver-Glenn, Elizabeth. 2018a. "Brokering Ties and Inequality: How White Real Estate Agents Recreate Advantage and Exclusion in Urban Housing Markets." *Social Currents* 5:350–68.

Korver-Glenn, Elizabeth. 2018b. "Compounding Inequalities: How Racial Stereotypes and Discrimination Accumulate across the Stages of Housing Exchange." *American Sociological Review* 83:627–56.

Krippner, Greta R. 2001. "The Elusive Market: Embeddedness and the Paradigm of Economic Sociology." *Theory and Society* 30:775–810.

Krippner, Greta R., and Anthony S. Alvarez. 2007. "Embeddedness and the Intellectual Projects of Economic Sociology." *Annual Review of Sociology* 33:219–40.

Krysan, Maria. 2008. "Does Race Matter in the Search for Housing? An Exploratory
Study of Search Strategies, Experiences, and Location." *Social Science Research*
37:581–603.

Krysan, Maria, and Michael Bader. 2007. "Perceiving the Metropolis: Seeing the City
through a Prism of Race." *Social Forces* 86:699–733.

Krysan, Maria, and Michael Bader. 2009. "Racial Blind Spots: Black-White-Latino
Differences in Community Knowledge." *Social Problems* 56:677–701.

Krysan, Maria, and Kyle Crowder. 2017. *Cycle of Segregation: Social Processes and Residential Stratification*. New York: Russell Sage.

Krysan, Maria, and Reynolds Farley. 2002. "The Residential Preferences of Blacks: Do
They Explain Persistent Segregation?" *Social Forces* 80:937–80.

Kuhri, Eric. 2013. "San Jose Real Estate Agent Who Scammed Friends and Family
Gets 15- Year Sentence." *Mercury News*, July 10, http://www.mercurynews.com
/2013/07/10/san-jose-real-estate-agent-who-scammed-friends-and-family-gets
-15-year-sentence/.

Kwate, Naa Oyo A., Melody S. Goodman, Jerrold Jackson, and Julen Harris. 2013. "Spatial and Racial Patterning of Real Estate Broker Listings in New York City." *Review
of Black Political Economy* 40:401–24.

Lacy, Karyn R. 2007. *Blue-Chip Black: Race, Class, and Status in the New Black Middle
Class*. Berkeley: University of California Press.

Lainer-Vos, Dan. 2011. "Manufacturing National Attachments: Gift-Giving, Market
Exchange and the Construction of Irish and Zionist Diaspora Bonds." *Theory and
Society* 41:73–106.

Lainer-Vos, Dan. 2013. "The Practical Organization of Moral Transactions: Gift Giving,
Market Exchange, Credit, and the Making of Diaspora Bonds." *Sociological Theory*
31:145–67.

Lainer-Vos, Dan. 2014. "Brothers' Keepers: Gift Giving Networks and the Organization
of Jewish American Diaspora Nationalism." *Socio-economic Review* 12:463–88.

Lamont, Michèle. 2012. "Toward a Comparative Sociology of Valuation and Evaluation." *Annual Review of Sociology* 38:201–21.

Lamont, Michèle, Stefan Beljean, and Matthew Clair. 2014. "What Is Missing? Cultural
Processes and Causal Pathways to Inequality." *Socio-rconomic Review* 12:573–608.

Lamont, Michèle, and Virag Molnar. 2002. "The Study of Boundaries in the Social
Sciences." *Annual Review of Sociology* 28:167–95.

Lands, LeeAnn. 2008. "Be a Patriot, Buy a Home: Re-imagining Home Owners and
Home Ownership in Early 20th Century Atlanta." *Journal of Social History* 41:943–65.

Lane, Ben. 2015. "Massachusetts Supreme Court Upholds Real Estate Agents' Employment Status." *Housing Wire*, June 4, https://www.housingwire.com/articles/34105
-massachusetts-supreme-court-upholds-real-estate-agents-employment-status.

Lareau, Annette. 2014. "Schools, Housing, and the Reproduction of Inequality." In
Choosing Homes, Choosing Schools, edited by Annette Lareau and Kimberly
Goyette, 169–206. New York: Russell Sage.

Lareau, Annette, and Kimberly Goyette. 2014. *Choosing Homes, Choosing Schools*. New York: Russell Sage.

Larson, Magali Sarfatti. 1977. *The Rise of Professionalism: A Sociological Analysis*. Berkeley: University of California Press.

Lauster, Nathanael T. 2010. "Housing and the Proper Performance of American Motherhood, 1940–2005." *Housing Studies* 25:543–57.

Leicht, Kevin T., and Mary L. Fennell. 2001. *Professional Work: A Sociological Approach*. Malden, MA: Blackwell.

Leidner, Robin. 1993. *Fast Food, Fast Talk*. Berkeley: University of California Press.

Lerner, Jennifer S., and Larissa Z. Tiedens. 2006. "Portrait of the Angry Decision Maker: How Appraisal Tendencies Shape Anger's Influence on Cognition." *Behavioral Decision Making* 19:115–37.

Levine, Jeremy R. 2016. "The Privatization of Political Representation: Community-Based Organizations as Nonelected Neighborhood Representatives." *American Sociological Review* 81:1251–75.

Levitt, Steven D., and John A. List. 2007. "What Do Laboratory Experiments Measuring Social Preferences Reveal about the Real World?" *Journal of Economic Perspectives* 21:153–74.

Levitt, Steven D., and John A. List. 2008. "*Homo economicus* Evolves." *Science* 319:909–10.

Levitt, Steven D., and Chad Syverson. 2008. "Market Distortions When Agents Are Better Informed: The Value of Information in Real Estate Transactions." *Review of Economics and Statistics* 90:599–611.

Lewis, Valerie A., Michael O. Emerson, and Stephen L. Klineberg. 2011. "Who We'll Live With: Neighborhood Racial Composition Preferences of Whites, Blacks and Latinos." *Social Forces* 89, no. 4:1385–408.

Lichtenstein, Sarah, and Paul Slovic. 2006. "The Construction of Preference: An Overview." In *The Construction of Preference*, edited by Sarah Lichtenstein and Paul Slovic, 1–40. Cambridge: Cambridge University Press.

Lichter, Daniel T., Domenico Parisi, and Michael C. Taquino. 2015. "Toward a New Macro-Segregation? Decomposing Segregation within and between Metropolitan Cities and Suburbs." *American Sociological Review* 80:843–73.

Lloyd, Richard. 2005. *Neo-Bohemia: Art and Commerce in the Postindustrial City*. London: Routledge.

Logan, John R., Andrew Foster, Jun Ke, and Fan Li. 2018. "The Uptick in Income Segregation: Real Trend or Random Sampling Variance." *American Journal of Sociology* 124:185–222.

Logan, John R., and Harvey L. Molotch. 1987. *Urban Fortunes: The Political Economics of Place*. Berkeley: University of California Press.

Logan, John R., and Brian Stults. 2011. "The Persistence of Segregation in the Metropolis: New Findings from the 2010 Census." Census Brief prepared for Project US2010, Brown University, http://www.s4.brown.edu/us2010.

Luken, Paul C., and Suzanne Vaughn. 2005. "'. . . Be a Genuine Homemaker in Your Own Home': Gender and Familial Relations in State Housing Practices, 1917–1922." *Social Forces* 83:1603–25.

Luken, Paul C., and Suzanne Vaughn. 2006. "Standardizing Childrearing through Housing." *Social Problems* 53:299–331.

Lynn, Michael. 1992a. "The Psychology of Unavailability: Explaining Scarcity and Cost Effects on Value." *Basic and Applied Social Psychology* 13:3–7.

Lynn, Michael. 1992b. "Scarcity's Enhancement of Desirability: The Role of Naïve Economic Theories." *Basic and Applied Social Psychology* 13:67–78.

Macaulay, Stewart. 1963. "Non-contractual Relations in Business: A Preliminary Study." *American Sociological Review* 28:55–67.

MacKenzie, Donald, and Yuval Millo. 2003. "Constructing a Market, Performing Theory: The Historical Sociology of a Financial Derivatives Exchange." *American Journal of Sociology* 109:107–45.

Madden, David, and Peter Marcuse. 2016. *In Defense of Housing*. New York: Verso Books.

Mantrala, Suryamani, and Edward Zabel. 1995. "The Housing Market and Real Estate Brokers." *Real Estate Economics* 23:161–85.

Marino, Vivian. 2017. "Manhattan Prices Stable in 2017, Even as Luxury Takes a Breather." *New York Times*, December 29, https://www.nytimes.com/2017/12/29/realestate/manhattan-prices-stable-in-2017-even-as-luxury-takes-a-breather.html.

Martin, John Levi. 2011. *The Explanation of Social Action*. Oxford: Oxford University Press.

Marwell, Nicole P. 2007. *Bargaining for Brooklyn: Community Organizations in the Entrepreneurial City*. Chicago: University of Chicago Press.

Massey, Douglas. 2005. "Racial Discrimination in Housing: A Moving Target." *Social Problems* 52:148–51.

Massey, Douglas. 2015. "The Legacy of the 1968 Fair Housing Act." *Sociological Forum* 30:571–88.

Massey, Douglas S., and Nancy A. Denton. 1993. *American Apartheid*. Cambridge, MA: Harvard University Press.

Massey, Douglas S., and Mary J. Fischer. 2006. "The Effect of Childhood Segregation on Minority Academic Performance at Selective Colleges." *Ethnic and Racial Studies* 29:1–26.

Mauss, Marcel. 1967. *The Gift: Forms and Functions of Exchange in Archaic Societies*. New York: W. W. Norton.

McCabe, Brian J. 2016. *No Place like Home: Wealth, Community and the Politics of Homeownership*. New York: Oxford University Press.

McCabe, Brian J. 2018. "Why Buy a Home? Race, Ethnicity and Homeownership Preferences in the United States." *Sociology of Race and Ethnicity* 4:452–72.

McPherson, Miller, Lynn Smith-Lovin, and James M. Cook. 2001. "Birds of a Feather: Homophily in Social Networks." *Annual Review of Sociology* 27:415–44.

Mears, Ashley. 2011. *Pricing Beauty*. Berkeley: University of California Press.

Mears, Ashley. 2015. "Working for Free in the VIP: Relational Work and the Production of Consent." *American Sociological Review* 80:1099–122.

Mele, Christopher. 2000. *Selling the Lower East Side: Culture, Real Estate, and Resistance in New York City*. Minneapolis: University of Minnesota Press.

Mendes, Elizabeth. 2013. "Americans Down on Congress, OK with Own Representa-tive." Gallup.com, May 9, http://www.gallup.com/poll/162362/americans-down -congress-own-representative.aspx.

Meyer, John. 2017. "Reflections on Institutional Theories of Organizations." In *The Sage Handbook of Organizational Institutionalism*, 2nd ed., 831–52. Thousand Oaks, CA: Sage.

Miles, Matthew B., and A. Michael Huberman. 1994. *Qualitative Data Analysis*. Thou-sand Oaks, CA: Sage.

Miller, Daniel. 1998. *A Theory of Shopping*. Cambridge: Polity.

Miller, Jonathan. 2014. "Manhattan Home Sales Are Not 80% All-Cash (They Are 45%)." *Matrix* (Miller Samuel blog), May 17, http://www.millersamuel.com /manhattan-home-sales-are-not-80-all-cash-they-are-45/.

Miller, Jonathan. 2015. "How Many NYC Apartments Are Bought With Cold Hard Cash?" *Curbed New York*, May 28, https://ny.curbed.com/2015/5/28/9956300 /how-many-nyc-apartments-are-bought-with-cold-hard-cash.

Mills, C. Wright. 1951. *White Collar: The American Middle Classes*. New York: Oxford University Press.

Minnesota Population Center. National Historical Geographic Information System, Version 2.0. Minneapolis: University of Minnesota 2011.

Mische, Ann. 2008. *Partisan Publics: Communication and Contention across Brazilian Youth Activist Networks*. Princeton, NJ: Princeton University Press.

Molotch, Harvey. 1972. *Managed Integration: The Dilemmas of Doing Good in the City*. Berkeley: University of California Press.

Moretti, Enrico. 2013. "Real Wage Inequality." *American Economic Journal: Applied Economics* 5:65–103.

Morris, Keiko. 2015. "Reviving the South Bronx Waterfront." *Wall Street Journal*, March 8, https://www.wsj.com/articles/reviving-the-south-bronx-waterfront -1425862978?mod=rss_newyork_real_estate.

Mortgage Fraud Blog. 2013. "2 Lawyers and Appraiser among 5 Indicted for Mortgage Fraud." August 29. http://www.mortgagefraudblog.com/2-lawyers-and-appraiser -among-5-indicted-for-mortgage-fraud/.

Muniesa, Fabian, Yuval Millo, and Michel Callon. 2007. "An Introduction to Market Devices." In *Market Devices*, edited by Michel Callon, Yuval Millo, and Fabian Mu-niesa, 1–12. Oxford: Blackwell.

Nadeem, Shehzad. 2011. *Dead Ringers: How Outsourcing Is Changing the Way Indians Understand Themselves*. Princeton, NJ: Princeton University Press.

National Association of Realtors. 2005. "A Buyer's and Seller's Guide to Multiple Offer Negotiations." https://www.nar.realtor/sites/default/files/policies/2005 /Multiple-Offer-Negotiations-Guide-2005–10–11.pdf.

National Association of Realtors. 2016. *2016 Profile of Homebuyers and Sellers*. https:// store.realtor.org/product/multimedia/2016-profile-home-buyers-and-sellers -download?sku=E186–45–16.

Newman, Katherine S. 1989. *Falling from Grace*. New York: Free Press.

New York State Association of Realtors. 2015. Code of Ethics. https://www.nysar.com /wingman/working-with-a-realtor/code-of-ethics.

Nuru-Jeter, Amani M., and Thomas A. LaVeist. 2011. "Racial Segregation, Income Inequality, and Mortality in U.S. Metropolitan Areas." *Journal of Urban Health* 88:270–82.

Obstfeld, David, Stephen P. Borgatti, and Jason Davis. 2014. "Brokerage as a Process: Decoupling Third Party Action from Social Network Structure." In *Contemporary Perspectives on Organizational Social Networks*, edited by Daniel J. Brass, Giuseppe Labianca, Ajay Mehra, Daniel S. Halgin, and Stephen P. Borgatti, 135–59. Research in the Sociology of Organizations 40. Bingley, UK: Emerald Group.

Ocejo, Richard E. 2014. *Upscaling Downtown: From Bowery Saloons to Cocktail Bars in New York City*. Princeton, NJ: Princeton University Press.

Ocejo, Richard E. 2017. *Masters of Craft: Old Jobs in the New Urban Economy*. Princeton, NJ: Princeton University Press.

Ody-Brasier, Amandine, and Freek Vermeulen. 2014. "The Price You Pay: Price-Setting as a Response to Norm Violations in the Market for Champagne Grapes." *Administrative Science Quarterly* 59:109–44.

Oliver, Melvin, and Thomas Shapiro. 2006. *Black Wealth / White Wealth: A New Perspective on Racial Inequality*. New York: Taylor and Francis.

Ondrich, Jan, Stephen Ross, and John Yinger. 2003. "Now You See It, Now You Don't: Why Do Real Estate Agents Withhold Available Houses from Black Customers?" *Review of Economics and Statistics* 85:854–73.

Orzechowski, Shawna, and Peter Sepielli. 2003. *Net Worth and Asset Ownership of Households: 1998 and 2000*. Report P70–88, US Census Bureau.

O'Shaughnessy, John, and Nicolas J. O'Shaughnessy. 2003. *The Marketing Power of Emotion*. Oxford: Oxford University Press.

Owens, Ann. 2015. "Assisted Housing and Income Segregation among Neighborhoods in U.S. Metropolitan Areas." *Annals of the American Academy of Political and Social Science* 660:98–116.

Owens, Ann. 2016. "Inequality in Children's Contexts: Income Segregation of Households with and without Children." *American Sociological Review* 81:549–74.

Owens, Ann. 2017. "Racial Residential Segregation of School-Aged Children and Adults: The Role of Schooling as a Segregating Force." *RSF: The Russell Sage Foundation Journal of the Social Sciences* 3:63–80.

Pager, Devah, and David Pedulla. 2015. "Race, Self-Selection, and the Job Search Process." *American Journal of Sociology* 120:1005–54.

Pager, Devah, and Hana Shepherd. 2008. "The Sociology of Discrimination: Racial Discrimination in Employment, Housing, Credit, and Consumer Markets." *Annual Review of Sociology* 34:181–209.

Pattillo, Mary. 2007. *Black on the Block*. Chicago: University of Chicago Press.

Pattillo, Mary. 2013. "Housing: Commodity versus Right." *Annual Review of Sociology* 39:509–31.

Perkins, Harvey C., David C. Thorns, and Bronwyn M. Newton. 2008. "Real Estate

Advertising and Intraurban Place Meaning: Real Estate Sales Consultants at Work." *Environment and Planning A: Economy and Space* 40:2061–79.

Peters, Ellen. 2006. "The Functions of Affect in the Construction of Preferences." In *The Construction of Preference*, edited by Sarah Lichtenstein and Paul Slovic, 454–63. Cambridge: Cambridge University Press.

Peterson, Ruth D., and Lauren J. Krivo. 2010. *Divergent Social Worlds: Neighborhood Crime and the Racial-Spatial Divide*. New York: Russell Sage.

Pixley, Jocelyn. 2004. *Emotions in Finance*. Cambridge: Cambridge University Press.

Pixley, Jocelyn. 2009. "Time Orientation and Emotion-Rules in Finance." *Theory and Society* 38:353–400.

Pixley, Jocelyn, Peter McCarthy, and Shaun Wilson. 2014. "The Economy and Emotions." In *Handbook of the Sociology of Emotions*, edited by J. E. Stets and J. H. Turner, 2:307–34. Heidelberg: Springer.

Podolny, Joel. 1993. "A Status-Based Model of Market Competition." *American Journal of Sociology* 98:829–72.

Podolny, Joel. 2005. *Status Signals: A Sociological Study of Market Competition*. Princeton, NJ: Princeton University Press.

Polanyi, Karl. 1944. *The Great Transformation: The Political and Economic Origins of Our Time*. Boston: Beacon.

Prus, Robert. 1989. *Making Sales: Influence as Interpersonal Accomplishment*. London: Sage.

Quinn, Sarah. 2008. "The Transformation of Morals in Markets: Death, Benefits, and the Exchange of Life Insurance Policies." *American Journal of Sociology* 114:738–80.

Quillian, Lincoln. 2014. "Does Segregation Create Winners and Losers? Residential Segregation and Inequality in Educational Attainment." *Social Problems* 61:402–26.

Quillian, Lincoln, and Devah Pager. 2001. "Black Neighbors, Higher Crime? The Role of Racial Stereotypes in Evaluations of Neighborhood Crime." *American Journal of Sociology* 107:717–67.

Rao, Krishna. 2014. "In Search of Affordability." Zillow, http://www.zillow.com/research/2013-q4-mortgage-affordability-6625/, accessed April 7, 2014.

Rawlings, Craig, and Clayton Childress. 2019. "Emergent Meanings: Reconciling Dispositional and Situational Accounts of Meaning-Making from Cultural Objects." *American Journal of Sociology* 124:1763–809.

Reardon, Sean F., and Kendra Bischoff. 2011. "Income Inequality and Income Segregation." *American Journal of Sociology* 116:1092–153.

Reardon, Sean F., Kendra Bischoff, Ann Owens, and Joseph Townsend. 2018. "Has Income Segregation Really Increased? Bias and Bias Correction in Sample-Based Segregation Estimates." *Demography* 55:2129–60.

Reardon, Sean F., Lindsay Fox, and Joseph Townsend. 2015. "Neighborhood Income Composition by Race and Income, 1990–2009." *Annals of the American Academy of Political and Social Science* 660:78–97.

Reardon, Sean F., Joseph Townsend, and Lindsay Fox. 2017. "A Continuous Measure of the Joint Distribution of Race and Income among Neighborhoods." *RSF: The Russell Sage Foundation Journal of the Social Sciences* 3:34–62.

Reich, Adam D. 2014. "Contradictions in the Commodification of Hospital Care." *American Journal of Sociology* 119:1576–628.

Reiss, Julian. 2009. "Causation in the Social Sciences: Evidence, Inference, and Purpose." *Philosophy of the Social Sciences* 39:20–40.

Rhodes, Anna, and Stefanie DeLuca. 2014. "Residential Mobility and School Choice among Poor Families." In *Choosing Homes, Choosing Schools*, edited by Annette Lareau and Kimberly Goyette, 137–66. New York: Russell Sage.

Rice, Andrew. 2014. "Stash Pad." *New York Magazine*, June 27. http://nymag.com /news/features/foreigners-hiding-money-new-york-real-estate-2014-6/.

Rich, Peter M., and Jennifer L. Jennings. 2015. "Choice, Information, and Constrained Options: School Transfers in a Stratified Education System." *American Sociological Review* 80:1069–98.

Ridgeway, Cecilia L., and Lynn Smith-Lovin. 1999. "The Gender System and Interaction." *Annual Review of Sociology* 25:191–216.

Rivera, Lauren. 2012. "Hiring as Cultural Matching: The Case of Elite Professional Service Firms." *American Sociological Review* 77:999–1022.

Rivera, Lauren. 2015a. "Go with Your Gut: Emotion and Evaluation in Job Interviews." *American Journal of Sociology* 120:1339–89.

Rivera, Lauren. 2015b. *Pedigree: How Elite Students Get Elite Jobs*. Princeton, NJ: Princeton University Press.

Rodríguez-Pose, Andrés, and Michael Storper. 2019. "Housing, Urban Growth and Inequalities: The Limits to Deregulation and Upzoning in Reducing Economic and Spatial Inequality." CEPR Discussion Paper DP13713. Available at SSRN: https:// ssrn.com/abstract=3383971.

Rohe, William M., and Michael A. Stegmam. 1994. "The Effects of Homeownership: On the Self-Esteem, Perceived Control and Life Satisfaction of Low-Income People." *Journal of the American Planning Association* 60:173–84.

Roscigno, Vincent J., Diana L. Karafin, and Griff Tester. 2009. "The Complexities and Processes of Racial Housing Discrimination." *Social Problems* 56:49–69.

Rosen, Eva. 2014. "Rigging the Rules of the Game: How Landlords Geographically Sort Low-Income Renters." *City & Community* 13:310–40.

Rosen, Eva. 2017. "Horizontal Immobility: How Narratives of Neighborhood Violence Shape Housing Decisions." *American Sociological Review* 82:270–96.

Rosen, Eva, and Sudhir Venkatesh. 2008. "A 'Perversion' of Choice: Sex Work Offers Just Enough in Chicago's Urban Ghetto." *Journal of Contemporary Ethnography* 37:417–41.

Rosenblatt, Peter, and Stefanie DeLuca. 2012. "'We Don't Live Outside, We Live in Here': Neighborhood and Residential Mobility Decisions among Low-Income Families." *City & Community* 11:254–84.

Ross, Stephen, and Margery Turner. 2005. "Housing Discrimination in Metropolitan America: Explaining Changes between 1989 and 2000." *Social Problems* 52:152–80.

Rossman, Gabriel. 2014. "Obfuscatory Relational Work and Disreputable Exchange." *Sociological Theory* 32:43–63.

Rothstein, Richard. 2017. *The Color of Law: The Forgotten History of How Our Government Segregated America*. New York: Liveright.

Roux, Caroline, Kelly Goldsmith, and Andrea Bonezzi. 2015. "On the Psychology of Scarcity: When Reminders of Resource Scarcity Promote Selfish (and Generous) Behavior." *Journal of Consumer Research* 42:615–31.

Rugh, Jacob S. 2015. "Double Jeopardy: Why Latinos Were Hit Hardest by the US Foreclosure Crisis." *Social Forces* 93:1139–84.

Rutherford, R. C., T. M. Springer, and A. Yavas. 2005. "Conflicts between Principals and Agents: Evidence from Residential Brokerage." *Journal of Financial Economics* 76:627–55.

Rutherford, Ronald, and Abdullah Yavas. 2012. "Discount Brokerage in Residential Real Estate Markets." *Real Estate Economics* 40:508–35.

Sallaz, Jeffrey J. 2009. *The Labor of Luck: Casino Capitalism in the United States and South Africa*. Berkeley: University of California Press.

Sampson, Peter. 2013. "Did Agent Mislead Buyer into Making Higher Bid?" NorthJersey .com, http://archive.northjersey.com/real-estate/did-agent-mislead-buyer-into -making-high-bid-1.602350, accessed October 21, 2013.

Sampson, Robert J. 2012. *Great American City: Chicago and the Enduring Neighborhood Effect*. Chicago: University of Chicago Press.

Sampson, Robert J., and Stephen W. Raudenbush. 2004. "Seeing Disorder: Neighborhood Stigma and the Social Construction of 'Broken Windows.'" *Social Psychology Quarterly* 67:319–42.

Schachter, Ariela, and Max Besbris. 2017. "Immigration and Neighborhood Change: Methodological Possibilities for Future Research." *City & Community* 16:244–51.

Schor, Juliet B., Connor Fitzmaurice, Lindsey B. Carfagna, and Will Atwood-Charles. 2016. "Paradoxes of Openness and Distinction in the Shared Economy." *Poetics* 54:66–81.

Schwartz, Alex. 2010. *Housing Policy in the United States*. 2nd ed. New York: Routledge.

Schwartz, Barry. 2004. *The Paradox of Choice: Why More Is Less*. New York: Harper.

Scott, Janny. 2006. "Report Alleges Bias by Real Estate Giant." *New York Times*, October 11, https://www.nytimes.com/2006/10/11/nyregion/11discriminate.html.

Sen, Amartya. 1973. "Behaviour and the Concept of Preference." *Economica* 40:241–59.

Sen, Amartya. 1993. "Internal Consistency of Choice." *Econometrica* 61:495–521.

Sewell, William. 1996. "Historical Events as Transformations of Structures: Inventing Revolution at the Bastille." *Theory and Society* 25:841–81.

Shah, Anuj K., Sendhil Mullainathan, and Eldar Shafir. 2012. "Some Consequences of Having Too Little." *Science* 338:682–85.

Shapiro, Thomas M. 2004. *The Hidden Cost of Being African American: How Wealth Perpetuates Inequality*. Oxford: Oxford University Press.

Shapiro, Thomas M. 2017. *Toxic Inequality: How America's Wealth Gap Destroys Mobility, Deepens the Racial Divide, and Threatens Our Future*. New York: Basic Books.

Sharkey, Patrick. 2013. *Stuck in Place: Urban Neighborhoods and the End of Progress toward Racial Equality*. Chicago: University of Chicago Press.

Sharkey, Patrick, Max Besbris, and Michael Friedson. 2016. "Poverty and Crime." In *The Oxford Handbook of the Social Science of Poverty*, edited by David Brady and Linda M. Burton, 623–36. New York: Oxford University Press.

Sharkey, Patrick, and Jacob W. Faber. 2014. "Where, When, Why and for Whom Do Residential Contexts Matter? Moving Away from the Dichotomous Understanding of Neighborhood Effects." *Annual Review of Sociology* 40:559–79.

Sherman, Rachel. 2007. *Class Acts*. Berkeley: University of California Press.

Sherman, Rachel. 2011. "The Production of Distinctions: Class, Gender, and Taste Work in the Lifestyle Management Industry." *Qualitative Sociology* 34:201–19.

Sherman, Rachel. 2017. *Uneasy Street: The Anxieties of Affluence*. Princeton, NJ: Princeton University Press.

Shi, Lan, and Christina Tapia. 2015. "The Disciplining Effect of Concern for Referrals: Evidence from Real Estate Agents." *Real Estate Economics* 44:411–61.

Shiller, Robert J. 2005. *Irrational Exuberance*. 2nd ed. New York: Broadway Books.

Shiller, Robert J. 2015. *Irrational Exuberance*. 3rd ed. Princeton, NJ: Princeton University Press.

Shiller, Robert J. 2019. *Narrative Economics: How Stories Go Viral and Drive Major Economic Events*. Princeton, NJ: Princeton University Press.

Shlay, Ann B. 2015. "Life and Liberty in the Pursuit of Housing: Rethinking Renting and Owning in Post-crisis America." *Housing Studies* 30:560–79.

Simmel, Georg. 1950. "The Triad." In *The Sociology of Georg Simmel*, edited by K. H. Wolff, 145–69. New York: Free Press.

Simmel, Georg. 1978. *The Philosophy of Money*. New York: Routledge.

Sisson, Patrick. 2017. "New South Bronx Waterfront Development Has Residents Asking Who It's For." *Curbed New York*, March 14, http://ny.curbed.com/2017/3/14/14915644/south-bronx-gentrification-waterfront-development.

Slovic, Paul. 1995. "The Construction of Preference." *American Psychologist* 50:364–71.

Slovic, Paul, Melissa Finucane, Ellen Peters, and Donald MacGregor. 2004. "Risk as Analysis and Risk as Feelings: Some Thoughts about Affect, Reason, Risk and Rationality." *Risk Analysis* 24:311–22.

Slovic, Paul, Melissa Finucane, Ellen Peters, and Donald MacGregor. 2006. "The Affect Heuristic." In *The Construction of Preference*, edited by Sarah Lichtenstein and Paul Slovic, 434–53. Cambridge: Cambridge University Press.

Small, Mario Luis. 2004. *Villa Victoria: The Transformation of Social Capital in a Boston Barrio*. Chicago: University of Chicago Press.

Small, Mario Luis. 2009a. "'How Many Cases Do I Need?' On Science and the Logic of Case Selection in Field-Based Research." *Ethnography* 10:5–38.

Small, Mario Luis. 2009b. *Unanticipated Gains*. Oxford: Oxford University Press.

Small, Mario Luis. 2013. "Causal Thinking in Ethnographic Research." *American Journal of Sociology* 119:597–601.

Small, Mario Luis, and Monica McDermott. 2006. "The Presence of Organizational Resources in Poor Urban Neighborhoods: An Analysis of Average and Contextual Effects." *Social Forces* 84:1697–724.

Smith, Charles W. 1989. *Auctions: The Social Construction of Value.* Berkeley: University of California Press.

Smith, Vicki. 2001. *Crossing the Great Divide: Worker Risk and Opportunity in the New Economy.* Ithaca, NY: Cornell University Press.

Spilerman, Seymour. 2000. "Wealth and Stratification Processes." *Annual Review of Sociology* 24:497–524.

Spillman, Lyn. 2012. *Solidarity in Strategy.* Chicago: University of Chicago Press.

Spillman, Lyn, and Michael Strand. 2013. "Interest-Oriented Action." *Annual Review of Sociology* 39:85–104.

Squires, Gregory D. 1994. *Capital and Communities in Black and White: The Intersections of Race, Class, and Uneven Development.* Albany: SUNY Press.

Squires, Gregory D., Samantha Friedman, and Catherine E. Saidat. 2002. "Experiencing Residential Segregation." *Urban Affairs Review* 38:155–83.

Squires, Gregory D., and Charis E. Kubrin. 2006. *Privileged Places: Race, Residence and the Structure of Opportunity.* Boulder: Lynne Rienner.

Stark, David. 2009. *The Sense of Dissonance.* Princeton, NJ: Princeton University Press.

Starr, Paul. 1982. *The Social Transformation of American Medicine.* New York: Basic Books.

Stellin, Susan. 2011. "The Buddy System, or the Buyer's Broker." *New York Times,* September 18, http://www.nytimes.com/2011/09/18/realestate/the-buyers-broker -getting-started.html.

Stets, Jan E. 2012. "Current Emotion Research in Sociology: Advances in the Discipline." *Emotion Review* 4:326–34.

Stevens, Mitchell. 2007. *Creating a Class.* Cambridge, MA: Harvard University Press.

Story, Louise. 2016. "U.S. Will Track Secret Buyers of Luxury Real Estate." *New York Times,* January 14, https://www.nytimes.com/2016/01/14/us/us-will-track-secret -buyers-of-luxury-real-estate.html.

Story, Louise, and Stephanie Saul. 2015. "Stream of Foreign Wealth Flows to Elite New York Real Estate." *New York Times,* February 8, https://www.nytimes.com/2015 /02/08/nyregion/stream-of-foreign-wealth-flows-to-time-warner-condos.html.

Stovel, Katherine, Benjamin Golub, and Eva M. Meyersson Milgrom. 2011. "Stabilizing Brokerage." *Proceedings of the National Academy of Sciences* 108:21326–332.

Stovel, Katherine, and Lynette Shaw. 2012. "Brokerage." *Annual Review of Sociology* 38:139–58.

Streitfeld, David. 2008. "Feeling Misled on Home Price, Buyers Sue Agent." *New York Times, January 22,* http://www.nytimes.com/2008/01/22/business/22agent.html.

Sullivan, Esther. 2017. "Displaced in Place: Manufactured Housing, Mass Eviction, and the Paradox of State Intervention." *American Sociological Review* 82:243–69.

Sullivan, Esther. 2018. *Manufactured Insecurity: Mobile Home Parks and Americans' Tenuous Right to Place.* Berkeley: University of California Press.

Suttles, Gerald D. 1972. *The Social Construction of Communities.* Chicago: University of Chicago Press.

Swedburg, Richard. 1994. "Markets as Social Structures." In *The Handbook of Economic*

Sociology, edited by Neil Smelser and Richard Swedberg, 255–82. New York: Russell Sage Foundation / Princeton, NJ: Princeton University Press.

Swidler, Ann. 2001. *Talk of Love: How Culture Matters*. Chicago: University of Chicago Press.

Tavory, Iddo. 2016. *Summoned: Identification and Religious Life in a Jewish Neighborhood*. Chicago: University of Chicago Press.

Tavory, Iddo, and Nina Eliasoph. 2013. "Coordinating Futures: Toward a Theory of Anticipation." *American Journal of Sociology* 118:908–42.

Tavory, Iddo, and Stefan Timmermans. 2013. "A Pragmatist Approach to Causality in Ethnography." *American Journal of Sociology* 119:682–714.

Tavory, Iddo, and Stefan Timmermans. 2014. *Abductive Analysis: Theorizing Qualitative Research*. Chicago: University of Chicago Press.

Taylor, Keeanga-Yamahtta. 2019. *Race for Profit: How Banks and the Real Estate Industry Undermined Black Homeownership*. Chapel Hill: University of North Carolina Press.

Taylor, Paul, Rakesh Kochhar, Richard Fry, Gabriel Velasco, and Seth Motel. 2011. "Twenty-to-One: Wealth Gaps Rise to Record Highs between Whites, Blacks and Hispanics." Social & Demographic Trends, Pew Research Center, July 26, http://www.pewsocialtrends.org/2011/07/26/wealth-gaps-rise-to-record-highs -between-whites-blacks-hispanics/.

Townsend, Nicholas W. 2002. *The Package Deal*. Philadelphia: Temple University Press.

Toy, Vivian S. 2012. "Buyer Confidence: Portent or Blip?" *New York Times*, April 15, http://www.nytimes.com/2012/04/15/realestate/buyer-confidence-portent-or -blip.html.

Tuckett, David. 2011. *Minding the Markets*. London: Palgrave Macmillan.

Turnbull, Geoffrey K., and Jonathan Dombrow. 2007. "Individual Agents, Firms, and the Real Estate Brokerage Process." *Journal of Real Estate Finance and Economics* 35:57–76.

Turner, Margery Austin, et al. 2013. "Housing Discrimination against Racial and Ethnic Minorities 2012." US Department of Housing and Urban Development, https:// www.huduser.gov/portal//Publications/pdf/HUD-514_HDS2012.pdf.

UC Berkeley's Urban Displacement Project and the California Housing Partnership. 2018a. "Rising Housing Costs and Re-segregation in Alameda County." http:// www.urbandisplacement.org/sites/default/files/images/alameda_final.pdf.

UC Berkeley's Urban Displacement Project and the California Housing Partnership. 2018b. "Rising Housing Costs and Re-segregation in Contra Costa County." http:// www.urbandisplacement.org/sites/default/files/images/cc_final.pdf.

UC Berkeley's Urban Displacement Project and the California Housing Partnership. 2018c. "Rising Housing Costs and Re-segregation in San Francisco." http://www .urbandisplacement.org/sites/default/files/images/sf_final.pdf.

Ultan, Lloyd. 2009. *The Northern Borough: A History of the Bronx*. New York: Bronx County Historical Society.

Uzzi, Brian. 1999. "Embeddedness in the Making of Financial Capital: How Social

Relations and Networks Benefit Firms Seeking Finance." *American Sociological Review* 64:481–505.

Uzzi, Brian, and Ryon Lancaster. 2004. "Embeddedness and Price Formation in the Corporate Law Market." *American Sociological Review* 69:319–44.

Velthuis, Olav. 2005. *Talking Prices: Symbolic Meanings of Prices on the Market for Contemporary Art*. Princeton, NJ: Princeton University Press.

Viscelli, Steve. 2016. *The Big Rig: Trucking and the Decline of the American Dream*. Berkeley: University of California Press.

Wacquant, Loïc. 1998. "Inside the Zone: The Social Art of the Hustler in the Black American Ghetto." *Theory, Culture & Society* 15:1–36.

Wacquant, Loïc. 2001. "Whores, Slaves, and Stallions: Languages of Exploitation and Accommodation among Boxers." *Body & Society* 7:181–94.

Wacquant, Loïc. 2008. *Urban Outcasts: A Comparative Sociology of Advanced Marginality*. Malden, MA: Polity.

Wacquant. Loïc. 2010. "Urban Desolation and Symbolic Denigration in the Hyperghetto." *Social Psychology Quarterly* 73:215–19.

Wacquant. Loïc, Tom Slater, and Virgilio Borges Pereira. 2014. "Territorial Stigmatization in Action." *Environment and Planning A* 46:1270–80.

Weber, Max. [1930] 1992. *The Protestant Ethic and the Spirit of Capitalism*. New York: Routledge.

West, Candace, and Don H. Zimmerman. 1987. "Doing Gender." *Gender and Society* 1:125–51.

Wharton, Amy S. 2009. "The Sociology of Emotional Labor." *Annual Review of Sociology* 35:147–165.

Wharton, Carol S. 2002. *Framing a Domain for Work and Family: A Study of Women in Residential Real Estate Sales Work*. Lanham, MD: Lexington.

Wherry, Frederick F. 2008. "The Social Characterizations of Price: The Fool, the Faithful, the Frivolous, and the Frugal." *Sociological Theory* 26:363–79.

Wherry, Frederick F. 2012. "Performance Circuits in the Marketplace." *Politics & Society* 40:203–21.

White, Harrison. 1981. "Where Do Markets Come From?" *American Journal of Sociology* 87:517–47.

Williams, Christine L. 2006. *Inside Toyland: Working, Shopping, and Social Inequality*. Berkeley: University of California Press.

Williams, David R., and Chiquita Collins. 2001. "Racial Residential Segregation: A Fundamental Cause of Racial Disparities in Health." *Public Health Reports* 116:404–16.

Williams, Jerome D., William J. Qualls, and Sonya A. Grier. 1995. "Racially Exclusive Real Estate Advertising: Public Policy Implications for Fair Housing Practices." *Journal of Public Policy & Marketing* 14:225–44.

Williams, Patti. 2014. "Emotions and Consumer Behavior." *Journal of Consumer Research* 40:viii–xi.

Wirth, Louis. [1928] 1998. *The Ghetto*. New Brunswick, NJ: Transaction.

Witte, Carl L., Marko Grunhagen, and James W. Gentry. 2008. "An Empirical Investi-

gation of Framing Effects in Negotiations: A Study of Single-Family Home Sales."
Psychology and Marketing 25:465–84.

Wolf, Eric R. 1956. "Aspects of Group Relations in a Complex Society: Mexico." *American Anthropologist* 58:1065–78.

Wynn, Jonathan R. 2016. "On the Sociology of Occasions." *Sociological Theory* 34: 276–86.

Yinger, John. 1981. "Search Model of Real Estate Broker Behavior." *American Economic Review* 71:591–604.

Yinger, John. 1995. *Closed Doors, Opportunities Lost*. New York: Russell Sage.

Yinger, John. 1997. "Cash in Your Face: The Cost of Racial and Ethnic Discrimination in Housing." *Journal of Urban Economics* 42:339–65.

Zaloom, Caitlin. 2006. *Out of the Pits: Traders and Technology from Chicago to London*. Chicago: University of Chicago Press.

Zavisca, Jane R., and Theodore P. Gerber. 2016. "The Socioeconomic, Demographic, and Political Effects of Housing in Comparative Perspective." *Annual Review of Sociology* 42:347–67.

Zbaracki, Mark J., and Mark Bergen. 2010. "When Truces Collapse: A Longitudinal Study of Price-Adjustment Routines." *Organization Science* 21:966–72.

Zbaracki, Mark J., Mark Ritson, Daniel Levy, Shantanu Dutta, and Mark Bergen. 2004. "Managerial and Customer Costs of Price Adjustment: Direct Evidence from Industrial Markets." *Review of Economics and Statistics* 86:514–33.

Zelizer, Viviana. 1979. *Morals and Markets: The Development of Life Insurance in the United States*. New Brunswick, NJ: Transaction.

Zelizer, Viviana. 1985. *Pricing the Priceless Child: The Changing Social Value of Children*. New York: Basic Books.

Zelizer, Viviana. 1994. *The Social Meaning of Money*. New York: Basic Books.

Zelizer, Viviana. 2005. *The Purchase of Intimacy*. Princeton, NJ: Princeton University Press.

Zelizer, Viviana. 2011. *Economic Lives: How Culture Shapes the Economy*. Princeton, NJ: Princeton University Press.

Zelizer, Viviana. 2012. "How I Became a Relational Economic Sociologist and What Does That Mean?" *Politics & Society* 40:145–74.

Zorbaugh, Harvey Warren. [1929] 1976. *The Gold Coast and the Slum: A Sociological Study of Chicago's Near North Side*. Chicago: University of Chicago Press.

Zuckerman, Ezra. 1999. "The Categorical Imperative: Securities Analysts and the Illegitimacy Discount." *American Journal of Sociology* 104:1398–438.

Zuckerman, Ezra. 2012. "Construction, Concentration, and (Dis)Continuities in Social Valuations." *Annual Review of Sociology* 38:223–45.

Zukin, Sharon. 1982. *Loft Living*. Baltimore: Johns Hopkins University Press.

Zukin, Sharon. 2004. *Point of Purchase*. New York: Routledge.

Zukin, Sharon, and Jennifer Smith Maguire. 2004. "Consumers and Consumption." *Annual Review of Sociology* 30:173–97.

Zumpano, Leonard V., and Donald L. Hooks. 1988. "The Real Estate Brokerage Market: A Critical Reevaluation." *Real Estate Economics* 16:1–16.

INDEX

Printed in the USA
CPSIA information can be obtained
at www.ICGtesting.com
LVHW050733010324
773206LV00005B/385